Silent Earth

David Israelson is one of Canada's most experienced and widely read environmental writers. The winner of two newspaper awards, he holds a law degree from Osgoode Hall and a B.A. from the University of Toronto. Currently the chief of the *Toronto Star's* bureau in London, England, he lives with his wife and their two children in central London.

THE POLITICS
OF OUR SURVIVAL

DAVID ISRAELSON

Penguin Books

PENGUIN BOOKS

Published by the Penguin Group

Penguin Books Canada Ltd, 10 Alcorn Avenue, Toronto, Ontario,
Canada M4V 3B2

Penguin Books Ltd, 27 Wrights Lane, London W8 5TZ, England

Penguin Books USA Inc., 375 Hudson Street, New York, New York
10014, U.S.A.

Penguin Books Australia Ltd, Ringwood, Victoria, Australia

Penguin Books (NZ) Ltd, 182-190 Wairau Road, Auckland 10,
New Zealand

Penguin Books Ltd, Registered Offices: Harmondsworth, Middlesex,
England

First published in Viking by Penguin Books Canada Limited, 1990

Published in Penguin Books, 1991

1 3 5 7 9 10 8 6 4 2

Map drawn by Jonathan Gladstone/j.b. geographics

Excerpts from *Silent Spring* by Rachel Carson.
Copyright © 1962 by Rachel L. Carson.
Reprinted by permission of Houghton Mifflin Co.

Silent Spring Revisited excerpted with permission from Briggs, S.A.
In *Silent Spring Revisited*; Marco, J.G.; Hollingworth, R.M.; Durham,
W., Eds.; American Chemical Society: Washington, DC, 1987; pp 5-7.
Copyright 1987 American Chemical Society.

Every effort has been made to acknowledge all sources of material used
in this book. The publisher would be grateful if any errors or omissions
were pointed out, so that they might be corrected.

Manufactured in Canada

Canadian Cataloguing in Publication Data
Israelson, David, 1954-
    Silent earth

Includes bibliographical references.
ISBN 0-14-012922-7

1. Pollution.   2. Environmental policy.   I. Title.

TD174.I77 1991   363.73   C90-094396-3

For Susan, Michael and Tessa

ACKNOWLEDGEMENTS

The world's libraries are full of apologies. So I'd like to add this one, and say how much I appreciate the patience and understanding I have received from my wife, Susan Elliott, and son, Jacob Michael Elliott Israelson. It would have been impossible to do this book without the support and editorial advice of my wife, and there is no way I could express my appreciation and love enough.

I am also deeply grateful to my friends Bill Harper, Beverley Slopen and Michael Perley, who read early versions of my manuscript (except, in Perley's case, material concerning himself) and offered valuable critical advice. I owe each of them extra *thank-you*s — to Bill for all his help with computers, to Beverley for being my agent and for being so encouraging and to Michael for sitting still long enough to be interviewed.

At Penguin, I'm grateful to the following people: Cynthia Good, Publisher, Editor - in - Chief, Vice-President of Publishing Division; Brad Martin, Vice-President of Sales and Marketing; Pat Cooper, Trade Marketing Manager; Karen Cossar, Assistant Publicity Manager (Hardcover and Trade Paperback Division) and Christeen Chidley-Hill, Senior Production Editor. My deepest appreciation goes to my copy editor, Cy Strom, and in particular to my two editors: Iris Skeoch, who supported this project and helped get it rolling and Laurel Bernard, whose dedication, commitment, wisdom and stamina saw it through. It may be a cliché to say it really wouldn't have been possible without these people, but it wouldn't.

There are many people at the *Toronto Star* to whom I am also thankful: John Honderich and Lou Clancy for supporting me as the paper's environment reporter; Ian Urquhart and Joe Hall for generously granting me a leave of absence; Peter Edwards, Don Sellar, Kelly Toughill, Janice Turner and Martin Cohn for enduring endless monologues about the work in progress; Susan Walker for her advice; and my own editor, Wayne Braun, for his patience and indulgence. Thanks also to Barti Ratanji and Frank Kennedy for their expert computer advice and support, and to Carol Lindsay and the ever-helpful *Star* library staff.

To my parents, Reeve and Barbara Israelson, who taught me to appreciate books, my in-laws Clifford and Maxine Elliott and next-door neighbours Janet and Richard Matte, I'm also thankful. This book could not have been written without their babysitting and other crucial assistance.

Thanks also to all the people who consented to interviews—especially to Jim Bradley and Tom McMillan, who were generous and co-operative when it wasn't necessarily in their career interests to be so. And to George Maddison and Jim Blake, for good advice, and Margaret Atwood, who took time from her busy schedule to talk about the issues and make me feel that what I've been doing is worthwhile.

And lastly, thanks to all the environmentalists. If I criticize you, it's because I want you to do a better job. Maybe some day we'll no longer need people to demand a cleaner world—but for now, we can't do without them.

David Israelson

SILENT EARTH

CONTENTS

There is no Silence in the Earth—so silent
As that endured
Which uttered, would discourage Nature
And haunt the World.
　　　　　　　—Emily Dickinson

INTRODUCTION

I come from a generation of North Americans – those born between 1945 and 1965 – that thrived on abundance. We had more of everything than anyone had before. We were taught to use things, enjoy them, and then throw them away. This was progress. It helped people earn their livings. As long as we threw things away, they could make more.

We benefited from great scientific advances. Our doctors wiped out polio. Our farms grew more food. It became easier to communicate over long distances, to fly across the oceans, to record our thoughts, to type this book. But when we were young, a few people started warning us that what we were doing was not altogether good. Eventually, if we kept making new things, we would run out of the materials we need to make them. And they said throwing everything away would make it harder to find places where the refuse wouldn't be noticed or cause some kind of harm.

By the 1960s it became hard to ignore all these things. The leftovers seemed to be everywhere; we started to think of this as pollution.

And it seemed that the supply of some of the things we thought we had plenty of – for example, wood – would not last forever. We saw that the dwindling of supplies was connected to other problems, such as animals becoming extinct or the fact that instead of taking half an hour to escape the city, it took two or three hours. We started to think of the connections as ecology.

We also learned that these kinds of problems were not confined to poor, crowded parts of the world, but in some ways were worse for us, because we were supposed to be wealthy enough to escape them. There was no escape. It seemed the whole world had one big problem, and we had just a part of it.

We called the problem the environment.

That understanding of the world was kind of a background noise for my generation: we would inherit the riches of the world, but we had to take better care of them than our parents did, or everything would be ruined. In the sixth grade, our teacher told us about a book called *Silent Spring* by Rachel Carson. This book said that in some places the environment was already so contaminated, when spring came the birds no longer sang.

With this impending problem—the environment—in the background, we grew up full of contradictions: rich but rebellious, acquisitive but dissatisfied. By 1970, when I was sixteen, we North Americans were concerned enough about the environment to demand that something be done. Using the vernacular of the day, we called this "consciousness."

This made the environment a political issue; it could be solved by politicians, if enough of us demanded a solution. So we demanded. World conferences were held. We got environment ministries and we got laws. We believed that because we had expressed concern and set up institutions, the political system would then take care of the problems. We called this pollution control. For a while, we forgot about the problems. The 1970s were supposed to be the environmental decade, but the environmental decade really lasted only five years.

By 1975, when I was twenty-one, North Americans seemed a bit tired of environmentalism. The environmentalists had outworn their welcome. Didn't all those laws and ministries mean they had won? What did they want now? Why did they persist? People thought they were strident, simplistic, left-wing utopians. They wanted everybody to wear sweaters, ride bicycles and eat brown rice. They were a cliché.

The only reason they were still tolerated at all was that despite all the protections we had brought in, there were still environmental problems. It seemed that we were running out of oil. There were accidents at nuclear plants. Whales were dying, right here in the St Lawrence River. The gap between our objectives for a safe environment and our achieving those objectives was filled by a whole new phenomenon: the politics of pollution. Somebody had to point out the problems.

Occasionally, some people did. In 1981, I was in journalism school in Ottawa. The president of the United States came to visit the city, and somebody held up a huge sign: Stop Acid Rain!

But we didn't do much about the environment in the early 1980s. In the United States, Ronald Reagan's administration set out to dismantle the regulatory system (the first effort was made by a task force headed by then-Vice-President George Bush). In Canada, we didn't have much of a system to dismantle, but a few unwise politicians tried anyway. Others grew angry about this, and we were indignant about acid rain and water pollution.

But this is not why I was angry.

I was angry because I didn't really understand the whole situation. If we had been concerned about the environment for twenty years, why was so little happening to fix things? What was happening? Was it getting better? Who was trying to improve the situation? Who, and what, made things worse?

In late 1985 I became the environment reporter at the *Toronto Star*, and I tried to answer these questions. I set out some simple guidelines: I would point out obvious truths; I would write stories that helped me understand what was going on—stories that I seldom could find elsewhere. I would make things as simple as possible. I wanted to do this because it seemed that whenever someone suggested a solution to an environmental problem, someone else would inevitably say: "It's not that simple." But maybe it is. Maybe it has to be.

By 1988, I felt there was more to say about the environment than perhaps could be said in a newspaper. The problems had grown more serious; things predicted by doomsayers in the 1960s had come true in the '80s, in many cases with terrible accuracy. Beaches were fouled, cities became less tolerable, lakes died, garbage piled up and scary chemicals seemed to be everywhere. We appeared to be running out of open space, and the doomsayers of the 1980s started warning us that it was going to get worse—a hot, dirty and crowded planet, where the sun could burn holes in your nose and kill you. This time, however, the environment was no longer in the background. By 1988—especially after a summer of frightening, weird weather—everyone seemed to be concerned about the environment.

The politics of pollution had become the politics of our survival.

The environment is now a mainstream issue, addressed by the top politicians and all the major corporations. Environmentalists no longer have to struggle to get in the door. But who are environmentalists? And when they get in the door, what do they have to say?

In the 1990s, people will have to look at what happened in the late '80s—what was predicted, who promised what, who had good ideas and who was playing games. This book is an attempt to move out of today's political and environmental thicket, to figure out what is going on so that we can change it.

It is my attempt to see that we don't allow silent spring to happen everywhere, so that we don't have a silent earth.

It was conceived in anger and born with difficulty and pain, so that it may live in an atmosphere of hope.

It was started when my son was born and completed when my daughter arrived—so that they may have a brighter future.

David Israelson
Toronto, 1990

PART ONE

FROM SILENT
SPRING TO
SILENT EARTH

CHAPTER ONE

The Most Polluted Creatures on Earth

Now small fowls flew screaming over the yet yawning gulf; a sullen white surf beat against its steep sides; then all collapsed, and the great shroud of the sea rolled on as it rolled five thousand years ago.
— Herman Melville, *Moby Dick*

In eastern Canada, about 180 kilometres east of Quebec City, the Saguenay and St Lawrence Rivers meet the sea. The subtle, pale light of the sky and the rolling hills, almost-but-not-quite mountains, play against the dark, choppy waters of the bay. It is the end of a long journey for the rivers; the larger one, the St Lawrence, is one of the continent's veins, carrying water from the centre of North America. Artists and nature lovers come to the Saguenay and the St Lawrence, to explore or to paint the landscape. Sometimes, those who go to the water's edge can come across a memorable sight: the stiff, beached body of a dead beluga whale.

When a whale dies, its wide, grey-white face is often fixed in an expression which, to humans, looks eerily reminiscent. Even after being washed up on a cold, stark shore, its eyes may remain open, punctuating its brow. And its huge,

3

expansive mouth is often turned up at the corners, forming
what appears to be a sly grin.

Belugas had been in the St Lawrence as early as 11,000
years ago, when the last Ice Age retreated. This is roughly as
long as the history of human life. They apparently thrived in
the river; the explorer Jacques Cartier was surprised to see
large numbers of them there when he arrived at the mouth of
the Saguenay in September 1535. The belugas were "a kind
of fish," he said, "which no man had ever seen before
or heard of." They were "shaped like greyhounds as to
the head and body, and they were as white as snow, and
without a spot."

Every year, about 15 dead belugas are found in the
Saguenay-St Lawrence estuary. The death toll is rising: in
1988, more than 20 of their huge carcasses washed up along
the St Lawrence shore. Some 350 to 500 remain alive—just
barely. They are the survivors of a herd that used to number
in the thousands.

Some scientists believe that whales, unlike other mammals, are capable of deep emotions. If so, the dead belugas
may indeed have been smiling in their last moments—from
relief. In life, they have been made sick by the waters they
swim in, which are full of the poisons of North America's
industry.

The dead whales are so full of toxic chemicals that their
bodies are classified as hazardous waste under Canadian
law. Their tissue contains twenty-four potentially deadly
contaminants, including cancer-linked chlorine compounds
and long-banned pesticides such as DDT. A dead beluga can
contain quantities of tar equivalent to the smoke of ten
billion cigarettes. Green garbage bags have been found
inside their bodies. Who knows what was inside the
bags?

It is possible, of course, that the whale corpses found each
year are the bodies of belugas that died of natural causes. But
it's not likely. Among the chemicals found in the belugas are
compounds called polycyclic aromatic hydrocarbons, or
PAHs. One particularly toxic form of these compounds is a
chemical called benzo(a)pyrene (BaP).

The dead whales' blubber has been found to contain PCBs (polychlorinated biphenyls) at levels of 576 parts per million—288 times higher than the level considered safe for fish eaten by human beings. PCBs, which have been linked to cancer, were once used as insulators in electrical products, but their production has been banned in most places, including Canada, since 1977. The whales absorb PCBs by eating contaminated fish.

The whales absorb pesticides in a similar way. A product called Mirex, which has been banned for years, has been found in their tissue. It was once used as a bug and rodent killer, a flame retardant in plastics and as an agent in the compounds used to generate smoke screens. Mirex, known to cause cancer, has been found in the sediment of Lake Ontario. Eels migrate from the lake toward the Sargasso Sea, where they spawn. They pass through the St Lawrence, where some of them are eaten by belugas. This is how the cancer-linked poison moves up the food chain.

A study of brain tissue from three dead belugas has found that the chemicals they ingested actually had altered the DNA in the whales' cells. DNA is the genetic code of life, which is passed from living beings to their offspring. If it is changed by chemical pollution, the offspring will be changed, too—they will be mutants. The effects of these mutations are little understood, but some of the other maladies affecting the whales are not hard to discern. Belugas have been found with burst ulcers, bladder cancer, pneumonia and in some cases, a breakdown of their immune systems similar to AIDS.

The whales—diseased, their blubber filled with chemical poisons—are metaphors for the degradation that is occurring across the continent. The survivors are living, breathing trash heaps, containing everything from disgusting raw sewage to complex chemicals that are dangerous in doses of a few molecules.

The belugas may be the most polluted creatures on earth, but they have competition for that title. And unfortunately, we are among the competitors.

—— I ——

It would be mildly reassuring to find that pollution in the St Lawrence-Saguenay area is an exception, that creatures in other waters aren't faced with the same threats as the belugas. But that's not the case. You can pick a spot nearly anywhere and find a problem. It's now almost possible to stick a pin in a nautical map—a map of any of the continents' coasts will do—and say with accuracy that whatever dwells beneath that pin is sick or dying.

The problems can be extremely unpleasant. Along the Atlantic coast, some 750 dolphins died mysteriously during 1987 and 1988 alone. *Time* magazine reported that "in many that had washed ashore, the snouts, flippers and tails were pocked with blisters and craters; in others, huge patches of skin had been sloughed off." Dolphins are among the smartest animals alive, but no amount of intelligence is enough to enable them to escape what threatens them: their environment.

Pollution is also threatening the fisheries of North America's coasts, and it has the potential to cause devastating economic harm. Canada's oceans in total contribute more than $8 billion a year to the economy and provide 140,000 jobs. In the United States, the commercial and recreational fisheries are worth nearly $3 billion (U.S.) alone. Part of the problem is overfishing and competition from foreign fleets, which have depleted fish stocks to the point where, in 1990 alone, 3,000 people in Atlantic Canada were laid off. But North Americans are aggravating the situation by poisoning the waters, with the cause and effect leading in a straight line right from the water to people's dinner plates.

In fashionable seafood restaurants, it's now common to see the names of exotic fish, such as mako shark, on the menu. But such offerings are not so much exotic as they are necessary—more familiar fish, such as flounder, are disappearing and fish once thrown back by fishermen as unsaleable are now finding their way onto restaurant blackboards.

These days, eating fish is more popular than ever—it's considered healthy. But considering the variety and quantity of the poisons in our oceans, it's hard to see how anything can be healthy that swims in them. Some of the worst situations are now well known, for example, the 37 million litres of crude oil that poured from the *Exxon Valdez* tanker and fouled Alaska's Prince William Sound. But in most cases, the problems are not as much the result of spectacular disasters as they are of everyday practice. In the year leading up to the *Exxon Valdez* spill, tankers poured four times as much oil into the oceans during "routine operations" such as loading and unloading.

Pollution is a byproduct of modern life. Each year, more than 4.5 billion kilograms of industrial chemicals enter North America's waters. We pour things down the drain, we flush the toilet, yet until recently we gave little thought to where all this contaminated water goes.

When we find out, our first reaction is, understandably, disgust. Offshore from New York harbour, 106 nautical miles from the entrance, there are dense, dark underwater clouds of sewage sludge. This is material that has already been processed by treatment plants in New York and New Jersey—so it was put there deliberately. The site, just beyond the continental shelf, is called Dump Site 106. It covers some 12,000 square kilometres of ocean. New Jersey Senator Frank Lautenberg flew over it and described it as "a dead sea spotted with mutated fish." Nearly 10 million tonnes of the sludge was dumped there from huge barges every year during the 1980s, until it was finally noticed by the U. S. Congress, which ordered a halt to the practice.

It's not just sea water that is full of filth. Our lakes and rivers—our drinking supplies—also contain vast quantities of chemicals and other contamination. The Great Lakes, which the Indians named "Sweetwater Seas," contain more than a thousand chemicals that react and combine in ways still poorly understood. Experts used to assume that the pollution poured into the water through sewer outlets and industrial discharge pipes. And it does. But the pipes merely form a section of a vast toxic cycle, in which chemicals move in many directions: leaching through soil, evaporating, forming clouds and falling as rain or snow, or simply settling with the dust. Acid rain—Canada's national pollution obsession—is just one type of pollution that is caught in this cycle. And acid rain alone has damaged 19,000 lakes in Ontario, in some cases rendering the water as acidic as battery acid.

The most significant aspect of this toxic cycle is the one we are only starting to understand: we are part of it. Pollution is not something we can avoid by staying out of the water or eating the right foods. It's in everything. We're breathing it. If you have a chronic sore throat, cough or bronchitis, it may be because of acid rain. This pollution is now suspected to be North America's third-leading cause of lung disease, after smoking and second-hand cigarette smoke.

The cause of such breathing ailments may, however, be the result of a more complicated part of the toxic cycle —toxic rain, the combination of hundreds of polluting chemicals that mix in the sky. It's a phenomenon that affects more than what we breathe. It is changing how we live, and may determine whether we survive.

Taken individually, chemical compounds emitted into the air are not necessarily menacing. We exhale carbon dioxide, for example. And ozone actually protects us when it's in the stratosphere, more than fifteen kilometres above us—it's a thin gas made of oxygen, whose pale colour is what makes the sky blue. But ozone at ground level causes smog, while carbon dioxide is building up in the atmosphere to the point where it is trapping heat and warming the earth. What makes such compounds dangerous today is that there are so many of them; they are being produced in quantities that upset the rough balance of nature, which has existed for thousands of years.

A major source is the automobile, the invention that has done more than any other to change the way we live. In Canada there are more than 450 cars for every 1,000 people; we are second only to the United States, which has more than 560 for every 1,000. On a per-person basis, each Canadian with a car drives an average forty-five kilometres a day. The exhaust pipes from these cars give off the gases that form ozone. And they spew out carbon dioxide, which is produced any time something is burned.

We have put so much carbon dioxide into the atmosphere, burning forests, running factories, driving cars, that we appear to have changed the weather. British scientists report that 1989 was the fifth-hottest year in the nearly one hundred years for which there are reliable records—bringing to a close a decade that had the hottest average temperatures ever recorded. The hottest year ever was 1988, when people began to notice mysterious, wild deviations from normal patterns that now occur regularly—record storms lashing the British coast and killing dozens, dirt-cracking droughts drying up Prairie farms, and so on.

The weather is largely determined by the tropical forests that circle the planet in a band around the equator. They make the difference between life on earth and no life, their leaves filtering the air, their roots and decaying matter nurturing the soil, their branches and trunks sheltering an immense variety of animal and plant species. Three-quarters of the rain that falls on these forests evaporates, forming clouds that cool the planet's hotter regions until they drift higher in the atmosphere and are carried to colder latitudes, where their vapour is released as warming rain. Without these forests, the temperature differences between warmer parts of the earth and colder ones would be much more extreme and unpredictable—which is what seems to be happening now. Yet if destruction of tropical forests continues at current rates, nearly all of these forests will be gone by the year 2040. The problem is compounded by one of the preferred methods of destruction—burning, which produces carbon dioxide. In South America, as many as 180,000 fires have been counted at one time.

Humans always dreamed that one day, it would be possible to see the entire planet at once, to look at the whole earth from some distant vantage point. But as we created the technology that enabled us to see our world from space, we also created the technology to change what we would see. When we look at the world from space, we can actually see the dense smog that covers an area like the Los Angeles basin, the ever-growing deserts of Africa and the smoke from the burning rainforests of Brazil. Our world has changed from what it was even a generation ago. We have created a different earth.

We have cut down forests indiscriminately, to the point where, even in an abundant land like Canada, it's uncertain whether or not we're running out of trees. To beat the heat, we have developed complex chemicals for use in air conditioners and refrigerators, not realizing that eventually they would start eating the upper ozone layer that protects us from the sun.

What's frightening is that it could easily get worse. Scientists warn, for example, that our warming of the earth may melt the polar ice caps. In some places this could trigger droughts more intense and vast than we have ever experienced. In others, such as Prince Edward Island or the Maldives in the Indian Ocean, there would be floods so high that all the land would be below sea level. The flooding, the fiery heat and the famine caused by drought may leave no place for us on the planet. The different earth we have created may in time become a silent earth.

—— **II** ——

The threat to our survival is so large that it seems overwhelming. Our environmental woes are turning out to be one big interlocking problem—too widespread for one industry to be blamed and too complicated to expect all the decisions to come from one part of society, such as consumers or the corporate world. To cope with fundamental problems like this, societies usually turn to government. But our environmental problem is too big for any one level of government to handle. It crosses borders, posing new challenges for international diplomacy, which have not been met. As things now stand, we haven't begun to practise the politics of our survival.

Our political system is locked in its own kind of toxic

cycle—a circular decision-making process that captures good intentions and contaminates them with short-term thinking and unfulfilled promises.

What appears to be movement is usually illusion. Improvements are pledged, money is spent, meetings are called, but the environment just seems to get worse. Politicians and bureaucrats move the problem along the political cycle using old, familiar tactics: blaming others, pleading that the cost of action is too high, taking vague measures rather than pinning themselves to specific goals and timetables.

Even when it's imperative for governments to break the pattern, they seem unable to do so. Municipal governments, for example, are supposed to keep our cities clean, collect the garbage and manage the local water supply. Yet, during the 1980s, all four of Toronto's sewage treatment plants broke the guidelines for how much bacteria from human waste they could pour into Lake Ontario, with the result that most of the city's beaches have been closed each summer since 1983.

Cities typically end up debating choices that are either short-term alternatives, such as expanding existing dumps, or unpalatable, such as burning the trash in smelly incinerators and causing air pollution. Until a few years ago, city garbage could be shipped far away. That became more difficult after the city of Islip, Long Island, tried to do this, putting its garbage in a barge. It travelled the Atlantic and Caribbean coasts for nearly six months and no port would accept its cargo. It brought the garbage home.

No level of government seems to cope with the environment. Theoretically, provincial or state governments should be able to sort out environmental squabbles among municipalities and establish tough, uniform protection over wide areas. Some jurisdictions, such as the Atlantic provinces, simply haven't bothered, but others, such as California or Ontario, have brought in strong regulations in recent years, only to find that this hasn't been enough. In some cases, regulations are routinely violated by polluters; for example, throughout the 1980s, between one and two out of every three large Ontario industries broke provincial water pollution guidelines, even though they had often negotiated these guidelines with the government beforehand. It wasn't until 1990 that the province ordered the temporary shutdown of a major factory because of pollution—and people had complained about pollution from this Uniroyal Chemical rubber and fungicide factory in Elmira since the 1940s. In other cases, one jurisdiction gets tough, but the neighbours don't co-operate; for years, American governments were unwilling to match Ontario's programs to cut acid rain pollution in half, since they didn't accept that the pollution was particularly harmful to the United States.

National governments have also failed to provide the kind of environmental protection that is needed. In the United States during the 1970s, environmental standards were drawn up and rules were made, but they have never been consistently enforced. For example, more than a hundred million Americans breathe air that is polluted at levels that exceed federal standards. In Canada, the situation is somewhat different—in most cases, there are no federal pollution standards. No matter what party has held power, Canadian governments have relentlessly pursued a policy of "promise anything, do little" when it comes to the environment. Where there is federal legislation, it serves chiefly to trigger federal-provincial disputes over jurisdiction—the political debate over the environment in Canada frequently consists of little more than legalistic arguments over who is responsible for which sewer pipes and who should pay to clean up contaminated dumps.

The results of this federal-provincial squabbling can be almost comical. In 1989, Canada was embarrassed by containers of PCBs (polychlorinated biphenyls) that belonged to Quebec and were heading over the Atlantic toward Wales aboard a Soviet freighter. The people in Pontypool, Wales, welcomed the shipment with makeshift Canadian flags, replacing the maple leaf with a death's head symbol. The cargo was turned away. The Canadian and Quebec governments agreed that the PCBs could be stored at a depot near Baie Comeau, Quebec, the home town of Prime Minister Brian Mulroney. This sparked a riot. Federal Environment Minister Lucien Bouchard vowed to stop such shipments of *federal* PCBs, but said that he could do little about provincial shipments. Pollution may have clearer constitutional rights than people.

As the Pontypool incident shows, environmental problems do not respect borders, and it would be logical to turn to international politics for solutions. But here, too, the solutions have been inadequate. Bilateral agreements depend on both sides enforcing all the rules, and sometimes the countries that sign them have different priorities and different ways of looking at things. There is an agreement between Canada and the United States to clean up hundreds of leaking toxic waste sites along the Niagara River. Canadians regard this issue as crucial to their heartland; the drinking water of as many as four out of ten Canadians is threatened by these dumps. But for Americans, it's just a regional priority, and when it comes to funding the cleanup, U.S. legislators have tended to see other regional issues as more important.

Of course, ultimately, global environmental issues will have to be dealt with through international agreements signed by many countries. And some such agreements have been signed over the past generation. Countries have pledged to control pollution of the oceans and to curb their use of chemicals that damage the ozone layer. And in the early 1990s, an international agreement is expected that will take measures to deal with the greenhouse effect. But while such documents are helpful in establishing principles, they're not particularly effective in practical terms. In order to get more countries involved, they tend to call for the weakest, most tentative measures possible. Even as the ozone agreement was being signed in 1987 in Montreal, the United Nations' top environment official was already calling it inadequate.

Even individuals who take action to improve the environment usually end up feeling that the odds are insurmountable. In the United States, people often launch lawsuits to see that pollution laws are properly enforced, but such cases can take years to resolve and cost millions of dollars, and, in the meantime, the pollution continues. In Canada, laws are often written so that the enforcement is left to the discretion of a minister, who may or may not decide to enforce a rule. This means that recourse to the courts is limited. And without the clout of the law, so are other options. "You can call a press conference, and that's about it," says Michael Perley, an environmental lobbyist who has spent ten years pushing for controls on acid rain.

—— **III** ——

Yet, hard as it is for individuals to make a difference for the environment, only individuals seem to manage to break the political cycle. Perhaps it is because there is no precise place for them in the political system. A citizen interrupting the government decision-making process can be like an uninvited guest who barges in at a dinner party—the crasher may be thrown out and the host may be angry, but it's impossible to ignore the unannounced visitor.

Leone Pippard barged in on the political scene and fought for two decades to save the most polluted creatures on earth. Her motivation was that slim possibility that maybe she could make a difference. In the early 1970s, while working as a Canadian Broadcasting Corporation radio producer, she found she couldn't stop thinking about the whales of the Saguenay-St Lawrence.

Pippard was first attracted to the region in 1973, when she was in her twenties. She was drawn from her downtown Toronto job by the moody beauty of the estuary. "Creative people, whether they be artists, writers or fashion designers, draw their inspiration from the bounties of nature," she says. What inspired her most, however, were the belugas. "I found them totally captivating, but also extremely threatening." She was drawn to them the way people are attracted to those they love—there is the promise of great rewards, but also upheaval and, quite possibly, heartbreak.

She discovered things about the belugas that she had never known. After three million years of evolution, they have developed a sophisticated sense of navigation, similar to the electronic sonar used by ships and submarines. Belugas communicate with each other by using a complex language, made up of high-pitched whines, squeaks and barks. They travel in groups of anywhere from two to a hundred, with offspring closely following the patterns of their mothers. These formations can turn sharply, with the precision of a dancing troupe, and they can roll over, swim upside down and move backwards, without breaking rank. It is believed that they have emotional preferences and attachments toward one another—friendships.

No one else had really noticed anything wrong. Before Pippard arrived, the whales were taken for granted, treated at different times as resources, nuisances or prey. She discovered that the hunting, or harvesting, of belugas began shortly after Jacques Cartier's 1535 visit, and continued well into this century. It's likely that their numbers declined drastically because of this, but as late as 1873 one observer noted that as many as 1,800 belugas were being caught in a good whaling season in the estuary.

However, by the 1930s the market for whale oil and hides was disappearing, and local fishermen considered the five thousand belugas a nuisance rather than a product. The fishermen thought the whales were eating the Atlantic salmon, depleting the stock and ruining the local catch. So they persuaded the Canadian government to offer a bounty: for every beluga tail brought in to the authorities, a fisherman would receive twenty-five dollars.

Between 1932 and 1939, 2,235 belugas were exterminated under the bounty program. It was then discovered that a ghastly mistake had been made. The belugas were not at all responsible for the depletion of the salmon stocks. Research revealed that their mouths were too small to eat the big fish, so the bounty was abandoned. But still the belugas were not safe. During the Second World War, the 22-foot-long whales were used for aerial bombing practice. "No one knows how many belugas were blown out of the water," Pippard says.

Yet after the bounty and the bombing ended, the whales continued to disappear: the turn-of-the-century population of 5,000 was down to 1,200 by the 1960s, moving each year toward the few hundreds that remain today. Even an untrained observer like Pippard could see that it did not make sense that the belugas were still disappearing. She became obsessed with their fate: "They were once as common as the whitecaps," she says. "Yet here, after three million years of evolution and another eleven thousand years in the St Lawrence, we were on the verge of losing them."

For three years, Pippard and a friend, Heather Malcolm, spent long hours in small boats in the waters where the whales lived and died. They drew delicate little sketches of the belugas and they photographed them. To get closer to the huge white mammals without frightening them, the researchers would put on scuba gear and dangle from the side of their boat, hanging on with their legs and sticking their heads in the water to watch. They gave them names—"Slash" for a beluga that had a long, ugly scar, "Complex" for one with a deformity so large that, from a distance, he looked like two whales. Pippard began to approach conservation groups and federal fisheries officials with her drawings, photos and notes, urging them to notice these abnormalities and look for causes.

Pippard's work paid off, at least in terms of political promises. By 1975 she was able to persuade the federal government to pay her to study them, and within a few years, established conservation organizations such as the World Wildlife Fund became interested in the whales. In 1979, the government recognized the belugas as an endangered species, and senior officials began to pay attention. Eventually, even Prime Minister Brian Mulroney took notice; after all, a good part of the whales' filth-ridden habitat was in his riding, and his home town, Baie Comeau, was not far away. In June 1988, Mulroney climbed aboard a ship in Montreal harbour and proposed to spend $110 million to clean up the St Lawrence, with $7 million of it to be spent on an underwater marine park where the river meets the Saguenay.

IV

Breaking the toxic cycle – and the political one – like this is a bit like solving a murder mystery. There are many suspects, and everyone in the room seems to be the culprit. Everyone also appears to have an alibi, yet if the culprit is not found soon, there will be more victims.

"There is a dawning realization that pollution in the St Lawrence may be threatening human health," says Pegi Dover of World Wildlife Fund Canada. She points to a ten-year study published in the 1981 *Journal of the Canadian Medical Association*. The study linked bladder cancer found in the belugas to cancers discovered in a group of aluminum workers in the Saguenay. If the toxic cycle is threatening the belugas' future, what is it doing to us?

We need to understand how the system we have established – these toxic and political cycles – works, and how it threatens to doom us. And we need to learn how to break the cycles.

"We are too ingenious," Pippard says, "because we are now using the burden of proof against ourselves. We somehow delight in saying, 'You can't prove it. You can't prove pollution is affecting these animals. You can't prove it's our chemical that's in that animal.... You can't attribute the higher incidence of illness in this area to our pollution.'"

Pippard now works full-time as an environmental activist. The fact that the political system finally started to acknowledge her concerns is what keeps her going. But if her heart is filled with hope, it is a qualified hope. Sometimes she despairs that it still takes so long to get people to understand that something has to be done.

She wishes there were a better way. "Some days I wish it would start raining red." Then we'd realize that the rain is contaminated. "We could see it falling out of the sky, and running red down the sides of our houses, across our driveways and into the streets."

CHAPTER TWO

THE GREAT GREEN WAVE

If environmentalism is just a fad, then it's the last one.
— Robert Hunter, former president of Greenpeace

The key factor in Leone Pippard's case was the change in public attitudes toward the environment. In the early 1970s, she says, "I remember how we were interviewed on "As It Happens" [the CBC radio interview show]: 'Now we have two friends of the whales.' It was tongue-in-cheek. It was not taken seriously." Now, she says, "I'm being regarded with a kind of awe and respect. It's all new." She was given a "Woman of the Year" award by the U.S. magazine, *Ms.*, in 1987. Radio and television shows started calling, begging for interviews, and she was appointed by the federal government to its "Round Table," one of the many panels of public sector and private industry experts appointed by various governments in the late 1980s. As for the belugas themselves, people who once did not know they existed now pay for sightseeing trips in the area just to watch them. Ultimately, political decisions are affected by these changes in public attitudes, partly because the politicians themselves are influenced by prevailing philosophies, and partly because if they ignore changing attitudes, they lose the next election.

Pippard first packed up and headed for the frigid, filthy river near the start of a great, green wave—a time of growing awareness about the environment and what threatens it. Toward the end of the 1960s, society developed a kind of "ecophobia," a fear that everything in the environment was somehow tainted, filled with chemicals. Politicians began to address this fear by talking about pollution as an issue that could be solved by legislative action. After an initial surge of interest there was a backlash, and people began to show more concern for the economy than the environment. Many people associated concern for the environment with economically marginal, politically left-leaning individuals and groups, the kind of people who ate brown rice and wanted to put warning labels on chocolate bars. But by the late 1980s, the green wave was on the rise again.

Society is not that different from an individual; you can't deny your experiences forever, and through the 1980s the degradation of the environment became less an abstract issue and more a fact of daily life. Toxic waste dumps leaked, water supplies were tainted, the air was dirtier and finally, in 1988, the weather got scary. This time, the Great Green Wave seems to be washing through the political structure. More than ever, it has the potential to turn the structure green.

If this is to happen—if we want politicians to actually do something about the environment instead of talk—then it's important to understand the philosophies and events that have created political and public concern. We need to know the history. What has made people so worried about the environment? How did the politicians respond when the wave began? How are they responding now? And what are the links between environmental consciousness and political action?

—— I ——

There is a direct relationship between our religious and social philosophies and the way we treat the environment.

But our philosophical attitude is ambiguous. Starting with the Bible, we have never seemed quite sure whether we were part of nature or its masters. In Genesis, God told Adam to "replenish the earth and subdue it: and have dominion." During the nineteenth century, the idea of dominion provided justification for this taming of nature; it was one of the driving forces behind the Industrial Revolution. Canada, one of the wildest, most "natural" lands, was even called a "Dominion" by the Fathers of Confederation.

Charles Darwin challenged the idea of a divinely inspired mankind improving nature in *The Origin of Species*, first published in 1859. Darwin argued that within all species, the individuals varied slightly. Some of the variations gave individual creatures a competitive advantage; since creatures tended to multiply at a faster rate than the supply of food, the most useful variations tended to be passed on through the generations. He called this natural selection, and further theorized that, over the years, species changed, or evolved. At the time—and to some extent, ever since—Darwin's theories were considered an enormous threat to religious belief, since they made humans just one more species among many. But his theories could also be interpreted as making man the end product of evolution, the top rung of the ladder, and his dominion over nature a right, by the process of natural selection. Science and industry were making the world better, pioneers were opening the West and explorers were discovering the jungle. It was only natural that humans dominate the earth, exploiting it and changing it. And it was good.

The theory of evolution also implied a certain brutality, suggesting that life was a desperate struggle for survival against competing forms of nature. So while poets, philosophers and painters may have extolled the beauties of nature, for most people nature was a place to get away from. A view of the natural environment as a more or less brutal place prevailed for all of the nineteenth century and most of the twentieth. Right up until recent days, people couldn't wait to move to the city.

This movement was particularly strong in the New World,

where nature was more raw than in the old one. North Americans have always been drawn to the idea of change for the sake of change. In his classic 1835 book *Democracy in America*, the French aristocrat Alexis de Tocqueville wrote that "America is a land of wonders, in which everything is in constant change and every change seems an improvement. The idea of novelty is there indissolubly connected with the idea of amelioration. No natural boundary seems to be set to the efforts of man; and in his eyes what is not yet done is only what he has not yet attempted to do."

Yet while it seemed obvious that taming the continent could only enhance it, by the middle of the nineteenth century, some were uneasy. "In wildness is the preservation of the world," the New England writer Henry David Thoreau wrote in 1851. "When I would re-create myself, I seek the darkest wood, the thickest and most interminable and to the citizen, most dismal swamp. I enter as a sacred place, a *Sanctum sanctorum*. There is the strength, the marrow of Nature. In short, all good things are wild and free."

Six years before he wrote those words, Thoreau set out to become as close as he could to nature, by moving to a simple hut, which cost him $28.12 to build, on the shores of Walden Pond in Concord, Massachusetts. He hoped to strip away the artifices of modern society, grow his own food (because he did, his grocery bills averaged only 27 cents a week), live a simple, solitary, Spartan life and record his observations. Actually, his life was not as Spartan as he made out; he often walked into town and tucked into a good meal at his mom's place. But his account, *Walden; or, Life in the Woods*, nevertheless remains a classic of American literature and philosophy. Highly influential, many of his observations have worked their way into modern thought so deeply that today we sometimes find ourselves accepting them without noticing. He popularized the term "civil disobedience" and wrote that "nothing is so much to be feared as fear." It is said that Franklin Roosevelt had Thoreau's book on his desk when he wrote, "The only thing we have to fear is fear itself."

Even in his time, Thoreau touched a nerve. Those who doubted progress had no political movement, and they did not really influence political decisions, aside from complaining about how the odd individual bridge or factory was ruining the scenery. There was no neat category to describe their concerns, either. But their concern about progress was really an early form of environmentalism.

Some of their complaints now seem prophetic. In 1863 a congressman and diplomat named George Perkins Marsh completed a book called *Man and Nature*, warning that "the earth is fast becoming an unfit home for its noblest inhabitant, and another era of human crime and equal human improvidence . . . would reduce it to such a condition of impoverished productiveness, of shattered surface, of climatic excess, as to threaten, the depravation, barbarism, and perhaps even extinction of the species."

Over time, the concerns became more focused. A sharp critique of what was wrong with modern thinking was developed by people like the naturalist John Muir. He was a saint-like visionary whose life foreshadowed the activism of today's environmentalists. And his vision led to one of the first political battles over the environment between the citizen and the state—and between two environmentalists.

In 1867, at age thirty-one, Muir walked fifteen hundred kilometres from Indianapolis to the Gulf of Mexico, carrying only a few personal items, the poems of Robert Burns, Milton's *Paradise Lost*, the New Testament and a journal, in which he wrote on the inside cover: "John Muir, Earth-Planet, Universe." He decided to take this journey after he was injured in an industrial accident, and on his trek he grew even more doubtful of the importance that people placed on modernity—and on the human race. "Why should man value himself as more than a small part of the great creation?" he wrote in his journal. The idea that humans are the most important creatures "is totally unsupported by facts." By the time Muir died in 1914, he had gained a worldwide reputation as a nature writer and activist. His work led directly to the preservation of huge tracts of wilderness like California's Yosemite Valley.

Muir's arch-rival was a man named Gifford Pinchot, who was born to one of the wealthiest families in the United States in 1865. He grew up in New York City, summered in France and studied at Yale, but in an iconoclastic move, decided to become a forester. This was unusual, for at the time forestry didn't exist as a profession in North America. Pinchot sought out European experts and eventually became an expert himself. He wrote extensively about forestry, and interest in the subject began to pick up. By the early 1900s, he was the first U.S. Chief Forester, responsible for 86 million acres of government-owned land.

Muir was the forerunner of the pure, uncompromising activists who hold sit-ins and pickets and won't budge an inch. Pinchot was an early version of the opposite—the environmental manager who wants to compromise for the greater good, the expert who doesn't insist on preserving resources, but doesn't want to waste them, either. It was Pinchot who popularized the word *conservation* in America. He warned in 1910 that American timber would last only thirty years at the rate it was being cut. "All the resources of the forest reserves are for use, and this use must be brought about in a thoroughly prompt and business-like manner," Pinchot said. To Muir, the idea of a "managed" forest was repugnant: "Any fool can destroy trees."

At first, Pinchot and Muir were friends. But the two men had fundamentally different philosophies. Today they are both regarded as conservationists, and what divided them is still one of the main divisions within the environmental movement that, as in their day, is often played out in the political arena.

The ultimate break between the two came when Pinchot advocated the damming of a valley called Hetch Hetchy in Yosemite National Park, to create a reservoir for San Francisco. Muir devoted much of his final years to opposing this plan, arguing that national parkland should never be tampered with. "These temple destroyers, devotees of ravaging commercialism," he wrote, "seem to have a perfect contempt for Nature, and instead of lifting their eyes to the God of the Mountains, lift them to the Almighty Dollar."

Muir lost. The valley was dammed after he died. But in some ways he won. The fight over land use in national parkland was so politically painful and intense that no one dared propose a similar scheme again in the United States. The organization Muir founded in 1892, the Sierra Club, grew into one of the most powerful environmental groups in the world, an effective lobbying organization with hundreds of thousands of members in the United States and Canada. Muir was the model for a certain type of modern environmental activist: impractical yet spellbinding, straddling the line between pest and prophet. His legacy is so far-reaching that late in the Reagan years, Interior Secretary Donald Hodel even suggested *undamming* Hetch Hetchy. (Most environmentalists ignored his suggestion, seeing it as a ploy to divert attention from the administration's environmental record.)

Both Muir and Pinchot influenced U.S. President Theodore Roosevelt, who became one of the first politicians to advocate conservation. He even held a conservation conference at the White House in 1908, where he declared: "The time has come for a change. As a people we have the right and the duty . . . to protect ourselves and our children against wasteful development of our natural resources."

The president was reacting to his times. As North America's frontiers closed at the dawn of the twentieth century, people began to long for the great outdoors. This was the time when the camping vacation first became popular. But it was a limited nostalgia—most of the time people wanted to hear about nature or visit it, not live in it. At the turn of the century, people were still worrying about pollution from horses and looking to industrial progress to solve it. The American political writer George Will points out that there were more than three million horses in North America, each of them producing as much as twenty-five pounds of manure a day. "Manure in the streets attracted swarms of flies until in hot weather, traffic ground it into dust that (a memoirist wrote) 'flew from the pavement as a sharp piercing powder, to cover our clothes, ruin our furniture and blow up into our nostrils.' Then came a solution," Will explains, "one of today's problems, the internal combustion engine."

Up to the twentieth century, the very idea of an "environment" was still at the fringe of Western thought. For example, it was not until a year before Muir headed to the mountains, in 1866, that a German scientist named Ernst Haeckel coined the term *ecology*. He defined it as "the science of relations between organisms and their environment." Nine years later, in 1875, an Austrian geologist named Eduard Suess wrote a book about the Alps, and in passing mentioned another new term, which described the various "envelopes" of the earth where there was life: the *biosphere*. Apparently, no one had needed to define such concepts before.

In Canada, where a small population felt itself spread thin across a huge wilderness, environmental ideas developed particularly slowly. In 1972, the Science Council of Canada looked back at the country's history, observing that "even intense local pollution, occasioned by an oil spill in a harbour, or by a mine in the wilderness, or by the smokestacks in coal- and wood-fired cities, was part of a scene in which some minor nuisances were taken as inevitable. There was always somewhere else to go, or else the nuisance wouldn't last long, or else the alternatives were, economically, quite out of the question."

To Canadians, the wilderness was hostile, vast and often deadly cold. The novelist and critic Margaret Atwood has pointed out in *Survival*, her study of Canadian literature, that the idea of huddling together in man-made surroundings—cities and towns—is essential to the Canadian identity: "Not surprisingly, in a country with such a high ratio of trees, lakes and rocks to people, images from Nature are almost everywhere. Added up, they depict a nature that is often dead and unanswering or actively hostile to man. . . ."

Canadians did occasionally worry that the country's resources were being wasted. At one point a prime minister of Canada looked out his window and bemoaned the endless piles of logs drifting down the Ottawa River. He wrote to the premier of Ontario that "we are recklessly destroying the timber of Canada and there is scarcely any possibility of replacing it." That was Prime Minister Sir John A. Macdonald writing to Premier John Sandfield Macdonald in 1871, when Canada was not yet four years old.

Atwood also says it's noteworthy that "Canadians were the first people to tell animal stories from the animals' point of view." The Canadians who came closest to being environmental advocates were the naturalist Ernest Thomson Seton, who wrote much-loved animal stories (from the animals' point of view), and, in the 1920s and '30s, a man named Grey Owl. Grey Owl was a popular author and lecturer who wrote about nature in lyric terms. He claimed to be an Indian from Ontario's Temagami region, but was really an Englishman named Archie Belaney, who had fallen in love with Indian lore and re-invented himself.

Canadians may have enjoyed the romance of the wild and liked hearing stories about the wilderness, but they didn't necessarily want to deal with *real* wildlife and *real* Indians.

Few worries were voiced in the nineteenth century, and concern in Canada for the environment was all but invisible during the first half of the twentieth, which saw a huge migration from farms to cities, two world wars and a depression. There were no Thoreaus or Muirs—or even prominent politicians like Theodore Roosevelt—to advance the cause of conservation. While America's national parks were forged out of a great philosophical battle over the wilderness, Canada's national parks were created for scenery; the first park, Banff, was set up in 1885 at the urging of William Van Horne, head of the Canadian Pacific Railway. He wanted to attract passengers for the new train line, so he envisioned a series of beautiful hotels in scenic areas. The Banff Springs Hotel, opened in 1888, is one of his creations.

There really were two Canadas—the Canada of the Imagination and the Canada of Reality, both of which are still thriving today. The Canada of the Imagination is the country Canadians themselves think of as theirs, but which doesn't quite exist. It's a sublime vision: a land of abundant, almost endless wilderness, where rivers tumble recklessly for thousands of miles, trees blanket the countryside and mountains shimmer beneath glassy skies. It's a country well taken care of by imaginary Canadians, a stoic-people who use the resources wisely, protect the wilderness and draw much of their solid, reserved character from the mysteries of the frozen North. It's the Canada on the back of the twenty-dollar bill, which depicts a part of Banff National Park called Moraine Lake.

The Canada of Reality is the one Canadians actually live in—a narrow, built-up area wedged between the U.S. border and the wilderness. It's less like the back of a twenty-dollar bill and more like the pictures on the old tens and ones. The tens, just recently replaced, depicted a huge industrial complex in Sarnia's "Chemical Valley"—actually a composite of several plants in the area, but based on the Polysar Ltd. facility, which began as a Crown corporation. This is reality: a brawny, industrial Canada built on government money. It's the Canada that subscribes to an approach to environmental issues known as "Iron Ring Disease." The term was coined by David Oved, who served as press secretary to Ontario's environment minister, Jim Bradley. It comes from the dull, unornamented ring worn by Canadian engineering graduates on their right baby fingers and refers to our excessive reliance on engineering to fix our environmental problems. Rather than ensuring clean drinking water by not polluting the sources, for example, the iron ring solution is to build huge treatment plants and add chlorine to the water—a costly and questionable one in terms of benefit to public health. The engineer's ring itself should suggest the limits to technology: the iron it's made of is supposed to come from a bridge near Quebec City that collapsed twice during construction, killing eighty-eight people.

The one-dollar bill, now replaced by a coin, pictured the Parliament Buildings from the Ottawa River, with a huge pile of logs being driven downstream—similar to what Sir John A. Macdonald saw from his window. It reflects another aspect of reality. It shows our resources being floated away, and polluting the water, under the noses of our politicians.

—— II ——

Despite the urgings of a few early conservationists, by the end of the Second World War there was very little public concern about the environment and therefore very little incentive for politicians to defend it. Iron Ring Disease was widespread, and most people believed that virtually any new technology was for the better. When Canada built its first experimental nuclear reactor at Chalk River in northern Ontario, even a warning by the powerful federal cabinet minister C. D. Howe that "the plant may entail hazards of a nature and on a scale beyond all previous experience" failed to stop it. When, on December 12, 1952, his warning came true and more than four million litres of radioactive water spilled into the reactor's basement, nobody raised an eyebrow about the safety of such facilities, and Canada's nuclear program went on unchecked.

A classic case of the prevailing climate was the suit against the Kalamazoo Vegetable and Parchment Company, or KVP, in the late 1940s. A private citizen went to court to fight the company, which had set up a pulp mill on the Spanish River at Espanola in northern Ontario. The mill's toxic pollution was more than a thousand times higher than the province's guidelines: fish died as far as fifty-five kilometres away. The citizen won an injunction against the mill, so in 1950 the Ontario government passed the KVP Act. This simple statute provided that "every injunction heretofore granted against the KVP Company Limited . . . restraining the Company from polluting the waters of the Spanish River, is dissolved." The premier at the time, Leslie Frost, later became a member of KVP's board of directors.

As an American reporter looking back on the years after

the Second World War said: "Nobody was worried about pollution. Conservation groups were bothered about parts of the wilderness . . . but that was an entirely different thing. That was an issue of esthetics, not health. Nobody seemed to mention air pollution or waste that might overwhelm the space in which to put it."

Then, in 1962, came *Silent Spring*, and people's indifference to the environment was truly shattered. The shock was administered by a soft-spoken author and biologist, Rachel Carson, who previously had been known mostly for her graceful descriptions of marine life. She offered up "a fable for tomorrow" – the story of a town actually killed by pollution. In this town, "which might easily have a thousand counterparts," children would be stricken while playing and die within hours. Birds "trembled violently and could not fly." Roadsides were lined with browned and lifeless vegetation. It was a "spring without voices," where "even the streams are now lifeless." Perhaps the most terrifying aspect of this imaginary place was that the people who lived there were doing it to themselves. "For the first time in the history of the world," Carson wrote, "every human being is now subjected to contact with dangerous chemicals, from the moment of conception to death."

The threats are so obvious now that there is a tendency to forget: it took a great deal of persistent, lonely nagging by people like Rachel Carson to get anyone to notice there was something wrong. The main point of *Silent Spring* was to warn of the dangers of the pesticide DDT (dichloro-diphenyl-tricholoroethane), a compound that was developed in 1874, but which was not used widely until the Second World War. In the 1940s, DDT was considered a godsend. A *Life* magazine feature in 1948 showed a photo in which "children romp in fog [of pesticide] after the fog truck" has sprayed a wooded area. "The fog covers everything with a submicroscopic and stainless film of poison, lethal to insects but harmless to humans, animals and food." Today, if we are appalled by this description, it is because of *Silent Spring*.

Carson was by no means the first to warn of the dangers of

pesticides. Concerns began to surface just after the heyday of DDT in the 1940s. Throughout the 1950s, as the Canadian conservationist Roderick Haig-Brown pointed out, "ornithologists at several universities had been observing, measuring and reporting the disastrous effects of DDT," and in 1961, the National Film Board produced a documentary on the pesticide controversy called *Deadly Dilemma*.

What made *Silent Spring* so different was the intense public reaction to the book. *Silent Spring* sold 40,000 copies in advance of its publication, with 200,000 more ordered before it came out. Its importance was recognized by President John F. Kennedy, who mentioned it during a press conference and appeared to be familiar with the material: people who knew him believe he had read excerpts in the *New Yorker* magazine. It also appeared just after the thalidomide scare, when the side-effects of a drug taken by pregnant women had led to children born with deformed arms or legs, and people were feeling a general fear of chemicals. *Silent Spring* was a comprehensive statement of this fear. As Carson said: "In each of my books I have tried to say that all the life of the planet is inter-related. We have already gone very far in our abuse of this planet. Some awareness of this problem has been in the air but the ideas had to be crystallized, the facts had to be brought together in *one place*."

Silent Spring was, in the words of one newspaper critic, "the year's great fright," and among those frightened were the chemical companies. Carson's biographer, Paul Brooks, speaking at a tenth anniversary celebration of the book's publication, explained that "the paradox is that the really hysterical reaction on the part of the chemical companies and so on was not because 'we can't sell so much DDT and our profits are going to fall.' DDT is a very small part of all this operation. The really scary thing was that she was questioning the whole attitude of industrial society toward the natural world. This was heresy and this had to be suppressed.... This is what caused a really hysterical reaction to *Silent Spring*, and it is the thing now that has made her almost a prophet among the young."

Carson's measured warnings aroused a storm of controversy. "Silent Spring is now noisy summer," said the *New
York Times* on July 22, 1962. The book had not even been
published yet, other than in the *New Yorker* excerpts. That
August, the Velsicol Chemical Corp. sent Carson's publisher
a five-page registered letter, complaining of "inaccurate and
disparaging statements" and suggesting that the publisher
might want to reconsider its plans. After *Silent Spring* was
published, Carson was subjected to vitriolic attack: chemical
companies questioned her data, her expertise and her
credibility. The president of one called her "a fanatic
defender of the cult of the balance of nature."

In 1963, she appeared at a U.S. Senate subcommittee
hearing, defending her views and demanding new laws to
restrict and control the use of pesticides. During a break in
the hearing, one agricultural expert spoke pointedly about
"emotional women in garden clubs." Another witness, a
professor who served as a consultant to the Shell Chemical
Company, joined in the attack. "Miss Carson is talking
about health effects that will take years to answer," said Dr
Mitchell R. Zavon, then Associate Professor of Industrial
Medicine at the University of Cincinnati. Pest sprays were
needed to grow food for hungry millions, he suggested, and
people like Carson were a threat to this food supply. "These
peddlers of fear are going to feast on the famine of the
world—literally."

A generation later, in 1989, Zavon still felt much the same.
He concedes that "*Silent Spring* alerted the public. [It] got
the public and the political community to pay attention to
the environment. [This is] something that more conservative
scientists had not been able to succeed in doing." But he
adds that "if you analyze *Silent Spring* you'll find that, in
terms of a scientific report, it's terribly padded."

Moreover, he still believes that the wave of environmentalism Carson unleashed with *Silent Spring* was misguided.
It led directly to what he considers panicky moves like the
evacuation of the Love Canal neighbourhood that had been
built atop a toxic dump. "I feel it's a tragedy that all these

people have had their lives disrupted. And there isn't a scintilla of evidence that anybody was ever harmed by it except for those few kids who got hold of phosphorous on the surface a few years back and got some burns. . . . I have a good friend whose husband just died, who worked across from the Hyde Park dump [another, larger dump near the Love Canal site]. I will never persuade her that the dust blowing from that site into the plant where he worked, did not cause his death. He died of a chronic myocarditis. And she will never convince me otherwise. So we've agreed not to discuss it any further.

"And that's the problem with many of these people. They don't have enough understanding of cause and effect."

Zavon, now living in Lewiston, N. Y., served for years as medical director for Occidental Chemical, the company that owns some of the most highly toxic dump sites along the Niagara River, including the Love Canal, and Hyde Park, one of the largest storehouses of dioxin in the world.

In some cases, attacks on *Silent Spring* were as virulent in Canada as they were in the United States. The book was called "inaccurate" and "exaggerated" by a University of Western Ontario professor, A. W. A. Brown. The *Toronto Telegram* reported his view that "proper use" of insecticides would not hurt wildlife. "Some of her statements are wrong and others are entirely misleading. She has harmed people doing a public service job with insecticides," he said. Without elaborating, he spun a vague conspiracy theory: "I think Miss Carson wrote herself into a mood after being influenced by 'certain people' against insect control."

Some of the criticism presaged the kinds of reactions that later became common in environmental battles: we sympathize, but you have to admit there are other factors. The *New York Times* reported that while most chemical companies "say they can find little error of fact" in *Silent Spring*, "what they do criticize, however, are the extensions and implications that she gives to isolated case histories. . . . The industry feels that she has presented a one-sided case and has chosen to ignore the enormous benefits in increased food production and decreased incidence of disease that have accrued from the development and use of modern pesticides." Companies were "annoyed also at the implications that the industry itself has not been alert." A research chemist from the Dow Chemical Company acknowledged that there were problems in the past, but accused Carson of indulging in "hindsight"—implying that by 1962, everything had been straightened out.

In spite of these attacks, there were some immediate political effects. In Canada, the book triggered much discussion in Parliament. Toronto Liberal MP (later Senator) Stanley Haidasz, a doctor, told the House of Commons in December 1962 that North Americans "have been stunned by the revelations" in Carson's book. "In this document," he said, "we find an indictment of the indiscriminate use of new chemicals which are contaminating our food and our whole environment. This should warn us to be careful, and to prod governments to review their legislation to ensure the safety of the public and the survival of nature." A British Columbia New Democrat, H. W. Herridge, also went on at great length about *Silent Spring*. "Any member of Parliament who is interested in the health of our nation and in the health of our wildlife should purchase this book," he told the House. "I can speak from personal experience . . . of having had cattle die on the range because of eating grass which had been covered by some of these insecticides. . . . I am one of those who believe that we are interfering with the balance of nature."

But it took seven more years for the pesticide to be banned in Canada. During that time, the problem of DDT was considered through the normal political channels, with the usual inconclusive result. Progressive Conservative MP Gerald Baldwin recounted for Parliament how, in the aftermath of *Silent Spring*, he had served on a committee in 1963, "with wide powers of reference to examine the impact of herbicides and pesticides on the environment, on the human existence. We invited Miss Carson to appear before the committee. Because of ill health she was unable to come to see us, but she sent us some documentation. We had a very full examination of this matter but toward the end of the committee's hearings the representatives of the agricultural chemical industry appeared before it. I am not faulting them. It was a lobby; there was no question about that."

The industry lobbyists didn't really have to press their case too forcefully. Many issues—not just environmental ones—get caught in the political cycle and remain there indefinitely, and that's what happened to DDT. In the tumultuous atmosphere of federal politics in 1963, the committee ran out of time. When Lester Pearson's Liberals took over from John Diefenbaker's Progressive Conservatives in mid-1963, the parliamentary committee recommended that a new committee be established, and the new committee, in Baldwin's words, "did nothing at all."

Much later, on November 3, 1969, a ban was announced in Parliament by Prime Minister Pierre Elliott Trudeau: "In the light of the persistence of DDT, its deleterious effects on wildlife, and lack of clearcut evidence about its long-term effects on man, it is prudent to curtail contamination of the environment by it." Shortly before Trudeau's announcement, a newly formed environmental group, Pollution Probe, had confronted Health Minister John Munro with facts about DDT, essentially the same data Carson had written about seven years earlier. Despite the parliamentary discussions, "the case had never been made [in Canada] for its immediate ban," said Probe's founder Donald Chant. "It was banned within a week. The officials of Mr Munro's department had failed in their duty of protecting our health and welfare." The move offered one of the first clues as to how to break through the normal political cycle—ignore it.

It was a rare exception for Canada to act ahead of other countries to protect the environment, but with DDT this was the case. It was not until 1972, ten years after the publication of *Silent Spring*, that DDT was banned in the United States. It is no longer in use in North America, but is still used by many developing countries; the United States exports as much as 18 million kilograms of DDT each year.

The fact was, what worked with getting DDT banned was an outside intervention, pressure from a force just beginning to gather momentum—the "wild-eyed environmentalists."

Once they came along, politicians who had mulled over the issue, studying the possible consequences of action while the consequences of inaction remained unchecked, suddenly moved to get things done. It was an important new technique and, at the time, it seemed like a new, easy way to do things: a few people get together, pick a name, gather facts and present their case, and all of a sudden the politicians pay attention to the environment. It was the beginning of the Great Green Wave.

Carson herself did not live to experience the wave she helped create. She died of cancer in April 1964. By then, she was already recognized as an environmental hero; the U.S. interior secretary was a pallbearer at her funeral, and Prince Philip sent the largest wreath. *Silent Spring* laid bare the toxic cycle, and it sketched the political cycle that made it difficult to bring about change from within the system. Carson didn't use such terms directly; ostensibly she was warning us about chemicals. But really, she was warning us about everything.

—— **III** ——

By 1970, The Great Green Wave had turned into a huge swell of public concern. At first, politicians feigned indifference—Prime Minister Pierre Trudeau dismissed environmentalism as "the latest kick"—but it soon became clear that no leader could afford to ignore it for long.

On April 22, 1970, hundreds of thousands of people took the day off work to celebrate the first "Earth Day." They collected trash, returned bottles, gawked at experimental electric cars that did not have smelly tailpipes. In Canada as well as the United States, they waved a stylized U.S. flag, with green and white stripes and an Earth Symbol in the corner where the stars usually went. Until then, the colour green had symbolized newcomers, envy or money; from this day, it began to symbolize the environment.

Earth Day was a worldwide mixture of protest and party, and it turned the environment into a full-fledged political issue. The *New York Times* remarked, with just a hint of cynicism, "Conservatives were for it. Liberals were for it. Democrats and Republicans were for it. So were the ins, the outs. . . . It was Earth Day, and, like Mother's Day, no man in public office could be against it."

In Buffalo, N.Y., civic officials paraded in front of city hall with brooms and shovels. In West Virginia, marchers picked up nearly five tonnes of trash along an eight-kilometre stretch of highway and dumped it on the steps of a courthouse. In San Francisco, a group calling itself "Environmental Vigilantes" protested against oil slicks by pouring oil into a reflecting pool at the office of the Standard Oil Company of California.

In Toronto, several members of the Ontario Legislature handed out packets of phosphate-free detergent to passersby and told them about how it was less harmful to lake water than ordinary suds. George Kerr, the province's resource minister, suggested that no-return pop bottles could soon be banned (they never were). A week before, he had announced that soon he would devote his full attention as a minister to pollution control, making him Ontario's first environment minister, while John Robarts, Ontario's premier, delivered a speech in which he focused on pollution and pledged to control it.

The movement spread into popular culture and philosophy. In a bestselling book called *The Population Bomb*, an American named Paul Erlich predicted almost gleefully that overpopulation would cause massive famines in the near future, which he said could kill as many as a billion people. Another influential work called *Small Is Beautiful* by E. F. Schumacher argued for a total reorganization of society, away from large-scale industrial growth in favour of locally produced goods and less emphasis on material well-being: "This implies, above all else, the development of a life-style which accords to material things their proper, legitimate place, which is secondary and not primary." And in 1972, a group of thirty scientists and academics known as the Club of Rome—an organization that is still influential today—warned that the earth's resources were running out, pointedly naming its report *The Limits to Growth*.

Newspapers described how people "listened to countless speeches by politicians, scientists and other leaders," and politicians responded to Earth Day in three ways: they talked, they made promises, and they unleashed a blizzard of legislation.

Former U.S. Vice-President Hubert Humphrey called on the United Nations to set up a worldwide environmental agency, a suggestion that was carried out within three years. "We can do things internationally, and we must," he said. Congress unanimously approved the Clean Air Act, which set national air quality standards for the first time and attempted to crack down on the industries and vehicles that fouled the air. Shortly before this, on New Year's Day 1970, President Richard Nixon had signed a law called the National Environmental Policy Act. It required U.S. government agencies to assess the "environmental impact" of any projects they proposed, and to provide alternatives. It also created a council to advise the president on environmental issues. It was one of the most sweeping pieces of environmental legislation ever passed, and it provided the legal framework for most of the environmental battles in that country over the next two decades. The legislation was later copied in Ontario in 1976, though not in Ottawa.

The Canadian Parliament did notice the environmental wave, however. All parties approved a measure that gave Canada more control over the frigid northern coast, the Arctic Waters Pollution Prevention Act. And in early 1971, Fisheries Minister Jack Davis talked in Parliament about a bill proposing a new Department of the Environment, which he would head. "It deals with the animate. It deals with the living. It deals with the renewable. It is primarily biological in its orientation. It puts the accent on quality rather than on quantity. It must often be soft-nosed, not hard-nosed. It must put ecology ahead of economics whenever a choice has to be made between the two. However, ecology and economic growth are not always opposed." There seemed to be a consensus that the time to protect the environment had come. In June 1972, the Science Council of Canada presented a report on the environment to the federal government titled *It Is Not Too Late—Yet*. Canada was "still a relatively minor contributor" to environmental problems, but "already there are many examples of local blight . . . ," it warned. "It may be later than we think." The consensus was worldwide. On June 5, 1972, representatives from 112 nations gathered in Stockholm to attend the World Conference on the Human Environment. The 1,200 delegates called for reducing pollution of air, water and food and proposed to set up an international network for monitoring the atmosphere. The 110 stations—3 of which would be in Canada, 4 in the United States—were to be built in relatively clean areas and would monitor dust, the earth's protective ozone layer and the buildup of carbon dioxide, which even then appeared to be warming the earth unnaturally. They called on governments to do more to prevent pollution from crossing borders, and it was in anticipation of the conference that most governments set up their first environment departments.

The green wave seemed unstoppable. Environmentalists gained influence. Newspapers and broadcasters paid attention to the groups they founded, and many of them captured the public's imagination. (Ironically, one of the best known groups, Greenpeace, began in Vancouver as the *Don't* Make a Wave Committee, in protest against testing of nuclear weapons at sea.) Monte Hummel, one of Pollution Probe's earliest members, recalls, "When we started there were no environmental ministries in government, no environmental protection acts, no environmental impact assessments, no environmental consultants, no university faculties or institutes of environmental studies." Attitudes had changed overnight and all the necessary legislation seemed to be in place.

—— **IV** ——

But by 1975, the green wave had begun to subside and, by 1980, there was Ronald Reagan. Many of the activists saw trouble coming almost as soon as the new laws and bureaucracies came into place. Just two months after Earth Day, Donald Chant complained that since founding Pollution Probe, he and his group were spending too much time dealing with unco-operative government officials: "Many have proved to be petty, narrow-minded worshippers of red tape who clutch their secret data on pollution, locked away from the very public whose servants they are supposed to be, all the while mouthing the standard reassurances that there is nothing to fear." All these environment ministries and meetings and conferences didn't seem to be achieving much. As Monte Hummel said, years later: "We must ask ourselves whether all this elaborate institutional claptrap, the careers and professional vested interest we've constructed has led to measurable improvement in the environment itself. If the measure of self-delusion is jargon, we're in serious trouble. If we continue to think we've actually solved problems by simply creating plans to solve them, we're finished."

These misgivings are significant because they came from people who wanted to do something about the environment. The public was likely to be even more sceptical, particularly as environmentalism became associated with the forced energy conservation of the 1970s. In 1973, the oil-producing countries started raising their prices, and by the end of the decade the price of fuel had quadrupled. People were encouraged – sometimes through regulation – to restrict driving and use less heat and electricity, and this made many unhappy. For the first time in four decades, North Americans felt their standard of living declining.

There was also a classic case in the 1970s that suggested the laws and agencies were more trouble than they were worth. In 1978, the U. S. Supreme Court prevented the Tennessee Valley Authority from finishing a multi-million-dollar power dam, although it was near completion, on the ground that it threatened an endangered species of fish called the snail darter. Few people had heard of the snail darter and, to many, environmental protection seemed to be good for fish, but bad for people.

Environmentalism began to be associated with left-wing, affluent, impractical academic types—leftover hippies (from an era many abhorred) who would be the least harmed if industries were closed. Putting limits on economic growth meant telling companies they couldn't expand, telling factories they couldn't make things that people wanted to buy, telling ordinary people there would be no new jobs. In North America, a potential backlash always lay beneath the surface, and to tell people in peacetime to do with less was to ask for political trouble, which politicians were quick to spot. "If there's ever a flat choice between smoke and jobs tilt toward jobs," Richard Nixon told his speechwriter, William Safire, later a newspaper columnist.

U.S. President Jimmy Carter was less well attuned. In the summer of 1979, he connected the energy shortage to a kind of national malaise. Speaking from the White House Oval Office, he said, "The true problems of our nation are much deeper, deeper than gasoline lines or energy shortages." He called it "a crisis of confidence . . . a crisis that strikes at the very heart and soul of our national will." Politically, it was making a fatal connection to associate conserving energy with bad things like gas lineups. Carter had generally supported laws to protect the environment, and as the 1980 presidential election approached, his Republican opponent did well by seizing upon this. Ronald Reagan accused environmentalists of "elitism" and argued that "the limits-to-growth people who are so influential in the Carter Administration are telling us, in effect, that the American economic pie is shrinking, that we all have to settle for a smaller slice." Reagan said it would be best for "government to get out of the way while the rest of us make a bigger pie so that everybody can have a bigger slice."

Reagan took this argument a step further. He questioned whether there was anything wrong with the environment in the first place, making his famous "tree" remark. "Approximately 80 percent of our air pollution stems from hydrocarbons released by vegetation," he said in 1980, "so let's not go overboard in setting and enforcing tough emission standards from man-made sources." The next week he said he had been misquoted. "I didn't say 80 percent. I said 92 percent, 93 percent, pardon me. And I am right." In fact, he was wrong. Industrial sources are believed responsible for up to 90 percent of the nitrogen oxides that blow across the continent, causing smog and acid rain.

It didn't matter. Reagan became president in 1981, and the signal for politicians was plain: abandoning environmental issues worked. Reagan put officials in charge of wilderness and environmental protection who explicitly questioned the need for such protection; he assigned Vice-President George Bush to a task force to look at easing regulations, and Bush quickly took aim at rules such as those controlling the dumping of toxic waste and requiring pesticides to be registered by their manufacturers.

In Canada, the anti-environmentalism backlash was less pronounced and most federal and provincial politicians kept up their pro-environment rhetoric. But from 1980 to mid-1985 no significant moves were made to protect the environment: there were no new laws of any consequence, and the few programs put forward were meaningless. In the case of some of Canada's most pressing environmental problems, the mood in the United States was critical, since American co-operation was needed in dealing with them. Acid rain pollution, for example, had declined by nearly 20 percent during the 1970s, but it remained constant or increased during the early 1980s.

—— V ——

In the late 1980s, at the beginning of a new decade, environmentalism rose again, more powerfully than ever before. Opinion polls showed an incredible swing in the public mood. According to an April 1988 survey by the Environics Research Group, nine out of ten Canadians believed pollution to be harming their health, and 93 percent feared they were being poisoned by substances that have not yet been identified. Another Environics survey that year found that 84 percent of Canadians wanted the government to do more to fight pollution, and 77 percent said they would prefer to buy environmentally safe products, even if they cost more. The figures were similar in the United States that year, where a CBS/*New York Times* poll found that 85 percent of those surveyed believed that pollution regulations could not be too strict and the cost could not be too high. In 1981, only 40 percent had agreed with this.

As the degradation of the environment during the 1980s has become more obvious with each passing year, the public has grown more restless and unforgiving of politicians who belittle their fears. In 1985 in northern Ontario, a car in which a pregnant woman was travelling was splashed by cancer-linked PCBs, which spilled from a truck. It happened during a provincial election campaign, and the Ontario environment minister at the time, Morley Kells, remarked that the amount of poison spilled would not harm a pregnant woman, only a rat. He lost the election, and analysts say his comment helped his party lose power after more than four decades in control of the province.

Ideas that once appeared strange now seem plausible and there is a new, cosmic attitude to pollution. In the late 1960s, a British scientist named James Lovelock put forward an elegant theory, which he called *Gaia*, after the Greek goddess of the earth. He said that we should think of the earth as one big biological system, a single living being that adapts to physical or chemical changes. "This is in contrast to the conventional wisdom which held that life adapted to the planetary conditions as it and they evolved their separate ways." One species can alter the environment; humans, say, can accomplish that by raising the temperature or cutting down trees. If it becomes hotter or more of a desert, this will be an extreme change for the human race—maybe too extreme for survival. But in terms of the earth's history the change will be minor. The planet will seek its own balance, and this sometimes involves the elimination of a particular species. Why not humans? After all, 99 percent of all the life forms that ever existed have become extinct. We could easily turn the planet into a silent earth.

In 1987, the United Nations World Commission on

Environment and Development issued a report called *Our Common Future*, which suggested *Gaia* was right. It said humanity was "changing planetary systems, fundamentally. Many such changes are accompanied by life-threatening hazards." This was "the new reality—from which there is no escape." The commission was headed by Norway's prime minister, Gro Harlem Brundtland, and included twenty-two members—two from Canada. "When the century began," it said, "neither human numbers nor technology had the power radically to alter planetary systems. As the century closes, not only do vastly increased human numbers and their activities have that power, but major, unintended changes are occurring in the atmosphere, in soils, in waters, among plants and animals and in the relationships among all of these. The rate of change is outstripping the ability of scientific disciplines and our current capabilities to assess and advise. It is frustrating the attempts of political and economic institutions, which evolved in a different, more fragmented world, to adapt and cope."

A year after the Brundtland report came out, the Canadian government sponsored a major international conference in Toronto on the greenhouse effect, called "The Changing Atmosphere." The name had several meanings. It suggested the changing chemical composition of the sky, which seems to be warming the earth. It also suggested the changing political atmosphere.

"I am an environmentalist—always have been," George Bush said during his 1988 presidential campaign. Around the same time, Prime Minister Brian Mulroney went on French-language radio as he prepared to call an election of his own, and mused, "We need a collective commitment . . . to give ourselves, as citizens, the best environment that could exist." Earth Day again triggered hundreds of events and demonstrations in April 1990, and the environment has once again become a motherhood issue.

We are on the crest of a new green wave that could be the springboard for political action against pollution. But history has shown that the wave may not be effective or lasting. How can we make it count? What are we up against?

Has anything been achieved already? With the environment apparently in more trouble now than ever, knowing what's wrong and who's trying to fix it may be the only way to avoid past mistakes and a bleak future. In a world of acid rain, trash-filled seas, dangerous weather and tainted food, what is the political record?

PART TWO

CYCLES OF DOOM

CHAPTER THREE

"WHO WANTS TO SWIM AMONG THE GALL BLADDERS?"

Mother, may I go and swim?
Yes, my darling daughter.
Hang your clothes on yonder limb.
But don't go near the water.

Nursery Rhyme

Among the many reasons why we're now more worried about the environment than ever is the fact that the mess is starting to cramp our style. While the problems always sounded frightening, they used to be distant and abstract. Newspaper editors would yawn at stories about things like toxic waste or dirty water. "What's the big deal?" one respected Canadian editor used to ask. "Why should we care? No one died."

His point was that even if the environment was in trouble, this wasn't necessarily a *people* problem. Environmentalists talked about how we'd all have to change our ways, but to most people, drastic adjustments didn't seem necessary. Nobody liked pollution, but in your daily routines you weren't particularly affected by it. If you came of age after the Second World War, you could eat, drink, breathe, work and play in 1980 much as you had done in 1960, and be reasonably sure that it was safe. Cleaning up the planet was a long-term project for the far away future; the environment wasn't going to come and get you.

Now, as the twenty-first century approaches, certain problems leap out at us, jumping quickly from theory to reality. We have started noticing all the garbage we threw away, because we seem to be running out of places to throw it. Our beaches are so polluted they're nauseating. It has come to the point where you literally have to step through blood and guts to get to the water—if you dare. These are no longer distant issues of passing interest. We need the answers, quickly, to some practical questions. Why do we make so much garbage, using products like disposable diapers? How did the beaches get so dirty? Why does our political system have so much trouble anticipating these problems and finding solutions? Maybe no one in our society has died yet from the environment—although that's arguable—but now we know why we should care. The environment *is* coming to get us.

Yet as the problems close in, the answers often seem farther away. Making everyday changes in the home might help, for example by recycling cans and bottles, but it won't help enough, because industries continue to make disposable goods and pour out waste. Telling industries to clean up is another approach, but this too has limits. To clean up without destroying the economy, companies turn to technology to manage their pollution and waste, and sometimes it's hard to see the improvement: fast-food containers used to be made of paper, using up trees; then they were made of plastic, which piles up in garbage dumps, and of foams that damage the earth's outer ozone layer. The alternative to technological changes is to shift away from the practice of making things that are supposed to be thrown away, but that would mean changing our industries and economy in dramatic, costly ways. We couldn't be a consumer society anymore. But we don't know how to be anything else.

This is where politics was supposed to step in, pushing us gently in the direction of change with sensible, balanced regulation to protect the environment. But of course, this hasn't happened. With people unsure about how far they wanted to go in their everyday sacrifices, and industries debating the merits of various technologies and how change might affect the bottom line, those who write and pass laws had little incentive to move quickly. Plans to reduce garbage or clean up beaches would come up for discussion, then the immediate threat would fade away, and so would the discussion. Then they'd come up again and the whole cycle would be repeated. We all helped create the situation.

The reason this seems unacceptable now is that the environment *is* a people problem. In a way, we're lucky that events made this clear in the late 1980s. Thanks to our garbage, we've been given a taste of how miserable life can be in a contaminated environment. And we're starting to see how difficult it can be to resolve even one aspect of our environmental problem, how hard it is to reconcile the competing interests of companies, environmental groups, politicians – and the rest of us.

—— I ——

The taste of misery came in the middle of 1988. It was The Summer of No Escape.

The heat was terrible. In the West and on the Prairies there was an awful drought. Forests burned, crops that should have been waist-high died after reaching a few sickly centimetres. And in the East, temperatures routinely rose above 30 degrees Celsius. The air seemed to burn, the cities stank. It was Toronto's hottest summer since 1949. It was Winnipeg's hottest summer ever. It was so hot, people stopped making jokes about the heat. It was as if, this time, the earth was laughing at us. One environmentalist explained, "This summer the environment appears to have reached and exceeded its carrying capacity."

There was the feeling that we were trapped, that the land was sour, and that environmental horrors were also closing in on us from the seas. It had never been a secret that we use the oceans as repositories for trash and poison. For years, scientists had monitored coastal waters and warned that the contamination would become intolerable. Now the water was a No-go Zone.

It happened so suddenly that it can even be pinpointed to the day: July 6, 1988, one of the hottest days of the most scorching summer in memory. On that day, people who headed to beaches on Long Island and northern New Jersey were met with a nasty surprise. In with the tide came tampons, syringes, bloodstained bandages, dead rats and human stomach linings that had been discarded by hospitals. There were also "greaseballs" – clumps of raw sewage two inches thick – and more than a hundred vials of blood. A few of these contained the hepatitis-B virus and at least five of them tested positive for AIDS antibodies.

The authorities tried to sound reassuring. "A beachgoer has a better chance of being hit by a meteorite than of contracting AIDS by touching this material," said an official from New Jersey's Department of Environmental Conservation. Others pointed out that AIDS and hepatitis viruses can't survive long in open water.

Officials vowed to track down the source. "We would love to pin it on somebody," said William Muszynski of the U. S. Environmental Protection Agency. A New York official, Marlene Gold, said the city was "looking at some medical facilities and fly-by-night clinics that have presented problems in the past." Finally, a medical worker was arrested, after bits of medical waste were found scattered outside a doctor's office. In New York, doctors are supposed to use special "red bags" to dispose of used needles, bandages and surgical tubing caked with blood. The allegation was that at this office, the red bag had been tossed into an ordinary green garbage bag. The implication was that this trash made its way into the water, and then to the beach.

New York's mayor at the time, Ed Koch, was optimistic that the arrest would help clear up the sickening pollution problem. "We don't have the smoking gun, but we're closer to the bullets," he said. If so, what was the answer to the crucial question: How did all that awful stuff get into the water? It couldn't have been just one person or one bag, and perhaps not even just one incident.

New York City hospitals alone generate more than 19 million kilograms of red-bag waste a year, and the garbage that goes into red bags is just a quarter of all the trash the hospitals throw away. Each day across the state, hospitals, clinics, nursing homes and labs toss out 113 tonnes of infectious waste. The red bags are supposed to be burned. Under state law, hospitals are required to burn half of all their red bags in their own incinerators. They can contract with private firms to burn the rest. Somebody decided not to burn the waste. Somebody—from either a private hauling firm, a lab, a clinic or a hospital—decided it would be easier to toss the garbage instead. Somebody may have just dumped it in the ocean.

Elements of the waste were traceable. Blood vials, for example, have brand names and come in numbered lots. But there was so much of the stuff. Within a month of the first discoveries, nearly two thousand needles, vials and blood-caked bits of garbage had been found. "It's like finding a ball at the bottom of the hill and there are thirty houses on the hill," said a Coast Guard official.

Different lifeguards also had different stories on how often they had seen garbage like this on the beaches. Some said they had often seen needles before among other garbage, but, remarkably, they hadn't given it much thought. Some said that this was something new, others said that it wasn't but they had never seen so many needles in such a short time. In that hot July of 1988, on the eastern shores of New York's Staten Island as many as seven hundred needles were being plucked from the beach each day.

But the precise details didn't really matter to most people. It was so nauseating. "The public is reacting with anger, disgust and fear," said Jacqueline Warren of the Natural Resources Defense Council, an American environmental organization. "Who wants to swim among the gall bladders?"

Testifying before a U.S. congressional subcommittee, she said that however small the risk, "wastes washing up on the beaches expose the public to risks from puncture and possible contraction of infectious disease." There was also the possibility of "additional symptoms, such as rashes, and disease carried by animals attracted to the wastes." Actually, in terms of physical risk, the danger posed by the needles and blood on the beach was probably minimal. In that sense, the experts who played down the threat weren't wrong. A report in the *Marine Pollution Bulletin*, a monthly journal that monitors contamination of the world's oceans, noted that "the amounts of wastes were not large and health officials did not consider the incidents a significant public health threat."

The U.S. government's Office of Technology Assessment held a workshop to figure out what what had happened. According to the report in the *Marine Pollution Bulletin* "experts seemed to generally agree that typical household wastes are more infectious than hospital wastes." Also, anyone could avoid trouble by simply staying away from the beach. All of this was intended to provide some kind of comfort. A civic official from a Long Island community predicted that "weeks from now, this may be a distant, hazy memory."

But it was not to be. As Warren said, public anger, disgust and fear prevailed. Politicians responded with unusual speed, some of them personally revolted, all sensing that the public mood was approaching panic. On August 9, about a month after the AIDS-infected vials were found, the U.S. Senate unanimously passed a law making it a crime to dump medical waste in the ocean. It called for phasing out the dumping of sewage sludge, the raw material of "greaseballs," by 1992. It established fines of up to $250,000 (U.S.) and five years in jail for violation of the waste-dumping ban. The Senate also voted to set up a demonstration project, to track medical wastes in the U.S. Northeast.

State governments got involved as well. They joined in the tracking program, agreeing that anyone involved in the disposal of medical waste would have to do better paperwork than in the past. They talked about building new medical incinerators, patrolling the coasts more often and doing more investigating of polluters who may be breaking the law.

The resort city of Asbury Park—Bruce Springsteen's home town—was hit with a million-dollar fine by the New Jersey government. The city's sewage treatment plant was obsolete; as a result, seven resort-area beaches had been closed. The fine was a record for the state, but public fear and resentment had reached new levels, too. The water at those beaches had been full of greaseballs, containing bacteria that could make swimmers ill with diarrhea, earaches and nausea.

When the blood-infested trash first turned up on the East Coast, the beaches were closed and the people were sent home. More than eighty kilometres of beach remained off limits temporarily. Some of them reopened, but they had to be closed when more of the medical mess washed in. Hospital waste was also discovered on the shores of Rhode Island and Massachusetts. Soon the authorities didn't have to bother closing beaches. At the few New York–area beaches that remained open during the rest of the summer, attendance dropped by more than 85 percent.

A year after the horrible washups, the *New Republic* reported that "most estimates place the amount of medical debris at only between one percent and ten percent of all debris that washed ashore last summer, with one [government] report comparing it to to one lunch bag's worth for every two five-ton truckloads of debris . . . 1988 was the year of the misidentified floating object. Cigar containers were reported as blood vials, animal fat became human organs, household rubber gloves became surgical gloves, sewer rats became laboratory rats." The stomach linings were animal guts, the needles were the kind used by diabetics. If so, the culprits were easy to determine. But, as the magazine noted, it was "much harder to bring [the culprits] to justice: social and cultural trends, weather patterns, and a failure to deal adequately with garbage disposal in general."

——— **II** ———

Even a few years earlier, such a swift official reaction might have satisfied the public that the situation was under control, but this was not a situation that could be cured by swift reactions. This lack of a garbage disposal plan was precisely the problem. As the report in October 1988 from the Congressional Office of Technology Assessment made clear, no one could be confident any longer that anyone was controlling the pollution. In her testimony to Congress, Jacqueline Warren pointed out the real reason all the sudden moves to clean up hospital waste were needed: "An effective national medical waste management system does not exist. A patchwork of laws and regulations exists at the state and local levels. But there is no federal program to ensure the proper packaging, treatment, transportation, disposal or tracking of medical waste."

Warren pointed to "critical gaps" in the U.S. sewage and trash disposal system, which was supposed to account for the garbage thrown out by hospitals and clinics. The U. S. Environmental Protection Agency insisted that the problem was regional, but eleven states and the District of Columbia were doing nothing to regulate medical wastes. "In the remaining states, the current system is simply not working very well," she said. States regulated their medical wastes by "confusing, inconsistent and inadequate regulations," the Office of Technology Assessment report observed. Things that are obviously medically-related sometimes don't count—for example, the 100,000 needles used each day by diabetics in New York. As Warren noted, "they throw them in the garbage."

The congressional report concluded that a few pieces of information about the waste were missing: along the lines of how much of it there is, the safest methods of treating it and how best to get rid of it. Some experts said it could be incinerated, others thought it should be dumped in landfills, but there wasn't any consensus. So it often just got thrown away. Since the 1970s, legislators had devoted much attention to classifying and controlling hazardous waste, but medical waste didn't get the same kind of attention. The U.S. Environmental Protection Agency wrote regulations for "infectious" material in 1978, but ten years later, the regulations hadn't become law. Without these rules and with the experts disagreeing, the people who were supposed to manage all this garbage were confused. What types of waste were hazardous? What types were ordinary garbage? The difference could be crucial for them, because under the few rules that did exist, it cost more to dispose of material that was legally defined as hazardous. Thanks to gaps in the law, one hospital changed its designation of infectious waste from thirteen categories, dropping it down to four and saving $250,000 (U.S.) a year.

In some cases, the law was not merely manipulated, it was broken. Between 1985 and 1988, New York's sanitation department prosecuted 194 illegal dumping cases against hospitals, doctors and haulers, winning 178 convictions. One New York-area company was indicted, accused of covering up the illegal dumping of 1,400 red bags. Another hauler, from Pennsylvania, was charged with filing false papers in connection with 5,000 bags collected from several New York-area hospitals. The bags were found in a warehouse. Some of them had been there as long as four years. "Investigators said they had to smoke-bomb the premises to kill clouds of flies before they could even approach the reeking bags," the *New York Times* said.

Often there seemed to be no connection made between the hazardous and repulsive nature of medical waste and where it went. If you ever wondered what happens to the blood and skin after an operation, Warren had a possible answer: "Astonishingly, the practice of pouring medical wastes down sewer drains remains one of the 'recommended' methods of disposal."

Even the few rules that did exist to control the disposal of such hazards seemed to be broken at will. New York City, for example, bans "potentially infectious waste" from its ordinary sanitation and landfill systems. But more than half of the city's eighty-three municipal hospitals have tossed syringes, blood vials and scalpels into the ordinary garbage, which is hauled to landfills in barges. In a high wind, as much as a tonne of garbage can blow off a barge. Even more slips into the water as the barges are unloaded by cranes. Only after the summer of 1988 did the U.S. government pass regulations requiring barges to be covered with nets.

In the end, it was impossible to point to only one source of the mess. "The variety of the wastes . . . suggests multiple sources of the debris," the *Marine Pollution Bulletin* said. "Those sources include 1. untreated sewage discharges resulting from sewage treatment plant failures and from combined sewer outflow systems overburdened by rainfall; 2. illegal disposal of wastes in the water or on the shoreline; 3. floating of debris from beaches that was previously washed ashore or that was left by drug users; 4. spills of solid wastes at shoreline or offshore transfer facility sites; and 5. dumping from boats."

Canadians may have felt secure in the knowledge that this disgusting tide of blood and body parts was washing ashore in another country. But they have little reason to feel protected. The laws that supposedly were written to keep Canada's shorelines clean are in many instances weaker than those in the United States. Many Canadian cities dump raw sewage right into their harbours. Various beaches across Canada—in the West, the Maritimes, on the Great Lakes—are regularly declared off limits because of contamination. And there is the unsettling knowledge that pollution doesn't respect borders, and pollution laws often ignore them. Garbage has floated across the Atlantic and it has been shipped from country to country. What is there to stop it from heading north?

As far as medical waste is concerned, the main thing stopping it from going north is the fact that it usually goes south. Ontario, for instance, ships 80 percent of its hospital waste out of the province for incineration, most of it to Cleveland and a small percentage to Quebec. Hospitals also burn some of their trash in their own incinerators, but the quality of their facilities is often criticized. The irony is that when such waste is burned in incinerators that function poorly, the chemicals go up the smokestack and end up in the toxic cycle. We may not have to swim in infected tissue or dump it in a pit, but we end up breathing it.

Many hospitals are trying to correct the situation, but much of the work began after the horrors of 1988. In Toronto, for example, the hospitals set up a task force in 1989. And apparently, some of the methods of shipping hospital waste are questionable, and possibly revolting. "Some of the stories would make your stomach turn," former Ontario Environment Minister Jim Bradley says. He does not care to go into details.

—— **III** ——

The fact that U.S. politicians responded quickly to the revelations of hazardous hospital waste was both a good sign and a scary warning. It was a good sign because it showed that many officials did care and could do more than just talk about the problems. The hearings and reports on the mess answered most of the questions about how it happened and the new laws and regulations aimed straight for the holes in the old ones. Thanks to political follow-up — and more favourable weather — the East Coast's beaches weren't plagued by nearly as much of this disgusting pollution the following summer.

But it was a scary warning because the investigations revealed a lack of garbage control of any sort and a huge problem, literally piling up. Those who downplayed the significance of medical waste were technically right: it was only a small portion of all garbage, falling in the "miscellaneous" category which makes up between 2 and 10 percent of all trash. We throw away so much that the quantities tend to be beyond what the average person can picture. Only when we can picture it, or we actually see it, do we get an idea of what level we've reached as a society. We're up to our ears.

New Yorkers toss out as much as 24,000 tonnes of garbage every day. The city uses barges to take the trash to its dumps, such as Fresh Kills, a 1,215-hectare site on Staten Island.

The garbage that comes is now being stacked in a pyramid, covering 162 hectares, which is already 40 metres high and will grow to more than 150 metres by 2005. The Great Pyramid at Giza, Egypt, stands about 137 metres and is much narrower and lighter, weighing 5.3 million tonnes. The garbage pyramid will weigh nearly 45 million tonnes and have a service road spiralling up its sides, paved with trash. It will be an engineering marvel. In the *New York Times*, Thomas C. Jorling, commissioner of the New York State Department of Environmental Conservation, described the pyramid as a "sharply-sided event." It will be the highest point on the Atlantic coast from Cape Breton to the tip of Florida. "The politics of the landfill will become apparent when it passes 200 feet," Jorling says. It is a typical "Iron Ring Disease" response to a political problem: no one wants garbage and there's nowhere to dump it in North America any more.

The garbage pileup New Yorkers are experiencing is part of a continent-wide pattern. Everywhere, cities, states, provinces and regions are running out of room, and they're finding that the few areas where space is still available are either too far away or don't want their trash. In Ontario alone, garbage is spread over more than 40,000 hectares of land, in an estimated 600 active dump sites, and this doesn't count the 2,500 that have already been closed. Toronto's two dump sites will be packed full before 1993, and authorities have warned that the day may come when trash is stockpiled in city parks. Canadians throw away more garbage per capita than any people on earth—an estimated 1.7 tonnes per person each year.

In the area of hazardous material, Canadians also produce more than 8 million tonnes a year—industrial waste, discarded consumer products that become contaminated, spilled chemicals and leftovers from laboratories and institutions. As in the United States, it is the best-regulated type of garbage. Theoretically, there is an elaborate nationwide system to control it: the Canadian Environmental Protection Act, passed in 1988, was called the toughest law of its kind in the world by the environment minister who introduced it, Tom McMillan. Both he and his successor, Lucien Bouchard, talked about "cradle to grave" management of toxic waste, particularly industrial material. This meant making sure that the authorities knew where the material came from, how it was used and where it went when industries finished with it.

In practice, where much of the hazardous material goes is anybody's guess. The federal law's effect is marginal. It establishes safety guidelines for only a handful of the more than 64,000 chemicals in commercial use. "They have us drawing up guidelines for pesticides that the companies aren't even marketing any more," says one federal official. "We're going to ban them." It takes about two years to come up with a guideline.

The law also does not effectively control the transport of toxic material across the border. Canada is both an importer and exporter of hazardous industrial waste, to and from the United States. There is a busy and lucrative free trade in such material, complete with its own free trade agreement.

In 1986, the two countries signed a deal to allow free movement of toxic shipments across the border. The next year, Ontario alone received 135,000 tonnes of U.S. wastes, while the province shipped 42,000 tonnes south. At least one jurisdiction, Halton Region near Toronto, sends its garbage to an incinerator in Niagara Falls, N.Y. In 1989, Congress took steps to cut off the bilateral garbage trade, and in response, two large Canadian waste disposal firms, Tricil Ltd. of Sarnia, Ontario and Stablex Canada Inc. of Blainville, Quebec, hired a Washington law firm and put together a lobby group to work against the legislation. They followed a tradition of lobbyists opposing pollution control laws by taking a name that sounded like an environmental group: the International Environmental Policy Coalition. In 1990, the garbage trade was still going strong, as the congressional bill to cut it off continued to be debated and studied.

Canada's national environment act and the toxic trade agreement are among more than twenty federal laws and another twenty provincial and territorial acts that set rules for waste disposal on land and in the water. But like the medical waste laws in the United States, they form a patchwork, ineffective at every level of government. The provinces have more jurisdiction than Ottawa over what happens to toxic waste, but even in the province with the strongest environmental laws, Ontario, it's not as if there's a working system. Governments find that even when they try to move quickly to deal with seemingly simple waste problems, they get stymied.

In the late 1980s, Ontario imposed a five-dollar tax on new tires, to pay for a safe way to get rid of old ones. Tires are an obvious problem. They litter the countryside, and anyone who has ever tried to bury large numbers of them knows that this is nearly impossible; they buckle and heave to the surface. Burning tires are notorious for their pollution; unless the incinerator is highly efficient, toxic chemicals from them escape into the atmosphere. The Ontario government considered using its five-dollar tax to set up a comprehensive tire recycling program, but while it was thinking about it, approximately 70 percent of Ontario's used tires – 14 million – piled up near a town called Hagersville at a depot called Tyre King Tyre Recycling Ltd. (The company was just called that; it didn't really recycle too many tires.) The Environment Ministry had ordered the owner, Edward Straza, to take basic precautions against fire, but as Environment Minister Jim Bradley said, "Instead of spending the money on the environment, he spent it on lawyers." Early in 1990, somebody torched the tires, causing a fire that burned for a week and forced hundreds of residents to move from their homes. Now known as the Hagersville fire, it threatened the water table with 21 million litres of toxic, molten chemicals and its effects on farmland, produce, water and air are still not known. Not all the politicians were as concerned as Bradley was. Treasurer Robert Nixon was said to have remarked that "now the problem is gone."

It is becoming harder and harder not to notice our garbage. In the late 1980s, we watched with dread and awe as trash-laden barges plied the seas for months, looking for a city, a state, a country—*anyone* who would take their loads. The best-known was the one that left Islip, Long Island, in March 1987 with 3,100 tonnes of garbage and spent nearly six months at sea, travelling nearly 10,000 kilometres, asking six U.S. states and three countries for dump space. "It really served as the Paul Revere of garbage," said the town supervisor, who in the end had to take back the trash, burn it and bury it. "The irony of all this," said the head of the hauling company that sent out the barge, "is that if we trucked the stuff into some of these places that have turned us down, they have no laws to reject it."

CHAPTER FOUR

THE DIAPER WAR

*Simply to toss away a used diaper and never see it again
seems the ultimate in convenience and practicality.*
— *Consumer Reports* magazine, 1968

We can blame institutions, companies or society as a whole,
but the fact is, a lot of our garbage is personal. It used to be
that a truck came down the street, picked up the trash, and
nobody cared where it went. Now North Americans have a
near obsession with garbage. People talk about composting
at cocktail parties. School children trek to McDonald's to
demand that their hamburgers be served on napkins instead
of in foam boxes. Recycling is popular. In Ontario, by 1990,
a million and a half households in 160 communities were
throwing cans, bottles and newspapers into "blue boxes"
handed out to them for recycling, and the provincial
government estimated that this saved more than half a
million cubic metres of landfill space, as well as 226,000
tonnes of paper, glass, steel and aluminum.

But the average Canadian still leaves behind about half a
tonne of "residential solid waste," or household garbage, a
year. (The industrial waste that gets discarded each year
works out to more than another tonne per person.) About a
third of the household garbage is food and yard waste, a

good deal of which could be eliminated by using it for compost. And as much as half of North America's garbage is packaging – the little baskets that hold tomatoes, the bubble packages that hold a dozen screws, and so on. North Americans use twice as much packaging per person as Europeans, and the amount we use is going up while they are using less. In the United States, more than half the paper and glass and about a third of the plastics produced will be used in items that will be in the garbage within a year.

Some people argue that we're too worried about this problem. William Rathje, an archaeologist at the University of Arizona, has been excavating landfills and analyzing their contents since the 1970s as part of a program called The Garbage Project. He marks off sections, and labels and photographs old bottles and table scraps the same way he catalogued Mayan burial ruins as a graduate student. The physical reality of landfills turned out to be different than he had imagined. He dug up 7,300 kilograms of garbage in Chicago, San Francisco and Arizona and found that nearly half of it was old paper, such as phone books and newspapers.

Plastic may be the best kind of garbage, not the worst, Rathje says. It can be compressed and it lasts for centuries in landfills, which means the toxic chemicals it contains won't go anywhere and can be accounted for. He acknowledges that there's a garbage problem. "If a municipal government wants to ban plastic packaging, more power to them . . . but I worry that we're going to go after the wrong targets."

But with so much garbage thrown away each day, shouldn't we be targeting every type of trash? Companies that produce disposable products frequently argue that, taken individually, their products are minor contributors to the garbage problem. Drink containers are only 2.5 percent. Batteries, paints, solvents and household cleaners that contain hazardous chemicals are only 2.3 percent, about 23 kilograms per person per year. Such arguments leave out crucial points, though. Plastic may be "good" garbage as Rathje suspects, but not when it catches fire at the dump, shooting poisonous fumes into the toxic cycle – which it does. And the paper he found in his excavations is the kind that would please an archaeologist – old newspapers, some of them dating back to the days of Harry Truman and Dwight Eisenhower. Nowadays, in more and more cities, people recycle newspapers. What goes into landfills today is not necessarily going there in the same proportions as what's already there. So much of it now is a matter of convenience.

—— I ——

Take the case of that most personal and convenient item of garbage, the disposable diaper. Ironically, disposable diapers have only come on the market and become popular since the early 1960s – almost the exact period in which the green wave came to be. According to Procter & Gamble Inc., one of the main diaper manufacturers, "the process began when a loving grandfather was babysitting for his first grandchild." It was "a job which, of course, included changing diapers."

Grandpa also happened to be a Procter & Gamble engineer, who hated cloth diapers. The cloth "bunched up, did not keep the baby dry enough, and required plastic pants which could irritate the baby's tender skin." As anyone who has used them will know, cloth diapers also meant getting your hands dirty; the putrid, sticky diapers had to be picked up, stored, washed, dried and folded, and in between they often were stored in a pail, where they stank. There was little alternative. Since the end of the Second World War, a few disposable diapers had appeared on store shelves, but they were not particularly easy to use; they were made of two pieces, and often required pins, just like cloth diapers. And they leaked. Grandpa figured "there had to be something better than cloth diapers."

Procter & Gamble did some market research and concluded that "obviously there was a real need for a better way of diapering." Since the war, the marketplace has been littered – in more ways than one – with products that never existed before, but for which there is now a "real need." The distinction between need and convenience has become blurred. Obviously, it's easier to use a disposable diaper on a baby than a cloth one with pins. But civilization managed to exist for thousands of years before disposables were invented. In fact, the old cloth ones hadn't been on the scene all that long.

Canadian Indians used to pack a type of fluffy, dry moss, called sphagnum, around their babies before placing them in their backpacks. Once soiled, the material was removed and simply tossed away; it may have been messy, but it was completely biodegradable. The immigrants who came to Canada before the turn of the century were not much more elaborate in their method. Their babies were swaddled in linen, not diapered in the formal sense, and then covered with hand-knitted wool soakers. Diapers came into widespread use in North America around 1900, and it was just during the 1950s that people started covering their babies' bottoms with plastic pants as well.

But being tuned to the thinking of North American consumers, Procter & Gamble's engineers were determined to meet the need they perceived. After fifteen months and at least one false start, they came up with a "radically new diaper design": a thin sheet of plastic covering an absorbent wad, made from pulp. It kept babies drier than cloth, and it could be thrown away, down the toilet. It was test-marketed only after "scientists studied new materials and checked them thoroughly for human and environmental safety."

A list of possible names were drawn up, among them "Tenders," "Dri-Wees," "Winks," "Tads," "Solos" and "Zephyrs." Finally, the company settled on "Pampers." It test-marketed them in Peoria, Illinois, in 1961, and began to distribute them across the United States five years later. In 1972, it introduced them to Canada. In the meantime, other companies had come up with their own disposable diapers. Kimberly-Clark Ltd. had improved on the original idea by adding adhesive fasteners to the sides of the plastic and pulp combination. And a Toronto company, Facelle Ltd., began an aggressive marketing drive to get its product into the

United States. Facelle's diapers were called "Flushabyes." Like most of the other disposable diapers during the late 1960s, they were meant to be flushed down the toilet after use.

Even though market research found people interested in trying disposable diapers, before about 1970 many parents still resisted switching. For one thing, the early disposables were thick, cumbersome wads of pulp, which made babies who filled them up seem as though they were hauling bags of wet cement, except that wet cement doesn't smell as bad. They were also expensive; the ones that were test-marketed in 1961 cost about ten cents each, at a time when each change of a cloth diaper worked out to about two and a half cents each. And virtually all of them were leaky.

Nevertheless, disposable diapers had undeniable attractions. The newer products with adhesives meant that parents no longer risked sticking their babies with sharp pins. The manufacturers also learned how to keep the diapers from leaking; the most up-to-date models, introduced in the mid-1980s, contain an absorbing material that turns liquid into gel and can suck up as much as fifty times its weight. Another significant attraction was that the used disposables hardly needed to be handled. As soon as they were off the baby, they could be tossed out. Even *Consumer Reports*, the sometimes grumpy U.S. magazine that tests products, remarked to its readers in 1968 that "simply to toss away a used diaper and never see it again seems the ultimate in convenience and practicality."

In marketing terms, by 1980, disposables were an idea whose time had come. Fathers liked them, which was an important consideration as more women entered the workforce and men had to do more around the house. So did mothers; by 1988, some 85 percent of Canadian babies were diapered with disposables. A product that had barely existed thirty years ago now did about $400 million a year in business in Canada and more than ten times as much in the United States.

But little thought had been given to what this meant in environmental terms. Procter & Gamble says its diapers are designed "so that the absorbent padding, which is similar to bathroom tissue, can be flushed away." This can be done after the outer covering, made of a synthetic fibre called polypropylene, is removed. When a soiled diaper is dipped into the toilet, "the fibres in the padding separate in seconds, forming a slurry which is easily carried through regular home plumbing into the sewage system." When this reaches the sewage system, "the fibres are treated in settling tanks and sludge digesters, where they are completely broken down in typical 30-day retention periods." The company adds that "the parts of the diaper which are not recommended for flushing are the polyethylene backsheet and the polypropylene topsheet." These parts, which make up about 25 percent of a diaper, "should be discarded in the garbage."

But all this is a fantasy. Even if disposable diapers were flushed down the toilet, in Canada there's no guarantee that those settling tanks and sludge digesters would be waiting for them at the other end. More than a third of Canadians live in communities that aren't served by sewage treatment plants, and many of the plants that do exist consistently break down. But who bothers washing and flushing these diapers, anyway? They're supposed to be convenient. A U.S. researcher, Carl Lehrberger, estimates that fewer than 5 percent of parents actually do this. So by the time a typical Canadian baby is toilet-trained, he or she will have contributed half a tonne each of gooey, foul-smelling wads of pulp, wrapped tightly in plastic, to a dump site outside a Canadian city or town. This is nearly 275,000 tonnes of diapers. The United States, with ten times Canada's population, throws away ten times this amount. One American has calculated that enough diapers are thrown away in the United States each year to stretch back and forth to the moon seven times.

This is obviously a problem worth tackling, and as the *Silent Spring* generation began having children in the 1980s, it has grown into a high-profile issue. So it was a natural issue for an environmental group to take up, and a promising one for a non-political, marketplace approach. In 1989,

Pollution Probe—the group that had successfully lobbied the federal government for the DDT ban—tried to work with a company directly. This led to the Great Diaper War.

—— **II** ——

If you turned on the TV in southern Ontario in the spring of 1989, you might have seen a commercial with a tall man and a short man standing together at a table, showing off products. The tall man, the one with glasses, was Dave Nichol, president of Loblaws. He was already well known as something of a marketing whiz, the man who turned Loblaws, a dowdy supermarket chain, into an attractive, popular, almost *fun* place to buy the weekly groceries. He had introduced new lines of products, from the low-cost "no name" line of generic goods to the Yuppie-friendly "President's Choice" line of upscale products. This latest line was also to be called "President's Choice," but it was "green." On the commercials, he wore a white sweatshirt with green lettering across the front that said "G.R.E.E.N." and below it, "Something *can* be done." The point of these products, he said, which included household goods as well as food, was that they were "environmentally friendly." The short man, wearing a suit, was Colin Isaacs, executive director of Pollution Probe.

There were several different commercials, for motor oil recycled from previously used oil, for non-chemical fertilizer and for a new kind of disposable diaper. Unlike other diapers, the green-brand product was made from pulp that was not bleached with chlorine. Chlorine bleaching creates dioxins and furans, chemical compounds that have been linked to cancer and that in some forms can be deadly. Dioxins end up in the water coming out of pulp mills, in the air and in the diapers. In September 1987, the U.S. paper industry revealed reluctantly that traces of dioxin could be found in their snow-white products: paper plates, coffee filters, sanitary napkins and diapers. Bleached white paper products are made the same way in Canada. "In the best of all worlds, everyone would use reusable cloth diapers," Isaacs said. But "diapers made with non-chlorine bleached fluff pulp are the next best thing."

Within two months, sales of Loblaws' green products topped $5 million. Harvard University asked permission to use the product launching as a case study in its business school. Advertising magazines hailed the TV promotion as "pure genius," and newspapers and magazines hailed a new era of environmental consciousness among corporations.

It sounded like the beginning of a time of amicable, non-political solutions, but many environmentalists were uneasy. Why was a non-profit group like Pollution Probe doing commercials with a big corporation like Loblaws, and were these new "green" diapers really all that good for the environment?

Isaacs had been concerned that in an age of pasta and power lunches, Pollution Probe was still stuck in the flower-power era. He felt the organization had to grow up. "I started to view us as a business," he told the *Toronto Star*. "If they [other businesses] sell widgets, we sell ideas, dreams, concepts of how to make change. And we have to interest the public as much as business does. I'm not interested in scaring people, I want to inform them."

Isaacs was also concerned that Pollution Probe's effectiveness was hampered by a shortage of cash. In 1988, the group worked out a deal with then-federal Energy Minister Marcel Masse to purchase its handsome downtown Toronto headquarters from the government for $175,000, about a fifth of market value. The implied catch was that Probe had to hold a garden party for Masse, who wanted voters to think of him as pro-environment, and it had to turn over a list of its 17,000 members to the federal government. To charges that this jeopardized the group's independence, Isaacs had a simple answer: "It was a question of how pure do you want your organization to be." Probe stood to gain as much as $150,000 from its deals with Loblaws—enough to pay off the mortgage on the house it had bought for $175,000. (A municipal grant had paid off $25,000.)

For its part, Loblaws had spent $6.5 million on

development costs and had drawn up a list of about one hundred products to include in the line, but it wanted the environmental group's backing for only a few. It meant that Loblaws could get a seemingly objective endorsement for a handful of products, but could call the whole line "green." As a result, the grocery chain's green products included many that had little or nothing to do with the environment: acid-free coffee ("contains fewer of the organic acids that can upset sensitive stomachs"), "lightly salted" popcorn and "high-fibre corn flakes." There were even "green" hot dogs, made with turkey meat, containing "No More Fat than Lean Ground Beef." It could be confusing; one product that was *not* part of the green line was an emerald-coloured dishwashing liquid labelled Green Soap.

The situation escalated rapidly into warfare between environmental groups, and between Pollution Probe and its head. In a *Globe and Mail* article, the Canadian chairman of Greenpeace, Michael Manolson, heaped contempt on Loblaws, and on green marketing in general, saying the grocery chain "makes more money and fools us into thinking that by buying such products as high-fibre corn flakes we are doing something to save the planet." Meanwhile, "industries, the real polluters, continue to pollute," he charged. "Corporate greening concerns green, all right, but make no mistake about it, it has more to do with greenbacks than with a green planet. Big business is exploiting environmental concern to make money. Loblaws' green line is a case in point. . . . What in heaven's name is truly environmentally green about disposable diapers?"

At the same time that Greenpeace was asking these questions, so was Isaacs' staff. While the Pollution Probe director was appearing on TV with stacks of diapers, the organization's magazine, *Probe Post*, featured a cover story: "Getting rid of disposable diapers." In early July 1989, Isaacs quit, charging that Pollution Probe "perhaps doesn't want to move as quickly in setting up alliances with business and government as well as with the public and consumers as I think is necessary to deal with our environmental problems."

The diaper dispute revealed serious weaknesses in the environmental movement and in the whole idea of corporate alliances outside the political structure. Pollution Probe damaged its own and other groups' credibility and did nothing to help the diaper dilemma. In the modern, real world, we need to enlist companies' co-operation in the fight to save the environment, but we also need to understand that there's a basic clash of aims. Companies are in the business of supplying our consumer habits, providing us with the products we demand and creating demands for new ones. A Canadian Tire employee explains the dilemma companies face: "Look, we want to do something for the environment. But if we do, what's going to happen? Say we cut down on our packaging, so when you buy four nails it doesn't come in a plastic pouch with cardboard. People will say that's good. But everything else we do is bad for the environment. We sell batteries, solvents, oil, gas. We fix cars. What can we do for the environment that will convince people we're sincere? Close?"

—— **III** ——

Maybe governments could set ground rules for companies that wish to become more green, but so far the political solutions are ineffective, too. At the municipal level, in November 1988, the city council in Peterborough, Ontario, passed a resolution calling for a complete ban on the sale and use of disposable diapers in the province. While this may sound encouraging, such municipal resolutions are unenforceable. What's to stop anyone from driving a kilometre or two out of town and buying a box of diapers? About four months later, the provincial environment minister offered to pay half the start-up costs for anyone who wanted to start a diaper service using cloth diapers that could be washed and re-used. But Jim Bradley's offer, made in a letter to a Peterborough activist, was so poorly publicized that virtually no one was aware it had been made. While the minister insists the offer is sincere, one well-placed official says that "the people in the ministry see it as a big headache" – a program created on a whim that the ministry's bureaucrats are disinclined to support. A lack of enthusiasm to actually *do* anything about the environment has been a long-standing problem in this particular ministry. "We have 2,300 people working for us," says another senior official, "and I think there are four we trust."

As far as any federal effort is concerned, at "The Changing Atmosphere" conference, held in Toronto in June 1988, Prime Minister Brian Mulroney announced an "environmentally friendly" program, in which the government would hand out its seal of approval to safe products. It was supposed to be working by January 1989, but as Colin Isaacs put it, the program was "a disaster." A panel of government and private sector experts was asked to come up with products that could earn the seal, but for nearly a year they dickered and decided that virtually nothing qualified. They changed the name of the program to "environmental choice," because after protracted debate they decided that nothing was truly friendly to the environment, and then finally came up with about a dozen types of products that would be eligible for the seal – things like construction materials made from recycled wood or paper. In March 1990, the panel proudly announced the first ten companies who had earned the seal, paying between $1,500 and $5,000 each for the right to use it for three years. The problem was that by the time this panel was ready, literally thousands of products were already claiming to be good for the environment, with their manufacturers not worrying about whether they needed to be certified as such.

Deciding what's environmentally good is not an undue interference with the marketplace; it's really not much different from having pure food laws. We ask the government to require that candy-bar makers not put rat hairs in their chocolate. In the 1990s, with the threats we face, it's not too much to expect rules that discourage products that harm the environment. Nor is it that coming up with a list is impossible; since 1979, the West Germans have had a consumer program called Blue Angel that includes 2,250 products in 50 categories. But if it takes the Canadian group a year just for the easy products, how long will it take for controversial ones—like the diapers Isaacs endorsed?

With diapers, the most successful independent initiatives have not been connected with either government, big companies or the environmental movement. In the Vancouver area, two cloth-diaper companies started up quietly in the late 1980s and grew phenomenally. One expanded by 100 percent per month during 1989, while the other shipped 80,000 dozen cloth diapers every month. One of their biggest promoters was not a consultant or a bureaucrat, but a volunteer from Peace River, Alberta, named Sharon Krushell. "I didn't even start out doing this for the environment," she says. A mother of two, she simply disliked spending money on paper diapers. She organized a nationwide program to hand out pamphlets on "alternatives in diapering" to new mothers in hospitals across the country.

As the diaper story indicates, the real question concerning all this garbage is not whether it's biodegradable or green, but whether we should be throwing it away at all. Every 2 percent adds up, and new landfills are rarely opened. So we're running out of room. Newspapers are full of stories about the NIMBY syndrome—neighbourhoods that say Not In My Backyard to proposals for new garbage facilities. There is also the NIMTOO syndrome—politicians who say Not In My Term Of Office. Approving a garbage dump is politically risky. In the end, there's no such thing as good garbage if nobody wants to take it.

CHAPTER FIVE

JUST ADD POISON AND STIR

Drink today, and drown all sorrow. You shall perhaps not do't tomorrow.

—John Fletcher (1579–1625)

It was a crisp, clear day when officals from Environment Canada called a meeting to talk about the Great Lakes. The department invited local activists and reporters to a restaurant in Queenston, Ontario, perched atop the Niagara Escarpment.

The escarpment is a craggy, four-hundred-kilometre ridge that juts out across southern Ontario's otherwise gentle landscape, stretching from Niagara Falls to the Bruce Peninsula. From its southern end, you can easily travel to Lakes Ontario and Erie, while the northern end divides Georgian Bay from Lake Huron. Out of the restaurant's large picture window, the people present at the meeting looked out over the Niagara River, one of the most polluted bodies of water on the continent. Just upriver is Niagara Falls, cascading to a turbid foam, full of chemicals that cause cancer. Above the falls, honeymooners and tourists strolled in a fine mist sprayed by the tumbling falls; a University of Toronto professor has done a computer analysis of the mist which suggests that it is full of toxic chemicals.

From the window, you could see across the troubled river to the United States, the source of most of the pollution. Just a few kilometres away—about ten minutes by car after crossing the border—is the Love Canal, where a whole neighbourhood was built on top of a poison dump containing 19.8 million kilograms of hazardous material. People who lived there smelled fumes, and they complained that sludge was seeping through their basement walls. Their dogs would drink from puddles and then lose fur and develop bleeding sores on their noses. Some residents complained of dizziness and breathing problems. Others developed breast cancer, and the rate of birth defects and miscarriages was much higher than normal. The dump is just one of 261 within thirty-two kilometres of the river, which runs through a deep gorge, with high cliffs that rest on cracked, porous bedrock. Waste dumps sit on top of this bedrock. At least four of them are leaking into the water. In some spots, you can see the poisoned water pouring in.

As the meeting commenced, Elizabeth Dowdeswell, then Environment Canada's Regional Director-General for southern Ontario, offered a few words of welcome. While the invited guests gazed moodily out the picture window, contemplating the scenic yet filthy waters that lay below, she said, "I hope the view doesn't distract us from what we came here for." Later, some of the guests ridiculed Dowdeswell's remark for its unintended irony. She was only trying to be polite, yet—as so often happens with environmental matters—if we think about her comment, we start to wonder. What *do* people come to these meetings for?

Our concerns about water have changed over the years. As recently as the early 1960s, people were less worried about whether water threatened our health than whether it could help our teeth. In cities across North America there were intense debates over whether to add fluoride to drinking supplies, since dentists discovered that the compound prevents tooth decay. Right-wingers said it was a Communist plot to poison us (in the movie *Dr Strangelove*, one of the American generals said that fluoride threatened "purity of essence"). Few people thought about the fact that we were already adding another substance, chlorine, to the water that comes from the tap. And still fewer wondered why.

It was—and is—to protect us from getting sick. Now, however, scientists are discovering more and more polluting chemicals, many of which are not filtered or neutralized by chlorine. Some experts say that we are only finding these chemicals because the detection equipment has improved, so we now find microscopic traces that can't harm us. Others say the new equipment may just confirm that there are worse things in the water than we thought. Whatever is in the water, there's no one protecting us from it: Canada doesn't have standards for tap water, but rather, discretionary guidelines. Bottled water, used by many households, is no alternative; the toxic cycle goes deep into the earth, and some of the springs where bottled water comes from may be affected by the same non-specific pollution sources as the lakes and rivers. In Canada, for the most part, testing what comes in bottles is left up to whoever wants to do it—a few municipalities, consumer groups and newspapers and magazines. In the United States, only about thirty states have testing standards for bottled water.

Just how much water we've managed to pollute is amazing. The worst example is the Great Lakes, our largest fresh water supply, 246,000 square kilometres of water or about six quadrillion gallons. They contain one-fifth of all the surface fresh water on earth. They also contain more than a thousand chemicals that were put there by human activities. About a quarter of these are toxic. From the headwaters of Lake Superior to the St Lawrence River, the lake system is a vast, thick vein of poison and filth. Nearly 40 million of us drink this water.

The fact is, we are killing these lakes. In November 1966, an article by Charles F. Powers and Andrew Robinson in *Scientific American* reported that the Great Lakes were not "aging" naturally. All geological formations have an aging process, determined by the natural forces that surround them. "The Great Lakes are so young that, biologically speaking, they must be considered in a formative stage," the authors said. But "the aging of the lakes is now being accelerated . . . by man's activities. Basically the destructive agent is pollution."

This movement toward an early, unnatural death is called "eutrophication," which really means "enrichment." During the life of a healthy lake, the water absorbs nutrients such as phosphorus and nitrogen from the streams that feed it. These make the lake fertile. Plants, fish and other marine organisms feed on the nutrients and grow, while the living organisms that die pile up on the bottom of the lake. Over a long period, the lake slowly gets shallower and the water gets warmer. Some forms of life disappear, for example, fish that prefer cold water such as trout and whitefish. Other species arrive, such as bass, sunfish and perch. Eventually, these too are replaced by frogs and mud minnows, as more plants grow on the bottom and start to fill the space where the water once was. Ultimately, as the vegetation takes over, the lake becomes a marsh.

The *Scientific American* article simply confirmed and amplified studies of Lake Erie that had been going on for more than a decade. In 1953, for example, a limnologist named Wilson Britt found that mayfly larvae— nymphs—had all but disappeared from a section of the lake bottom. This was significant because they were replaced by sludge worms, which thrive in spots where there is little oxygen, like swamps. Five years later, a scientist with the U.S. Bureau of Commercial Fisheries found a 2,600-square-mile patch of Lake Erie bottom water where there was no oxygen at all.

The Niagara meeting was part of a continuing process to deal with the water pollution. It was an information session the government arranged to explain the elaborate procedural and scientific work and how it was coming along, and it demonstrated that the problems aren't being ignored. The finest researchers and the top politicians are paying attention to them—right up to the prime minister and the president—and there's an elaborate network of legislation, regulations, international agreements and cleanup programs, which all aim to eliminate the contamination in the water. But it's as bad as ever—maybe worse.

Like the view out the picture window, the policies and programs—the politics—mask an ugly reality. The pollution evaporates, mixes with clouds and falls as toxic rain on farmers' fields, getting into food. Birds are born deformed and fish grow large, grotesque tumours. Each day, the pollution pours into the water in tonnes, in many cases in complete accordance with the law.

Meanwhile, in Canada, politicians and their senior officials spend an inordinate amount of time going off on tangents—fighting bureaucratic turf wars and picking on their own field workers. It's as if they want to *not* confront the questions that really concern the public—how bad the water is and what that means—even when their own studies give them answers. The Great Lakes have been the focus of a series of scientific investigations and of the most intensive political activity in the history of environmental diplomacy. We have at least five Canada-U.S. agreements to clean up the Great Lakes already—the first one more than eighty years old—yet still they are polluted. The way we have dealt with the Great Lakes should make people think twice about what agreements do and what they fail to do.

—— I ——

In the mid-1970s, scientists from the Canadian Wildlife Service noticed something was wrong with birds that lived on the Great Lakes. The eggs of some colonies of herring gulls on Lake Ontario wouldn't hatch. One biologist, Mike Gilbertson, had tried to incubate gull eggs from an island at the south end of Prince Edward County, near Picton, Ontario. He packed them in a beer cooler with a hot-water bottle and took them to the lab, as he had done with gull eggs from Lakes Huron and Erie. Only a few of the Lake Ontario eggs would hatch. Many of those that did produced deformed, mutated chicks. Gilbertson became concerned and so he followed up by marking 180 gull nests along the Canadian side of the lake. When he came back at hatching time, he found that only one in five nests contained a live chick. About a third of the eggs had rotted. Some had dead chicks inside. They were science-fiction creatures, hideous mutants. Some had tiny, abnormal eyes, others had little bird feet growing out of their knee joints. Others had deformed beaks – the top bill crossed over the bottom one. The defects showed up in eggs along Lake Ontario from Toronto to Kingston.

More follow-up work by the Canadian Wildlife Service showed that the herring gulls had not reproduced properly on Lake Ontario for about eight years, between 1966 and 1974. The scientists suspected that the culprit was pollution, but they could only guess as to just how the contaminated water affected the eggs. So in 1975 they turned to a man named Doug Hallett, a chemist and biologist.

His task on the herring gull project was to figure out what chemicals had made their way from the lake into the eggs, and which of these had killed them or turned them into monstrosities. Until the mid-1970s, most people thought of water pollution as "lumps and colours" – easily identified contaminants such as lead, mercury and the phosphorus that fed the stinky, oxygen-eating algae in Lake Erie. This pollution was obvious and it was relatively easy to trace. But by mid-1976, it was obviously a case of more than lumps and colours: Hallett had identified three hundred different contaminants in the eggs.

They included unsurprising ones, such as mercury and DDT. They also included unexpected pollutants, such as the pesticide Mirex, which later turned up in the belugas of the St Lawrence River. This was surprising because Mirex was used to kill fire ants that eat cotton plants in the South, but never used in Canada or the northern United States. The pollution also included PCBs, which were beginning to worry health experts. PCBs, consisting of chlorine, carbon and hydrogen, have been around since 1881. The compound does not burn well (notwithstanding an infamous PCB fire in Saint-Basile-le-Grand, Quebec, in 1988) and does not conduct electricity well, so it makes an excellent insulator, which is why it was first made. But PCBs started to cause alarm in 1968, in Yusho, Japan, when they leaked into cooking oil at a food processing plant. Some 1,200 people ate rice that was cooked in the oil, and they became seriously ill. Scientists figured out later that what poisoned them were furans, the chlorine-based chemicals that are produced as a byproduct when PCBs are burned incompletely, as they would be when rice is fried. They are known to cause chloracne, an ugly, painful skin condition suffered by people who work too closely with chemicals. They have also caused liver damage and have been linked to cancer. Because of such links, most countries banned their manufacture in 1977, including Canada and the United States.

Hallett was as concerned as anyone would be to discover that hundreds of pollutants were in the lake. But the levels of these chemicals were very low, not enough to kill gull eggs or disfigure the chicks. In such low concentrations, only one compound could be so lethal—the worst form of dioxin, 2,3,7,8-TCDD.

This chemical is now commonly referred to in newspapers as "the deadliest chemical known to man." But industries dispute the threat, noting that there are 75 different types of dioxins and 135 types of furans (compounds that are similar in their chemical structure). Both types of compounds are based on rings of benzene—molecules made of hydrogen and carbon. The rings are joined by oxygen atoms: furans have one, while dioxins get their name because they have two. The rings become dioxins or furans when one or more of the hydrogen atoms is replaced by chlorine. The numbers 2,3,7,8 refer to the positions of the chlorine atoms. Both dioxins and furans are unwanted byproducts of combustion, created by virtually anything that burns. Dioxins have been around "since the advent of fire," the Dow Chemical Company says. "Coal-burning power plants, wood-burning stoves, gasoline and diesel powered automobiles and trucks all create trace amounts of dioxins. For that matter, so does cigarette smoking!"

The reason dioxins are referred to as deadly is that the worst form, 2,3,7,8-TCDD, is ten thousand times more deadly than DDT. A dose of one two-hundredth of a drop can kill a seventy-kilogram man or woman. By contrast it would take four hundred drops of arsenic to do in the same person, or a half-cup of bleach. Data are sketchy and controversial on the compound's exact effects on human beings, but lab animals given a dose of one-trillionth of a drop of the worst form sicken and die. It also causes birth defects.

While Hallett was working away, a series of frightening dioxin stories began to surface. In St Louis in 1971, some material containing dioxin spilled onto the dirt floor of a horse arena. It quickly killed hundreds of sparrows; later, horses exposed to it died in agony. In 1976, about two kilograms of the less lethal forms of dioxin dusted an Italian community called Seveso. While there seem to have been no long-term effects, at the time children in the area developed symptoms of acute poisoning, such as nausea and skin rashes, and plants, birds, rabbits and chickens curled up and died. It was a lot like that town in *Silent Spring* where "a strange blight crept over the area and everything began to change."

In other places, dioxin damage has led to lawsuits. Forest workers in New Brunswick are still seeking redress for exposure to dioxin contained in the pest sprays they used. And there was the Agent Orange case, a lawsuit launched on behalf of 16,000 American Vietnam War veterans who were exposed to a form of dioxin used to burn away jungle hiding places, and later complained about health problems. (The case ended in 1984 with a court-imposed settlement of $250 million.) Most spectacularly, dioxin contamination led to the evacuation of two communities: Times Beach, Missouri, not far from the horse barn where the material was spilled, and the Love Canal, which was frighteningly close to the lake that was home to the gulls whose eggs Hallett was studying.

To find out if the dioxin was in the gull eggs, Hallett had to program a machine to detect it, by giving it a "taste" with a crystal of the deadly material. He obtained a lab sample and worked in a locked, specially ventilated facility in the slab-like Environment Canada office complex in Hull, Quebec. "I had a crystal of 2,3,7,8-TCDD in the lab. I was holding it in the tweezers. We were testing it using a mass spectrometer—the same device used to analyze the lunar rocks. For a split-second, I lost the crystal in the tweezers. My heart jumped. I thought, here's enough to wipe out thousands of people."

A few weeks after this, Hallett was able to confirm that there were traces of dioxin in the herring gull eggs, and in November 1980 it was officially announced that the deadliest chemical was in Lake Ontario.

—— II ——

The fact that we were polluting the Great Lakes was never a secret. As far back as 1918, a team of Canadian and American investigators described many parts of the Great Lakes basin as "gross" and "foul." They said that "the situation along the frontier is generally chaotic, everywhere perilous and in some cases disgraceful." Since the lakes belong to both Canada and the United States, the prevailing view has been that to save the water, both countries need an agreement. In 1909, Elihu Root, the U.S. secretary of state, signed an agreement called the Boundary Waters Treaty with James Bryce, the British ambassador to Washington. Bryce was acting on behalf of the Dominion of Canada, which had not yet acquired treaty-making powers from the British Parliament. The treaty had been suggested three years earlier by another British negotiator, Sir George Gibbons, as a way of resolving disputes over shared waterways, such as the Columbia River in the West and the Great Lakes-St Lawrence River system in the eastern and central parts of the continent. While there had not been many disputes, it became necessary to deal with these waters as the West was settled and the Industrial Revolution advanced. People on both sides of the border wanted more and more water for irrigation, shipping and hydroelectric power.

The treaty had fourteen sections, or articles, as they were called. A preliminary article defined the term "boundary waters" as "the waters from main shore to main shore of the lakes and rivers and connecting waterways . . . along which the international boundary between the United States and the Dominion of Canada passes, including all bays, arms and inlets thereof, but not including tributary waters. . . ." This meant that although the water was not international water, it was in some way shared, right up to the edges of the cities and towns that lined the shores. The treaty concerned itself with issues like water levels, protecting Niagara Falls and dam-building.

Article 3 dealt with diversions of water. This could be done by either side, but each side had the right to complain and take legal action if a diversion caused harm. And at the end of Article 4 there was the following sentence: "It is further agreed that the waters herein defined as boundary waters and waters flowing across the boundary shall not be polluted on either side to the injury of health or property on the other."

To police the treaty, Canada and the United States set up the International Joint Commission, made up of three Canadians and three Americans. The commission, then and now, was envisioned as a joint dispute-settling mechanism, much along the lines of what was planned under the 1989 Free Trade Agreement between Canada and the United States—although the joint commission has more authority over water than the trade panel has over trade. Under free trade, a dispute-settling panel has the power to decide whether each country is applying its own laws fairly, but it can't strike down these laws. The joint commission can make binding decisions about water if the governments ask it to do so—not that that has ever been done.

The joint commission's first meeting was in 1912, and it was during that same year that the first concerns about water quality were raised. By the 1950s, the commission had dealt with pollution issues many times, but it was not until 1964 that the Canadian and American governments asked the commission to determine whether the lakes were indeed polluted and if so, what could be done. The answer to the first question was painfully obvious, particularly after the Cuyahoga River in Cleveland actually caught fire.

Like many legendary pollution events, the burning on June 22, 1969, of this river, which feeds into Lake Erie, was not as widely noted as it would be later. Even at the time, however, it was hard to ignore water so contaminated that it could be ignited. For several kilometres flames shot up from the water—if the badly polluted liquid could still be called that—and a fireboat had to rush to the rescue. In coffee houses, folksingers sang: "Burn on, mighty river."

In 1970 the commission reported that the Great Lakes were indeed polluted, and it identified the main sources and types of contamination. The commission suggested that it be allowed to supervise a cleanup, which it was estimated would cost (in 1968 dollars) $1.3 billion on the American side and, since the population was smaller, $211 million for Canada. (The estimates later rose to $2 billion and $250 million respectively.) Two years later, on April 15, 1972, President Richard Nixon and Prime Minister Pierre Trudeau responded by signing the Great Lakes Water Quality Agreement at a brief ceremony in Ottawa. There had been talk about signing the agreement in Toronto, but officials feared a bad reception—the Vietnam War was going strong and Toronto was home to thousands of American draft dodgers and deserters. The agreement was hailed in the *Toronto Star* as the beginning of "a new era of environmental diplomacy." The chief feature was a commitment to a five-year cleanup, with the goal of a 50 percent reduction in pollution of the lakes. The "general objectives" were that the waters should be "free from substances that directly or indirectly enter the water as a result of human activity," including material that "will settle to form putrescent or otherwise objectionable sludge deposits," or "floating materials such as debris, oil, scum and other immiscible substances." In other words, things that make the water look brown or smell bad or make people sick.

The day after Trudeau and Nixon signed the agreement, the *Toronto Star* published a map of the lakes showing where the cleanup would take place, and when. The map, following details of the agreement, showed only Lakes Huron, Erie and Ontario, and it indicated that work was to be done only on the latter two lakes, from Detroit to Rochester. It said the Detroit River would be 90 percent cleaner by 1976 and Cleveland's harbour "should be normal in [the] mid-'70s." Its forecasts were just as hopeful for Lake Ontario: the Niagara River would be "much cleaner by 1980," and by 1976 things would be better in Rochester as well as along the shore from Hamilton to Toronto. The accompanying article added that "swimmers will be less susceptible to ear, eye and nose infections. And the clean-up will help make Ontario a good place to work." It ended by answering a question it posed at the beginning: "Yes, we really can save the Great Lakes."

The *Star* also offered, accompanying another article, a cartoon of Trudeau and Nixon standing together in a rowboat, fishing a tire out of the water with a gaff hook – a portrayal of friendship and co-operation between the two men that proved to be about as close to reality as the hopes for the agreement itself.

The main type of pollution to be controlled under the agreement was phosphorus, which was largely responsible for the increase in nutrients that threatened to kill the lakes. Many people thought laundry detergent was the main contributor of phosphorus, because the detergents of the 1960s were made with complex molecules designed to produce more suds. It was true that when, with much publicity, soap companies phased out their high-phosphate detergents, phosphorus levels in the lakes declined. But phosphorus also poured from sewage plants and was discharged by industries like sugar refineries and match companies: by 1972, Lake Erie alone was receiving 30,000 tons of phosphorus each year. The agreement aimed to control these larger sources as well as peoples' washing suds, calling for a reduction in Erie to 16,000 tons by 1976.

The phosphorus program is a good example of one of those 1970s pollution laws that improved the environment, but not enough: it worked well in the '70s, then was less successful in the '80s. In 1989, the commission noted that

phosphorus levels were again on the rise, particularly in
Lake Ontario. The problem with the agreement was that it
had gaps. Each country was expected to find its own way of
managing the environment: so, while all the state governments in the United States imposed various but similar
phosphorus limits for detergent, Canada's limit has been
more than four times higher than any of them. Under the
Canada-U.S. agreement, a meeting was supposed to be held
between the two countries to discuss this problem. But as of
mid-1990, there had been no such meeting.

The 1972 agreement was a positive development. For
example, it pushed more communities on the lakes to use
waste treatment plants before they sent their sewage into the
water. At the time, only 5 percent of the population on the
American side had sewage treatment facilities, compared to
60 percent in Canada up to the Ontario-Quebec border
(after which the percentage was much lower). Today, most
Ontario and U.S. communities have sewage treatment. The
agreement also contemplated research into "non-point"
sources of pollution—contaminants that weren't coming
from any specific place, but were mixing with rain and snow
or runoff water from farms, entering the toxic cycle—and it
strengthened the international commission, relying on it to
co-ordinate the cleanup.

—— III ——

The 1972 Great Lakes agreement was supposed to last five
years. The idea was that either the cleanup would be well
underway by then or the deal would be renegotiated. It took
only three years, however, for the International Joint
Commission to report that progress on cleaning up the lakes
was "generally slow, uneven and in certain cases, disap-
pointing." The plan to reduce phosphorus was taking effect,
but much more slowly than the two countries had promised.
Nixon had set back the plan to build sewage plants in the
United States by impounding billions of dollars that
Congress had allocated for the work. He thought it was too

expensive—although the Americans ended up spending $5 billion on sewers once the impoundment conflict was resolved. The two countries still believed it was good to have an agreement, and they agreed that they needed to renew the one they had, but as the expiry date approached, each country complained that the other was not doing enough.

While the Canadian negotiators complained about Nixon's impoundment of funds, the Americans complained that they had spent far more than Canada on the cleanup. True, the United States has more people on its side of the lakes, and consequently more pollution to deal with, but Canada wasn't pulling its weight. Canadians like to smirk at Cleveland, but the Americans pointed out that cities like Toronto and Thunder Bay had filthy harbours, and that the biggest emerging problem in such harbours wasn't sewage, but industry. And the industries on both sides of the border were about even in the damage they were doing to the water, while they were uneven in the way they tried to deal with the damage. The agreement allowed officials from the Ontario Environment Ministry to sit down with industrialists and work out how much pollution their factories could pour into the water, and so the government issued—and still issues—documents called "certificates of approval." The conditions spelled out in these certificates have become tighter over the years for most companies, but until the mid-1980s, industries could more or less dictate their terms. "We weren't really the environment ministry," says one official. "We were the ministry of pollution permits."

The system, in the United States differed in that it set specific goals: water that would be "fishable and swimmable" by 1983 and total elimination of deliberate polluting by 1985. While neither of these goals came even close to being reached, just having them gave everyone something to live up to, to measure their progress. In addition, the pollution standards in the United States were far stricter than those in Canada. In the case of many substances, there were no Canadian standards at all, only unenforceable guidelines, and sometimes these guidelines were as much as ten times weaker than the legally enforceable standards in the United States.

As the five-year deadline for renewing the 1972 agreement approached, American negotiators were understandably irritated with this double standard—or rather, a single standard on one side, and no standard on the other. They wanted Canada to adopt real pollution controls, not guidelines, and they wanted any new agreement to deal not only with the Great Lakes, but with the rivers and streams that feed them. But Canadian officials said no to both suggestions, arguing that tougher controls weren't needed in Canada and that in any case, the Ontario government wouldn't want to get tough with the province's industries.

The negotiations were difficult, and it took until the end of 1978 to reach a new agreement to replace the one that, technically, had run out a year before. But the new pact was an improvement. For the first time, it referred to the Great Lakes as an "ecosystem." This was not simply an attempt to keep up with trendy new jargon. It was a leap of faith.

Taking an "ecosystem approach" meant that both countries officially recognized that the pollution that was choking the lakes affected all living things in the region, including the people. The nations agreed that "restoration and enhancement of the boundary waters cannot be achieved independently of other parts of the Great Lakes Basin Ecosystem. . . ." meaning that tributaries and streams had to be considered in any cleanup. They also agreed to work more co-operatively, so that eventually there would be common standards and common programs. Most importantly, however, a few new words were added to the new agreement: "The purpose of the Parties is to restore and maintain the chemical, physical, and biological integrity of the waters. . . . In order to achieve this purpose . . . the parties agree to make a maximum effort . . . to eliminate or reduce to the maximum extent practicable the discharge of pollutants into the Great Lakes system." This meant stopping pollution, not just controlling it—a tough goal for a society afflicted with Iron Ring Disease.

—— **IV** ——

Unfortunately, once Ronald Reagan came to power, the Great Lakes agreement – as well as the lakes – were ignored by politicians on both sides of the border. Reagan's new Environmental Protection Agency administrator, Anne M. Burford, was unequivocal in her support for the industry view that there was too much pollution regulation already. (She later came under fire in an agency scandal which led to her resignation in 1983.) In Canada, Pierre Trudeau and the Liberals were re-elected after a nine-month Conservative hiatus in 1979, and the government focused its attention on writing a constitution for the country. By 1981, both countries were in a recession, and the green wave was at its low point.

The paradox was that for government scientists like Doug Hallett this was a kind of golden era. The Liberal government was so uninterested in what the scientists were doing that they could do more or less whatever they wanted. For several years, both Canada and the United States didn't even bother to appoint people to the International Joint Commission; at one point, the six-member commission was down to one. Canadian scientists operated under two ministers: first John Roberts, viewed as sympathetic but anxious for a cabinet promotion, and then Charles Caccia, who was strongly supportive but had little influence in cabinet. Hallett, working at the government's Toronto office, had a free hand.

But by 1984, he was not the only one with a free hand. In September of that year, Brian Mulroney swept into power, winning 211 seats to the Liberals' 40 and the New Democrats' 30 (there was one independent). It was such a lopsided victory that the government took up seats on both sides of the House of Commons. During the election campaign, Mulroney had made a promise to fight acid rain, but he didn't really address any other environmental issues. So when he won, he too could more or less do what he wanted.

The new finance minister, Michael Wilson, announced a

series of budget cuts on November 8, 1984, totalling $4.2 billion. About 1,500 civil servants would be laid off. He did not mention it at the time, but a quarter of them were to be cut from Environment Canada as part of a $46-million budget reduction. Those whose jobs were to be eliminated included 84 people who worked for the Canadian Wildlife Service, among them those who studied the poisoned herring gulls. Most of the Environment Canada administrators who did paperwork in Hull were not affected.

Cancelling the herring gull program proved too controversial, and it was partly restored later, with a fifth of its former budget and resources. But the original move sent a powerful political signal that had an important bearing on scientists like Hallett, and more importantly, affected how Canada has dealt with water pollution ever since. The environment minister at the time, Suzanne Blais-Grenier, suggested strongly that the federal government was not particularly interested in protecting the environment. In Ontario, the Conservative provincial government was caught at election time covering up information about pollution. Officials said the data weren't ready, although one remarked privately, "It's funny. The reports are all bound and have green covers on them, and they're sitting in boxes." Just before the May 1985 election, the *Globe and Mail* mockingly referred to the government's environmental information policy as "Silent Spring," a remark that reflected the rising concern with the environment. Both governments got caught in the green wave. In Ontario, the Liberals came to power in June and appointed Jim Bradley as environment minister; he released all the information. Then in August, Blais-Grenier was demoted and replaced by Tom McMillan, an MP from Prince Edward Island.

Blais-Grenier was so disliked by the environmental movement that McMillan's appointment was universally praised. The feeling was that Ottawa would now be more sensitive to environmental issues. But right around the time McMillan was appointed, somehow a valve was left open at the Dow Chemical plant in Sarnia, Ontario. Canadians learned a new term for pollution: the blob. The open valve allowed 11,000 litres of a dry-cleaning fluid called per-chloroethylene to pour into the St Clair River, covering an area about the size of a basketball court. Perchloroethylene looks like water, but since it's dry-cleaning fluid, it sucks up dirt. The spilled fluid did just that, sucking up sediment from the river bottom that contained a healthy sampling of all the pollution Dow had been pouring into the water for forty years.

The spill itself was not unusual. During the thirteen years since 1972, there had been at least 275 spills in the Sarnia area alone, where about two dozen plants, mostly petro-chemical factories, line the forty-mile river just south of Lake Huron. In ten of those years alone, in just 32 of those spills, more than 11,500 tonnes of contamination slipped into the river—of which 70 percent was never recovered. Beneath the Sarnia area there is also a vast storehouse containing 8 billion litres of toxic waste, in wells and salt caverns. In one notorious incident in 1972, a slimy ooze bubbled up in a laneway behind the city's movie theatre on the main street. You could go in and watch a horror movie, but the reality outside could be worse. Almost every time there was a spill, violators were warned, not prosecuted.

People were alarmed because the St Clair blob contained dioxin. It wasn't the most deadly variety, but it hit them with the clearest case of environmental cause and effect most people had seen. A few months after the blob made headlines, tiny traces of dioxin were discovered downriver in drinking water. The traces appeared to be too small to pose a health risk, but it was the first time the toxic chemical was found in water that had already been treated for drinking.

With public concern running high, both the federal and provincial governments sent teams of experts to monitor the blob: divers to swim through it daily to collect contaminated sediment and scientists to analyze what they brought back. Pressured by the close scrutiny and by public opinion, Dow spent more than $1 million sucking the tarry material from the bottom of the river using a giant vacuum perched on a barge, and then burned the material in its incinerator at the

Sarnia plant. The ashes were put into a landfill. The company also spent more than $50 million to improve its facilities, in order to capture more toxic material before it enters the air and water. However, while the company may have tested the incinerator in which the blob was burned to see if its smoke contained dioxins and furans, there was no official monitoring of this. Ontario officials pointed out that the law provided them with no legal grounds for insisting on the measure. So it's likely that the same poisons that so concerned the regulators when they found the blob went up the smokestack, into the toxic cycle. Dow pleaded guilty to causing the blob and was fined $16,000. "I'll have a cheque tomorrow," the company's lawyer responded when sentence was passed.

The new federal and provincial environment ministers were both anxious to appear in control of the blob situation, but the two men responded differently to the public's growing awareness that the lakes were poisoned. Bradley confronted the issue, while McMillan tried to minimize it. Evidence mounted that something was seriously, chronically wrong with the water. In December 1985, about four months after the blob was discovered, a group of scientists from the Royal Society of Canada and the U.S. National Academy of Sciences held a news conference in Toronto. They announced that they had examined whether the 1978 Great Lakes agreement was curbing pollution. They came out with a stunning statement: people living near the Great Lakes are likely ingesting more toxic chemicals than anyone else in North America.

"We do feel strongly that the long-term effects from exposure to and accumulation of these compounds are cause for concern," said one of the scientists, zoology professor Henry Regier of the University of Toronto. "We are also particularly concerned about results from studies of PCB levels in breast milk." He added that the group feared "that the current levels of contaminants out there will have an effect, in cancers and other things, that will only become apparent decades from now, with the children growing up in these areas." Another member of the team, Jennifer

Ellenton, explained that "we can't define the risk. We know that there is a concern and that the main thing is to control the problem." There followed a classic example of the Canadian government's approach to environmental problems.

—— **V** ——

Jennifer Ellenton was Doug Hallett's wife. Around the same time, Hallett provided his own research for a federal government pamphlet called *Storm Warning*, which said essentially the same things as the report his wife had helped prepare. Hallett's boss, Jim Kingham, authorized its release, and Tom McMillan was furious. In Parliament, the environment minister was trying to ease fears about the blob, and here were his officials handing out pamphlets saying that we could get cancer from the water. After one tense meeting with his Toronto officials, McMillan emerged and vowed "to string them up by their balls."

The message the government was trying to convey about pollution was that Ottawa was taking care of the problems. "We may not win the pollution battle," McMillan had confided to one of his officials. "But at least we'll win the public relations battle."

Storm Warning was not a good weapon. It dealt with the toxic cycle. "What goes up must come down—and does, often in our food and water," it warned. "More and more disturbing information about airborne toxic substances is coming to light. . . . Toxic substances are also found in the bodies of Ontarians who live far inland, and do not draw their drinking water from Lake Ontario. Chemical substances such as PCBs and DDT have been found in mothers' milk and are passed along to nursing babies. Toxic chemicals are found in the body tissue of individuals who eat little or no fish from the Great Lakes. . . . Scientists agree on the dangers of these substances, have a fairly good idea of how they behave in the environment, and of what effects they can have on human and environmental health."

Doug Hallett himself, as a government wildlife scientist

enlisted in the 1970s, was part of a new kind of hybrid species—the scientific bureaucrats. While there had long been government fisheries and health experts, the class of civil service environmentalists grew rapidly in the wake of *Silent Spring*, and they came of age as environment ministries started up after Earth Day.

There were—and still are—good environmental bureaucrats and bad ones. The bad ones have the right scientific credentials, but they try to please the politicians they work for, who are worried about controlling budgets as well as pollution. Or they may minimize the problems because they are so familiar with them, the way a doctor is reluctant to believe his children are too sick to go to school because he sees so many worse cases at the hospital. Hallett was one of the good ones. That turned out to be his problem. He believed he was supposed to fight pollution, and he talked about this publicly: "People seem to regard the environment as the environment and then there's us and we're clean. You can't say there's the pollution, and it's bad, but here I am and I'm okay."

To the government, this meant Doug Hallett was not okay either. Within two weeks of *Storm Warning*'s release, the deputy minister, Genevieve Sainte-Marie, ordered the pamphlet withdrawn from circulation.

The government gave various reasons for suppressing the booklet. McMillan said that it was "riddled with errors." But in early December 1985, Hallett was summoned to talk with officials from another department, Health and Welfare. The health department said it didn't like environmental officials talking about pollution in food, because food purity was a health department responsibility. According to government records, a health official, Stan Winthrop, told Hallett and the others responsible for *Storm Warning* that "credibility problems are created for the government of Canada when more than one department is speaking on health issues." Nearly two months later, to stress this point, Health Minister Jake Epp wrote McMillan, calling it "unfortunate that this information [in *Storm Warning*] was released to the public in a federal publication before it had been thoroughly vetted by my officials."

There was some bureaucratic logic to this dressing-down. A government can look silly if one department says one thing without checking what the others say. But apparently neither McMillan nor the health department had done any research on these problems. More pages of documents were produced concerning what to do about *Storm Warning* than concerning what to do about the pollution issues it raised. Nor did every official agree with the ban. In one memo, a Toronto-based Environment Canada official named Jeanne Jabanoski wrote Kingham and his superior, Assistant-Deputy Minister Robert W. Slater. "Attempts perceived as restricting information are viewed suspiciously and negatively," she pointed out. "The minister should state the real reason the publication was withdrawn." However, this was not done, and before long, the government's environmental performance began to look as bad under McMillan as it had under his predecessor. At one point, when McMillan came to talk to citizens in the Niagara area, a local activist, Margherita Howe, introduced him by saying, "He hasn't done much, but he has good teeth and hair." McMillan had lost his public relations battle as well.

The government went on to implement a plan to trim Environment Canada's budget by 6 percent over five years and eliminate about six hundred jobs. It was just a matter of streamlining operations, Slater said. It was all to be done quietly. Deputy Minister Sainte-Marie wrote in an in-house newsletter that "there will be no grand announcement" of any changes. Within weeks of his being called on the carpet, Hallett resigned from Environment Canada and his boss, Jim Kingham, was reassigned to a job in which he complained he had nothing to do. A year and a half later he accepted a prestigious position with the Ontario government, writing McMillan that "cumulative decisions by senior management have fundamentally altered the conditions under which a meaningful contribution can continue to be made to protect the environment."

Finally, in 1987, *Storm Warning* was re-released with a

two-page error sheet stapled to the front cover. "The department has made a judgment that it would be in the best interest of the public to reissue the booklet," it read. Most of the corrections on the error sheet were technical, but the first one changed that controversial statement about scientists agreeing on the dangers of pollution. "That statement has been corrected to read 'Scientists agree on the dangers of these substances and have a fairly good idea of how they behave in the environment; however, scientists are uncertain of the effects these substances have on human health and the environment at the low concentrations they are being detected in the environment.' " A team of Jesuits would have trouble explaining the importance of this change, but it ended nearly two years of bureaucratic anxiety.

The irony was that in the late 1980s, the federal water pollution control record also improved—but only on paper. Ottawa negotiated an agreement with the United States to try to reduce the poisons going into the Niagara River. And in late 1987, McMillan signed the toughest Great Lakes agreement yet with the United States. Its wording aimed to force both countries to report more frequently on what they're doing—or not doing—to clean up.

Meanwhile, Ontario and Quebec brought in ambitious programs that intended to discourage industries and municipalities from putting pollution into the water in the first place. These plans were far from perfect, but at least they were plans. The Quebec program involves building sewage treatment plants, in many cities for the first time. The Ontario plan, which took full effect at the beginning of 1990, increases the number of polluting chemicals monitored by the government from only a few to nearly two hundred, and ultimately it will require the province's industries to stop pouring out the worst ones.

—— **VI** ——

In 1989, the International Joint Commission met in Hamilton to discuss progress in cleaning up the Great Lakes.

The commission said bluntly what *Storm Warning* had only dared suggest: "More emphasis must be placed on the preventative aspects of ecosystem management, rather than waiting for adverse impacts and then reacting." Its scientific panel denounced "the current framework for policy decisions [that] requires one-by-one 'proof' of harm before an industrial chemical is banned," calling it "dysfunctional and unscientific." The scientists also noted that few of the 65,000 chemicals in use in North America have been tested for adverse health effects, and said that dickering over absolutes can only lead to "costly errors" in judgment. "Random changes" to the environment "have a high probability of being harmful," it said.

Another commission panel, the Great Lakes Water Quality Board, noted that pollution standards are still different on either side of the border and that for all the talk about conclusive evidence of harm, four out of ten laboratories had trouble measuring the most basic pollutant, phosphorus. "Based on information provided thus far by the governments, the board finds that it is unable to fully assess the health of the ecosystem or to properly evaluate the adequacy of programs."

In recent years, even the commissioners, long criticized by activists as faceless political hacks, have started to show their frustration. They invited Greenpeace to give the keynote speech at their 1989 meeting, a departure from the usual practice of hearing from dignitaries such as the governor-general of Canada. During a luncheon, Greenpeace Great Lakes co-ordinator Joyce McLean was ushered to the podium by members of the group who wore papier-mâché masks of birds with twisted beaks. They played a tape of a funeral march and carried a coffin, from which emerged two more group members, one dressed as a dying eagle, the other a dying beaver. The symbolism was hard to miss.

McLean noted that bald eagles in parts of the Great Lakes basin have ingested so much pollution that they can't reproduce. And beavers have seen their wetland habitats around the lakes shrink by two-thirds. Of fifty-nine recommendations made by the International Joint Commission in 1978, only twenty-nine had been implemented a decade later. "There's an old saying," she told them. "Once the last tree is cut and the last river poisoned, you'll find you cannot eat your money."

The day before this meeting, two private research groups, the Canadian Institute for Research on Public Policy and the U.S. Conservation Foundation, announced that they too believed that living near the Great Lakes may add to the risk of cancer, birth defects or brain damage. They warned of "subtle alterations" in human thinking and behaviour, a development that "may be far more significant than even cancer or gross physical defects." The information reconfirmed existing findings, but the significance of the report was that it demonstrated that environmentalism was becoming part of mainstream thinking. The U.S. group that co-wrote the report had been headed by William Reilly, who was later appointed by President George Bush to head the Environmental Protection Agency. Reilly appeared at the press conference where the report was released and praised it. However, Tom McMillan's successor as Canadian environment minister, Lucien Bouchard, was on a tour of Europe looking at pollution on the Rhine River.

In place of Bouchard, Ottawa sent a videotape of Health Minister Perrin Beatty, who announced that the government would keep studying what *Storm Warning* already said. He promised to spend $125 million over five years to examine the problem and clean up some trouble spots on the lakes—about one-fourth the cost of one sewage treatment plant these days. The announcement was a political victory, though—for the federal health department. *They* got to announce the program, not the environment department.

CHAPTER SIX

FOOD, DANGEROUS FOOD

We live in a chemical society.

—Tom McMillan

Everything gives you cancer.

—Joe Jackson

Chemistry teachers like to tell their students how the human body is really just a collection of inexpensive chemicals — hydrogen, potassium, carbon and so on. But a biopsy of a typical North American will invariably turn up a few that nature didn't count on. Our hair, nose, blood, bones and nails contain polyaromatic hydrocarbons, the same PAHs found in the belugas of the Saguenay-St Lawrence. Our brains contain traces of the same compound, as well as aluminum, which is believed to cause Alzheimer's disease. Our fat contains dioxins and furans, dry-cleaning solvents, PCBs and vegetable, fruit and grain insecticides long out of use.

When some people hear this and look at their groceries, they can already envision the doctor explaining that the chemotherapy starts next week. The scientists who warn that people living near the Great Lakes, for example, are ingesting pollution aren't just worried about the water—they're worried about food. A 1989 study of the

Great Lakes basin said that "both wildlife and humans are at risk because of accumulation of toxic substances in the food web." Those most at risk from the region's chronic pollution are "human embryos, infants and children whose parents have consumed contaminated fish and wildlife." The area's wildlife had "significantly more birth defects, tumours, embryo abnormalities, enlarged livers and inexorable weight loss" than other areas, the study said, adding that "the same contaminants are found in both animal and human tissue, and the parallels are disturbing."

Nothing illustrates the toxic cycle better than the relationship between water, pollution and food. Sewage and contaminants pour from pipes into lakes and rivers, and the chemicals that are sprayed on farmland wash into the ground and the waterways with the rains. Then the water evaporates and the pollution rises with the forming clouds, mixing with the contaminants of thousands of factories and blowing with the wind. Then it rains again, on our farms—which of course have already been sprayed with pesticides. Then we eat, go to the bathroom, flush the toilet, and send more sewage to mix with contaminants in the pipes from industries and farms; this flows again to the water, where we catch fish. The fish that swim in the poisoned water are eaten, and they are ground up for fertilizer and meal for livestock.

It's not a matter of moving to a "clean" part of the world. We have to eat, and the contamination can be found virtually everywhere nowadays. Even when one type of pollution is stopped, that pollutant lingers in the toxic cycle for decades; traces of pesticides banned in the 1970s are still showing up in produce and fish. Pollution travels thousands of kilometres. DDT wafts across the continent from Mexico and South America, where it is still in use, and settles on our fields and water. It gets into everything, including us. In the 1960s, health food fanatics used to say, "You are what you eat." If that's the case, then we have a problem: our meat is spiked with antibiotics, and deep in the water, our fish feed on toxic waste. Nobody can say conclusively what all these chemicals in our food do to us or how much we should worry.

This is a major problem. North Americans looking into their pantries don't know what to eat, because not all scientists agree what's in there or what it means. Experts have been arguing fiercely about chemicals in food since the days of *Silent Spring*. "We suffer from a crisis of credibility," said Jim Kingham, shortly before he resigned from Environment Canada. "Think of finding dioxin in a glass of water at ten parts per quadrillion. How much is ten parts per quadrillion? Well, you can compare it to one second in 31 million years. Or you can think of it as three billion molecules in a six-ounce glass of water. One sounds like next to nothing, the other sounds like an awful lot. But nobody can say with certainty what it really represents. No one can say credibly that ten parts per quadrillion is absolutely safe, but no one can say that it is definitely dangerous either."

As many as three hundred different pesticides go into North American produce, leaving residues, and most of these have never been tested exhaustively to see if they cause cancer or birth defects. Chemical and food companies maintain that these substances help feed the world by increasing productivity and improving the quality of food, and some scientists insist that our fears of such chemicals are unjustified. "The pesticides we are eating are 99.99 percent natural," says Bruce Ames, the leading have-no-fear advocate and chairman of the Biochemistry Department at the University of California at Berkeley. "Tens of thousands of these natural pesticides have been discovered, and every species of plant contains its own set of toxins, usually a few dozen. . . . It is probable that almost every plant product in the supermarket contains natural carcinogens."

This may or may not be so: *Consumer Reports* magazine points out that Ames's analysis of many of these "natural" dangers is sketchy and imprecise. His examples of both synthetic and natural hazards are selective, and he overestimates the amounts of some foods people eat—for example, a gram of dried basil each day. And in some cases, he misclassifies as natural carcinogens materials that are man-made, such as the chemical byproducts produced by nitrite in bacon.

On the other hand, a two-year scientific study commissioned by the U.S. Natural Resources Defense Council found that government estimates of the cancer risk from pesticide residues were based on adult eating patterns and may underestimate the risk to children by several hundred times. "Between 5,500 and 6,200 preschoolers might get cancer solely as a result of their exposure by age 6 to the eight common carcinogenic pesticides in fruits and vegetables analyzed in the study," says one of the environmental group's senior lawyers, Al Meyerhoff. Based on population size, this would translate into 500 to 600 Canadian children, since most of the same pesticides are used on both sides of the border.

Ellen Silbergeld, senior toxicologist for another U.S. lobby group, the Environmental Defense Fund, points out that erring on the side of caution is probably wise: on health issues, the scientists who don't are often wrong. She notes that at one time, experts downplayed the dangers of things now known to be bad, such as asbestos and tobacco, and, of course, DDT.

But we have a system that deals poorly with substances already in use. To get rid of them, the proof of danger must be overwhelming. Every once in a while, the public outcry is strong enough to get a particular substance removed, but the public can't possibly keep up with the hundreds of different chemicals used to grow food, let alone what their potential side effects may be.

— I —

Even when a link between health and chemicals in food is established, getting action can take an excruciatingly long time. Early in 1989, concerns about the pesticide Alar, which makes apples redder, were featured on CBS-TV's "60 Minutes." The pesticide, actually called daminozide, was first registered by Uniroyal in 1963—the same year *Silent*

Spring became a bestseller. It was used extensively, even though in the 1970s five separate studies linked it to cancerous tumours in lab animals. After the CBS show, the U.S. government took steps to ban Alar, and later that year its manufacturer, Uniroyal Chemical, took it off the market. In Canada, however, Health and Welfare officials refused to ban Alar even after the U.S. action; the Canadians argued that the pesticide traces in apples were not at health-threatening levels. But the marketplace spoke and shoppers refused to buy apples or feed their babies apple sauce until these products were Alar-free. Finally the company withdrew its pesticide, and so Canada didn't have to do anything.

Although its record is far from admirable, the United States does tend to be quicker to deal with suspect pesticides, and some effort has been made to investigate alternative methods of farming. A report to the U.S. National Research Council finds that chemical-free agriculture can be just as productive as farming that relies on pesticides and synthetic fertilizers. "Wider adoption of proven alternative systems would result in ever greater economic gains," it concludes. There is clearly a market for chemical-free produce; although organic food grabs just a tiny 0.2 percent share of the market in Canada, stores that specialize in these products say they can't keep them on the shelves. Toronto's Big Carrot health food store sells ten thousand dollars' worth of organic produce a week, and expected its 1989 gross sales of organics to rise by 50 percent over the previous year. Some of the larger grocers have noticed the trend; in 1989, four regional chains in the United States and Montreal-based Provigo Inc. announced that they will phase out pesticide-treated food by 1995. Many others now offer consumers a choice of chemically treated or chemical-free food.

The evidence is strong that pesticides as currently used do little good and lots of harm. As Al Meyerhoff, the Natural Resources Defense Council lawyer, points out: "The bugs are winning. At least 20 different species of insects have mutated to a form that nothing will kill. We now lose roughly the same percentage of crops to pests as we did during World War II. The farmers? Well, they're losing. A comprehensive 1987 National Cancer Institute study of Kansas farmers found substantially higher rates of soft tissue sarcoma and lymphoma due to exposure to herbicides. And increasingly, pesticides are turning up in ground water."

North America and Europe export many of the chemicals considered too dangerous for domestic use to Third World nations, which then ship us their food. The Natural Resources Defense Council tested imported coffee beans in 1983 and found "multiple illegal pesticide residues" on every sample taken. And in the countries that use substances banned here, pesticides are not merely a threat: they kill. The Oxfam relief organization estimates that 750,000 people are poisoned every year by pesticides and as many as 10,000 die – amounting to half of all the poisonings that occur in the Third World. Two American researchers who have documented the international trade in pesticides, David Weir and Mark Shapiro, call it the "circle of poison" – a concentric, commercial version of the toxic cycle.

Canada deals even more poorly with pesticides than the United States does. First of all, it's not clear who's in charge. It's the same problem that came to light when *Storm Warning* was banned. The Health and Welfare Department monitors food purity and Environment Canada sets pollution standards for the chemicals. To make matters worse, a third department is involved, Agriculture, which has a "very stringent registration system that exerts rigorous control over our chemicals" – a system that's "just fine the way it is," claims federal Agriculture Minister Don Mazankowski. That must be why it permitted apples to be sprayed for more than two decades.

The grading system that labels fruits and vegetables as Canada No. 1 or Extra Fancy is also set by the Agriculture Department, and it is based not on purity, but appearance – the shiny reds of apples that only chemicals like Alar can produce. "It is difficult," Mazankowski says, "to imagine an agriculture industry without chemicals." But that's because the deck is stacked. Farm credit policies are set up to push farmers to maximize their production, which

they can only do through chemical pest control and fertilizers. Intensive farming has weakened the soil to the point
where a Canadian Senate committee found that organic
material—the dirt things grow in—has declined by as much
as 50 percent in the worst areas, costing the nation's farmers
one billion dollars a year in lost income.

Canadian federal and provincial governments do little
other than to react after the damage has been done. The
Ontario Environment Ministry's temporary closing of
Uniroyal's fungicide factory at Elmira in early 1990 came
too late to prevent a chemical byproduct from the plant from
getting into local wells and reservoirs, including the water
used by a major apple juice manufacturer. More than one
hundred thousand cans of juice had to be recalled.

As recently as 1986, the Canadian government was still
resisting the idea of studying pollution in food. This changed
when Kate Davies, then a public health official for the City
of Toronto, got a ten-thousand-dollar grant from the
International Joint Commission and did some research of
her own. While federal bureaucrats were sending memos
back and forth about *Storm Warning*, she conducted a study
that supported the findings of the supressed pamphlet. She
was concerned that Toronto-area residents did not have
enough information, and she had a willing supporter at the
commission in Doug Hallett, who was being hounded out of
Environment Canada but still served as a scientific adviser
to the international board.

Davies started her research by going shopping. She
bought a typical food basket of fresh produce from southern
Ontario and divided the food into five groups: fruit, leafy
vegetables, root vegetables such as carrots or beets, milk, and
finally eggs and meat. Then she put the food into centrifuge
machines, which whirled it at high speeds, enabling its
chemical content to be separated and analyzed. She released
her findings at an international scientific meeting at
Mackinac Island, Michigan, an idyllic button of land about
sixty miles south of Sault Ste Marie in the strait where Lakes
Superior, Michigan and Huron meet. The scientists had
chosen the spot to talk about the pollution of large lakes
around the world, but Davies told them that what she found

in her grocery bag was more disturbing. One activist summed up her results as "an apple a day may land you in the cancer ward."

Her findings were not quite as explicit as that, but they were worrisome, nevertheless. Davies' food basket contained dozens of toxic chemicals, including DDT, PCBs and traces of dioxin. As much as 86 percent of the toxic chemicals people are exposed to come from food, only 10 or 11 percent from water. There is no way anyone, anywhere, could avoid ingesting these materials, she said. "Ontario food is no more contaminated than food from anywhere else – or no better. You could stop eating Ontario apples and switch to pears from Mexico, but they'd probably contain DDT."

Davies was the first to admit that her tests were not conclusive. The contamination levels were close to the bare minimums the equipment could detect, and people's eating habits differ, so the contaminants wouldn't affect everyone in the same way. But her research made the need for further study inescapably obvious, and she persuaded the federal health and welfare department to hire her and let her continue. Follow-up studies done since her pilot project have brought wildly varying results, but they all indicate a tendency that had been predicted with stunning accuracy by Rachel Carson in *Silent Spring*: the tendency for pollution to spread everywhere, into everything. "As crude a weapon as the cave man's club, the chemical barrage has been hurled against the fabric of life," Carson wrote. Davies takes up the same broad theme. "People seem to have missed the message of the study, because they're concentrating on the fact that we found dioxin in food. The message is that we need to further reduce pollutants and look at where they are coming from."

— II —

Davies is right. Food pollution is not just a matter of pesticides or of dioxin. Pollution has become so pervasive that there is really no particular place where it starts; the smoke, sludge and sewage that pour from individual sources are like riders that hop aboard a merry-go-round. The Ontario government estimates that as many as 12,000 industries and municipalities are sources of pollution. Metals, paints, chemicals, drain cleaner and anything else poured down a sink or toilet also go into sewage plants, and there is little, if anything, done to treat them. Small factories often use the ordinary sewer lines, too, and while it's illegal for them to pour pollutants into the sewers, it's also hard to catch them.

Most cities in the United States and in Canada west of Quebec have sewage treatment facilities, but many are old, inadequate and breaking down. There is an old story about a New Yorker who came back from a Florida vacation with souvenirs for a friend: baby alligators. The friend grew tired of the reptiles, so he flushed them down the toilet, and the huge reptiles grew in the sewer system, terrorizing people. The story is apocryphal, but, because of inadequate treatment, what's actually in the water may be worse.

Scuba divers talk of swimming through "black mayonnaise"—clouds of wispy toilet paper and half-dissolved human waste, lying above bay bottoms covered with a foul layer of sediment, toxic chemicals and sewage. When such pollution is poured out by coastal cities, it may not harm drinking water, but it enters the toxic cycle just the same. There are dead zones off the coasts as big as eight thousand square kilometres, where up to a million fish have been killed by contamination. The slimy mixture creates red and brown tides, explosive blooms of algae that block the sunlight. This leads to eutrophication, similar in its effects to the fish-choking pollution that harmed Lake Erie.

In most cities that have treatment plants, when you flush your toilet the water and sewage go into what is euphemistically known as a "sanitary" sewer, separate from the storm sewers that collect rain and melted snow. New suburbs usually have such double systems, as do downtown business districts of big cities, where the sewers are improved when new office towers go up. But in older residential neighbourhoods, sometimes the water from the toilet and the rain are combined and sent toward the sewage treatment plant. This is all right in dry weather, but after a storm it can flow right through the plant, sending brown, smelly, pulpy liquid straight into the water.

In a modern treatment plant, if the system doesn't fail, the sewage is caught by huge screens and bars that trap the largest clumps of material, best left undescribed. Sewage still gets through, however, and is sent to large tanks, where it remains until the solids settle to the bottom. The remaining liquid flows into tanks where it is aerated, much like an aquarium with an air bubble machine. Bacteria love the mixture of air, water and sewage, and they eat the sewage voraciously and multiply. The whole mess then flows to another tank, where the bacteria settle to the bottom. Some of them are sent back to the aerated tanks to eat more sewage. The rest move on to de-gritting facilities, which remove sand and gravel, then to "gravity thickeners"—pools about the width of a hockey rink where more solids sink to the bottom. The newly thickened material then goes to covered pools where bacteria that *don't* thrive in air eat more sewage, munching away for nearly a month. The sludge that's left at the end of this process is then either incinerated, producing dioxins and furans, or landfilled, adding to the fears of running out of dump space that most cities are now experiencing.

When it works, this treatment is a reasonably efficient way of taking care of the most obviously offensive aspects of sewage. But while this is going on, the liquid that was separated is simply laced with chlorine and returned to the lake or river after a few hours of treatment. In many cities, these systems can't handle all the sewage that comes to them. Toronto's beaches were closed during the 1980s because storm water mixed with sewage and flowed through the treatment plants into Lake Ontario. In New York City, officials estimate that as much as 10 percent of the city's sewage—more than 227 billion litres—overflows into the water each year. U.S. cities were supposed to comply with a law requiring their sewage plants to work by July 1, 1988, but on that day, thirty-four cities along the East Coast could not meet the rule. Their sewage plants could only screen out large, floating objects.

Congress has voted more money to help U.S. cities improve their facilities, overriding a presidential veto in the waning days of Ronald Reagan's administration. But in Ottawa, pleas by municipalities for help have fallen on deaf ears. The cities say the nationwide bill for properly upgrading treatment plants, sewers and the roads that will have to be rebuilt over the new pipes will run as high as $15 billion. Municipalities and provinces say they can't afford to pay the entire bill, but the Canadian government argues that this is not a federal problem—a questionable constitutional nicety that the environment won't respect.

An even bigger problem, however, is that existing sewage treatment plants can't stop the relatively small but possibly dangerous quantities of toxic compounds that travel through the sewers and end up raining on our food. Some jurisdictions, most notably Ontario, are trying to prevent this pollution with new regulations that will require companies to purify their waste water before it can reach the sewers, but many jurisdictions haven't come this far. This is most noticeable on the coasts, where many of our most succulent seafood delights are now loaded with poisons.

—— III ——

In the United States, a third of the country's shellfish areas were closed in 1987. "Bacterial contamination is a significant problem nationwide," a congressional study reported. The problem is growing in fast-developing areas such as the Gulf of Mexico coast and the southern Atlantic states. At Long Island, N.Y., the clam and scallop harvest has declined since the 1970s from $110 million a year to less than half of that today. In New Bedford, Massachusetts, a total of 7,300 hectares of harbour have been closed to lobstering because of PCBs that were dumped there for thirty years, as recently as 1977. In Chesapeake Bay, one of the world's richest estuaries, the U.S. Environmental

Protection Agency concluded that the entire area was in
decline because of pollution.

In Canada the situation is equally bad, and certain
industries stand out as major polluters of the fisheries. In
1989, an Environment Canada study obtained by Greenpeace found that across the country, 122 pulp mills
discharged their wastewater directly into rivers, lakes and
ocean bays. Of these, 71 were virtually unregulated, and 30
of them were responsible for more than 70 percent of the
known water pollution in Canada. The report said that
"virtually every mill" in Canada could be charged if federal
regulations were strictly enforced. Most mills, of course,
remain open, few have been charged and fewer still have
been convicted. None have been ordered to shut down if
they can't clean up.

In November 1989, the federal government closed seven
British Columbia fisheries because the shellfish were
contaminated by pulp mills. Commenting about the
pollution caused by these pulp mills in Howe Sound, just
north of Vancouver, John Reynolds, then British Columbia's environment minister, said. "If you want to go to Howe
Sound to eat crab with me, I'll take you anytime. They are
very safe to eat." He must not have seen the crab caught by a
commercial fisherman off Gambier Island in the sound. The
crab's leg had a claw with two pincers, which is normal, but
out of one of these pincers another claw had grown. It had
been exposed to the deadliest form of dioxin, which pours
out of the wastewater from a pulp mill at Port Mellon, B.C.
In March 1990, he was asked again if he'd eat crab from the
sound. "Only the commercial fishery was closed," he replied,
adding that he still would eat crab he caught on his own – a
distinction perhaps only he understands.

Just up the bay, between two pulp mills, an underwater
photographer named John Pennington has taken photos for
an activist group called Environmental Watch; he has since
described what he saw: "The team remarked on the very
noticeable foul after-taste and pungent odour of the sound's
water. It was unlike anything we had experienced elsewhere
in Vancouver's coastal waters. On our fifth and final dive, I

came upon a red snapper, the first fish I'd seen! As I slowly reached out to touch this colourful fish, he turned and looked at me with his one good eye. The other eye was deformed and looked to be tumorous." Snappers are normally people-shy, but this one lingered, Pennington recalls. "I felt as if he wanted me to tell the world about his pain."

Under British Columbia law, pulp mills that knowingly continue to pollute above their legally established limits can be shut down and fined up to three million dollars, and the individuals responsible for the pollution can be thrown in jail. "The government could charge most mills with breaking the law every day," Environmental Watch says. The British Columbia government even announced it would bring in tough new pollution control standards for the province's twenty-four mills by the end of 1991, which would require the mills to put in secondary treatment systems similar to those at municipal sewage plants. But the laws are almost never enforced.

One of the two mills at either end of the area where Pennington swam, the Western Forest Products Ltd. facility at Woodfibre, B.C., did have twelve charges laid against it, but it has been allowed to continue its present mode of operation until the cases have been completed. The other one, a Canadian Forest Products Ltd. mill at Port Mellon, was checked for air pollution—which also enters the water through the toxic cycle—five times in May 1989, and found to be breaking the legal contamination limits each time. Instead of laying charges, however, the British Columbia government changed the rules in a clever, sophisticated way that enabled the pollution limits to remain the same on paper, but allowed the pollution to increase.

The amendment, called the "bubble system," lets the Port Mellon mill measure the emissions coming from all of its smokestacks and average them. Every other industry in the Vancouver area must measure each smokestack's pollution individually.

The British Columbia government favours the pulp industry over the fishery because it is worth more than the fishery: province-wide, the pulp industry is worth $6 billion per year and produces more than 8 percent of British Columbia's gross provincial product, compared to the $11-million fishing industry. In effect, British Columbia has a system that allows companies to exercise the right to make money even if it hurts others' livelihood and poisons a food supply.

Other industries besides pulp mills cause harm. Off the B.C. coast, in the water north of the Vancouver area, there are radioactive mine tailings and waste. Many experts are also concerned that there will be growing pollution in the province from undersea oil drilling, which the provincial government is considering allowing. The pollution there from existing industry is bad enough already—in 1987, scientists performed an autopsy on a whale that washed ashore in British Columbia, and found that the poor creature's liver had the highest level of mercury ever recorded in any animal, anywhere. Mercury is released by pulp mills.

Pulp mills are a problem on the East Coast, too, but in the Maritimes it's the pollution caused by urban sewage that tends to be more noticeable. Beaches are posted with signs warning people not to harvest shellfish because, as Environment Canada warns, of "the presence of sewage in coastal waters and estuaries."

—— IV ——

In the Maritimes, the number of closed beaches has gone up steadily since 1940. While this is partly because more areas have been examined, the department notes that "it is significant that by 1983, more than 40 years after the problem was recognized, over 250 shellfish closures were in effect, closing over 100,000 hectares to commercial harvesting." In 1987, a year after this was reported, more than 300 Atlantic shellfish areas were closed. "Diseases in the Atlantic marine system include blooms of *Gonyaulax*, causing shellfish to become toxic (which can cause fatalities in humans . . .)," Environment Canada says. "There are suggestions that the incidence of *Gonyaulax* blooms is increasing and that this might be attributable to more sewage in coastal waters." In the Gulf of St Lawrence, large Canadian hydroelectric projects add to these kinds of pollution problems. The projects have altered the ratio of spring to winter runoff, affecting the nutrient supply for creatures such as lobster.

Third World-style sewage treatment exists as far inland as Montreal, which poured 2 billion litres of raw waste into the St Lawrence each day right through the 1980s. The city was just getting around to building its first treatment plant late in the decade. To its credit, the Quebec government has also promised to spend more than $4 billion to build plants for other cities in the 1990s. This will bring the percentage of Quebec cities with sewage treatment to where most of the continent was in about 1973. During the 1980s, only 6 per-cent of the province's population was served by sewage treatment plants.

Governments find sewage pollution a tough habit to break. Even seemingly innovative ideas can get bogged down in a mire of local opposition and political hesitation. In the Halifax area, for example, people have used the harbour as an open sewer for 240 years. When he was environment minister, Tom McMillan called the harbour a sewer; many residents were offended. But it's the harbour that's offensive. Each day, forty sewer lines send out 38 million gallons of putrid water, toilet paper, tampons and the like—a volume of filthy, stinking water the size of a thirty-storey office building. "In the winter people sort of get calmed down about it," says Lois Corbett of the Ecology Action Centre, a local activist group. "But in the summer you can really smell it."

Attempts to change this have been like parodies of actual pollution cleanup programs. In 1973, the city of Halifax slapped a "pollution control" charge on water bills, but the city spent nearly all of the $26 million it earned from this on new pumps and pipes for industrial parks, so the water—still not cleaned or treated in any way—could move more efficiently into the harbour. Finally in 1988, with both the federal and provincial elections about to take place, the two governments announced an ambitious cleanup plan that they said would cost $195 million.

It was dubbed the "petro-poop" plan, because it envisioned turning sewage sludge into oil. First, water is mechanically squeezed out of the sludge, so that the sewage becomes 40 percent solid. Then the material is heated to 350 degrees Celsius in an oxygen-free environment and dried until it's 95 percent solid. Oil and gas are produced from this. The process mimics the way nature produces crude oil from the fossilized remains of dinosaurs, except the new technique takes thirty minutes instead of several million years. Canada could produce 700,000 barrels of oil a year from sludge, saving $20 million in energy costs and cleaning up harbours in the process.

As promising as this may sound, the plan is full of ifs and maybes. In early 1989, once the federal and provincial elections were safely over, the whole program was put on hold. The petro-poop plant was to be built in a town of thirteen hundred inhabitants called Herring Cove, and residents there objected. "The people of Herring Cove don't think they should have to deal with Halifax and Dartmouth's shit," Corbett says. They were heard: the local representative in the provincial legislature was Premier John Buchanan, who promised public hearings, changed his mind, then changed it again. Finally he appointed a task force to study the plan. "It takes the heat off the government," explains Corbett. "Whatever happens, they can say the task force recommended it."

That is, if anything happens. It's a good example of how governments put a high priority on talking about the environment, but a low one on doing anything about it or even figuring out what is right to do. For despite all the promise of this new technology, there are things it is unable to do—clean up the harbour, for example. Petroleum can only be made if the sewage is partially treated, so a secondary treatment facility should be added. But since the $195-million plan was announced, the estimated cost has already gone up to $850 million. If secondary facilities were added, the cost would soar to $2 billion. And even full sewage treatment won't filter out the chemicals that pour into the harbour from industry.

In the meantime, officials set up a Halifax Harbour Cleanup Corporation to handle the money promised before the elections, and the corporation came up with its own solution. It wants to lengthen the sewer pipe, so the sewage–still untreated–will not drain so close to Halifax's Historic Properties tourist area.

As Corbett explains it, the trouble with the petro-poop plan is the usual one. With federal, provincial and local governments involved, plus a task force, it's hard to determine who is running things. "Whenever you get more than two people from government involved, you get problems," she says. It's another case of Iron Ring Disease. As Corbett observes, "technology is the horse leading the cart. . . . Sometimes you get other problems that turn out to be bigger than the ones you started with."

Yet it wouldn't be that difficult to stop the continuing pollution of the harbour if simple–and cheaper–solutions were tried. "Most of the volume of sewage is water," Corbett says. "Water conservation is not a sexy topic, but if we could conserve two-thirds of the water we now use, we could save two-thirds of the cleanup money. It's not as if the people of Halifax and Dartmouth are pooping up a storm."

— V —

Sewage is also damaging fisheries farther out in what Corbett calls "the big toilet"–the Atlantic, where Canada's once-lucrative fishery languishes in a sea full of toxins and trash. To make matters worse, through a series of mistaken assumptions and bad judgments, Canada has jeopardized the future of the fishery by permitting overfishing. In 1977, when the federal government extended its authority offshore to two hundred miles, new technology enabled Canadian trawlers to extend their cod-fishing areas farther north, through the ice to spawning areas. A federal task force on Atlantic fisheries headed by Liberal Senator Michael Kirby reported in 1983 that "we face the happy prospect of a 50 percent increase in the groundfish catch between 1981 and 1987." Instead, catches declined by nearly 80,000 tons between 1982 and 1989, leading to a loss of three thousand jobs. The two main fishing companies lost $20 million each in 1988 and 1989.

Overfishing by foreign vessels helped cause this; stocks of twenty-seven out of thirty species in the North Atlantic have declined, with some, like halibut, dropping by 90 percent. But much of the problem was our own doing. As Kirby acknowledges, scientific advice was "seriously in error," which caused officials to overestimate what the Canadian fleet could catch without endangering the fishery. New limits on catches were imposed in 1990 out of fear that the fish will disappear altogether.

Overfishing appears to be the main cause of declining fish stocks, but pollution is playing its part. Even when contamination isn't killing large quantities of fish, it's preventing them from multiplying. The water of San Francisco Bay, for example, is so polluted that some species of fish are failing to reproduce. Significantly, Kirby also points to what may be the biggest threat: "Even today, the abundance of fish will always depend on large-scale fluctuations in the ocean environment, of which we have very little knowledge. The big question today is whether there has been some permanent environmental change—for example, a much larger seal population, or an unknown source of pollution—that will cause a permanent reduction in available stocks."

CHAPTER SEVEN

FROM SEA TO FILTHY SEA

Containing an oil spill is no great trick.
> —Exxon magazine ad, 1974

The seas make up 71 percent of the earth's surface. They were formed some 2 billion years ago. Life was born in them. They can be majestic, tranquil, wild and threatening, or awe-inspiring. They have enticed explorers to dare their waves; others have been drawn to study their depths. They cover steep slopes that plunge for distances greater than the highest mountains on land, and they contain deep canyons that may never be seen by humans. A single wave can inspire a poet or a painter; the vast ocean expanses have spawned legends of continents lost beneath the waves. The seas feed a large portion of humanity, and they are a main source of our oxygen, our weather changes, our rain.

The water itself, without poisons, is a complex mixture of chemicals; a single cubic mile contains 150 million tonnes of salts alone. But humanity is putting mercury into the water at two and a half times the natural rate, manganese at four times, zinc, copper and lead twelve times, antimony thirty times and life-choking phosphorus eighty times. The famous oceanographer Jacques-Yves Cousteau warned in the late 1970s that "poisoning the sea will inevitably poison us." If he is right – and there is no reason to dispute him – then we are well on the way to our destruction.

No part of the ocean is free from pollution any more; there are globs of tar floating in the middle of the Pacific. In Antarctica, the fat of penguins has been found to contain DDT, even though the pesticide, obviously, was never sprayed on the snow and ice. Pollution is turning up in polar bears and arctic whales. Water travels everywhere, of course – and so does the contamination it contains. In ninety years, every single drop that is now in the Mediterranean, Caribbean and North Seas will have flowed to other seas. They're all filthy.

So far, the open oceans are generally in better shape than inland or partly-enclosed waters, though as Cousteau warned in 1985, "that may not be true in 10 or 20 years. We face a catastrophe." We have certainly not treated them well. Perhaps it is because we don't drink sea water that we have long considered the oceans to be receptacles. Back in 1895, there were accounts of swimmers in New York drifting into table scraps. A magazine called *Metropolitan* noted that "for many years bathers at all the resorts within one hundred miles of New York were wont, while paddling outside of the ropes, to come into violent contact with a watermelon rind, or perhaps, worse, to bunk noses with the refuse end of a cucumber, both of which had more than served their usefulness in New York."

It's more than a matter of cucumbers nowadays. It's even more than a matter of local sewage plants overflowing. In Galveston, Texas, beachgoers wade into tides that bring plastic bags and garbage all the way from Norway. There are seas of plastic; it has been estimated that every day, more than five million plastic containers are thrown overboard around the world. According to the U.S. National Academy of Sciences, each year more than 20,000 tonnes of plastic packaging are tossed into the water by fishermen, who also manage to lose or discard about 123,000 tonnes of plastic nets, lines or buoys. It's not surprising; in the North Pacific alone, along the migration route of Canadian and Alaskan salmon, Japanese, South Korean and Taiwanese fishermen have spread enough driftnet to circle the earth, and they lose at least several hundred kilometres a year.

Then there are the packing pellets, those little bits of polyethylene and propylene that are used to protect shipping goods. In some parts of the North Atlantic, South Atlantic and Pacific oceans, one to four thousand of these pellets are floating on every square kilometre of surface. Environment Canada notes that "plastic wastes, known as 'persistent plastics,' are found in all of the oceans, and there is growing concern that these discarded materials are seriously harming marine life." They certainly are "persistent": they last indefinitely. There are only two ways to destroy plastic—by burning it or making it biodegradable. Incineration either pollutes the air or creates tonnes of incinerator ash, or both, and ships don't have incinerators, anyway. Biodegradable plastic decays only with exposure to light—which varies in intensity and is too weak to act on plastic just below the sea's surface. Marine mammals and birds often mistake plastic for food, or they get caught in plastic netting and debris, and then they die. As many as one million seabirds and approximately a hundred thousand cetaceans (whales, dolphins and porpoises) die each year because of plastic pollution. And worldwide plastic production doubles every twelve years.

— I —

"Every Canadian should expect a clean and healthy marine environment and safe products from the sea," Environment Canada says. And in fact, there are laws and international agreements that aim to meet these expectations. One of the country's earliest environment-related laws, the Navigable Waters Protection Act, was passed in 1873. At least twenty other federal laws deal with environmental protection of the seas and the estuaries and rivers that feed them. The main ones are the Fisheries Act, the Canada Water Act, the International River Improvements Act, the International Boundary Waters Treaty Act, the Northern Inland Waters

Act, the Arctic Waters Pollution Prevention Act, the Canada Shipping Act, the Canada Oil and Gas Act, the Transportation of Dangerous Goods Act and the Ocean Dumping Control Act.

Both individually and collectively, they don't work properly. A report by officials from Environment Canada (which administers some, but not all, of these laws) says, "It is evident ... that the number of controls is minimal [and] the existing controls are inconsistent." Another government report notes more specifically that "the defintions of various types of waters contained in these acts differ from one to another. The geographic extent of the application of these statutes also varies. Several of these statutes contain cross-reference to others, explaining their mutual application. This abundance of legislation has produced confusion as to the occasions on which it is appropriate to use each statute." In the Arctic, the legislation is so confusing that "federal officials themselves have difficulties in understanding where their respective responsibilities begin and end."

The system can fail in many ways. For example, the Ocean Dumping Control Act of 1975 is supposed to curb the practice of hauling incinerator ash and garbage to sea. But in July 1988 – at the same time that the medical debris hit the eastern shores of the United States – municipal and regional governments were pressuring federal officials to allow ash and sludge to be dumped in the water. Southam News reported that they wanted to follow "the example set by London, England, and New York City."

Jim Kingham, the former Environment Canada official who authorized *Storm Warning*, was instrumental in drawing up the Ocean Dumping Control Act. He offers another example of how the laws don't work. When an oil slick pollutes a fishing zone, the Canadian Shipping Act provides a compensation fund, the Maritime Pollution Claims Fund, that could help people who suffer damages. "The Canadian system is supposed to respond," he says. "Except somebody will find a loophole. They'll say, 'We can't apply the Maritime Pollution Claims Fund, because we don't have the money to deal with this problem.' Or: 'This incident has resulted in damages which are unspecific. The fund was intended for people who are damaged in terms of their livelihood, namely loss of fishing gear or fishing vessels or fish, to let them make a specific claim for compensation.'

"No matter how well you design systems, they break down."

Governments around the world have long talked about who is responsible for keeping the seas clean, and they've long avoided coming to precise conclusions. In 1926, an international meeting was called to discuss "oil pollution of navigable waters," but nothing really came of this. One of the main concerns was not the environment, but the fact that oily water would blow against ships and dirty the sailors' clothes. Until the 1950s, ships regularly, and deliberately, discharged ballast—the water held in empty fuel tanks—which soon becomes an oily mess. There were no rules to stop the practice.

Finally, in 1954, an international agreement called the Oilpol Convention was reached, and it took effect four years later. It forbade the discharge of ballast close to shore. In some congested areas, such as the Mediterranean Sea, it's supposed to be forbidden entirely. But the oceans still absorb as much as 6 million tonnes of oil each year, which must come from somewhere. No one is exactly sure; while some experts say up to 90 percent is washed into the seas from activities that take place on land, others say as much as half comes from sea-based operations—ships cleaning their bilges and offshore drilling platforms. The big discharges attract much attention. A 1969 oil well blowout that fouled the shoreline at Santa Barbara, California, helped create the green wave, turning many people into instant, dedicated environmentalists. People turned on their TVs and saw shuddering, oil-soaked seabirds, moving a step closer to painful death with each desperate flutter of their caked, sticky feathers. Another blowout in the Gulf of Mexico in 1980 lasted nine months, spilling 3 million barrels of oil. (A barrel contains 35 Imperial gallons, which equals 42 U.S. gallons or nearly 160 litres.)

Many people believe that the biggest problem in the oceans comes from oil spills, but spills contribute less than a third of all the oil that comes from sea-based activities. From the everyday activities of shipping alone, nearly 1.5 million tonnes of oil are discharged into the water each year. Even before the *Exxon Valdez* spill, the cost of handling this mess was about half a billion dollars a year (U.S.) in damages paid by shipping companies and in loss of fisheries and shellfish beds around the world.

Oil is so prevalent in the oceans that oil slicks have even been mapped worldwide. Between 1975 and 1978, the United Nations sponsored a survey, which involved nearly one hundred thousand visual inspections of the sea surface, to look for floating pollution. Slicks and floating tar were found all along the major tanker routes, and petroleum residues were detected almost everywhere. Yet as the U.S.-based World Resources Institute notes, because spills are more spectacular, "the major sources of oil pollution are virtually unnoticed by the public."

Spills also tend to highlight flaws in the legal structure. In 1967, an incredibly large tanker spill occurred in the English Channel, when *Torrey Canyon* ran aground and released nearly a million barrels of oil. The oil ruined beaches in both England and France. But when the authorities tried to collect damages, they ran aground legally. The ship was registered in Liberia, insured in England and owned by the American Oil Company, which leased it to another American firm, Barracuda Tanker Corporation. Barracuda subleased it to Union Oil, also American, which subleased it again to Petroleum Trading Ltd., a subsidiary of the British Petroleum Company. It had an Italian crew. Who should sue whom? Who was legally responsible for the mishap? The Cousteau Society's *Almanac* noted sarcastically, "While the sale of the *Torrey Canyon*'s oil might have been everybody's profit, the British and French authorities discovered the spill was nobody's fault." Nearly a decade later, in 1976, a similar situation arose just forty kilometres south of Nantucket, Massachusetts, when the *Argo Merchant* ran aground, spilling 200,000 barrels of fuel oil. The biggest shipboard spill ever was the 1979 grounding of the *Amoco Cadiz* tanker off the coast of France, which spilled 1.3 million barrels and generated a decade of legal proceedings.

Canada has gotten off relatively easy when it comes to spills. Until late in 1988, the last tanker accident that had occurred entirely within Canadian waters was in 1979, when the British tanker *Kurdistan* broke up in the Cabot Strait, between Nova Scotia and Newfoundland. Another Canadian disaster had taken place in 1970 – the sinking of the *Irving Whale* in the Gulf of St Lawrence, about fifty kilometres northeast of Prince Edward Island. It has been more of a problem. Almost twenty years later, the federal government acknowledged that its cargo of more than half a million gallons of oil (about two million litres) was still leaking slowly into the water. There's virtually nothing anyone can do to stop it.

Nevertheless, since the 1970s it has become a bit easier to clean up at least some of the legal issues after a spill. There are now several international agreements that set standards for training crews and deal with liability, the protocol for cleaning up and compensation for the damage that is done. If all these procedures are followed, the courts have less to deal with later; if they're not, the courts know where to look to find out what went wrong. Authorities in the United States have even tried to come up with "replacement costs" for birds. Figures have ranged from one dollar per bird – an amount set arbitrarily in 1969 after the Santa Barbara blowout – to two hundred dollars for the whistling swans of Chesapeake Bay.

But when it came to the kind of accident that everyone feared would happen and that the rules had been made to guard against, the environmental safety measures, the laws and the political response all proved hopelessly inadequate. This was true even though the spill occurred entirely within the territory of one country – which is what happened when the *Exxon Valdez* hit a reef.

—— **II** ——

The facts of the *Exxon Valdez* accident have been the subject of endless talk and speculation, in official investigations, in the media, in ordinary conversation, even in jokes. Given the subject matter – an oil spill – the stories inevitably involve black humour. "Now fish sticks will come in leaded and unleaded." A cartoon depicted a seal, caked with oily slime, saying, "Remember when they used to just bludgeon us?"

The sick jokes, the hearings, the official statements and the post-mortems don't obscure the fact that the *Exxon Valdez* accident was actually quite straightforward. Early in the morning of March 25, 1989 – Good Friday – an oil tanker that was as long as three football fields was bound for Long Beach, California, but it went aground in Prince William Sound, a sensitive marine area about thirty-three kilometres south of Valdez, Alaska. The crash ripped open a six-metre gash, allowing eight of the tanker's thirteen compartments to leak. There were 1.26 million barrels of crude oil in the tanker, more than 200 million litres. Roughly one-sixth of this, more than 37 million litres, poured into the water, at the rate of about 5.7 million litres an hour. This was a relatively small spill – less than one-fifth the volume of the *Amoco Cadiz* spill – but it spread over a distance of more than 1,600 kilometres and an area of about 2,500 square kilometres, forming a pool about the size of the state of Rhode Island. The crude oil coated every living thing in its path with a deadly ooze. It killed some 33,000 seabirds, nearly 1,000 sea-otters and caused extensive, perhaps permanent, damage to a salmon and herring fishery worth some $150 million a year. It created a new symbol for Americans – the bald eagle soaked in crude oil. At least 138 of them died in this way. It was the biggest oil spill in North American history.

There was evidence that the ship's captain, Joseph Hazelwood, had been drinking before the *Exxon Valdez* ran aground; he was charged with criminal negligence, but the prosecutors could not prove he had been drunk. Hazelwood was convicted on a lesser charge and ordered to pay $50,000 in restitution and help in the cleanup of the spill. Exxon fired him, but how much his drinking contributed to the accident, and what were the ultimate causes of the spill, are still to be determined by some of the more than 150 civil and criminal cases now in the courts. However, it already seems clear that many others demonstrated impaired judgment when it came to the spill, starting with the Exxon Corporation.

In 1974, Exxon ran magazine ads touting a device for cleaning up oil spills—a fence to surround them and drag them away, called a "bottom-tension boom." "Containing an oil spill is no great trick," the ads said. "The tricky part is containing it in rough water. And we're pretty sure that Exxon has developed a device that can be used in rough water. . . . Tests show that the bottom-tension boom works." Apparently, there's no substitute for practical experience: the company found it hard to locate a 1,600-kilometre long boom. Contingency plans for a mega-spill like the 1989 disaster were actually drawn up in 1977, when the Trans-Alaskan pipeline was completed, enabling supertankers to load up with oil at Valdez. The plans called for double-hulled tankers, but, because the companies complained they were too expensive, nobody ever made them a requirement. The plans also called for a quick cleanup response.

It took Exxon four days to take serious action. In the early 1980s, the company had cut 80,000 people from its 180,000-strong workforce; among those cut were its spill specialists. (After the spill, however, Exxon claimed it still had on hand 1,000 people trained to handle spills—1 percent of its workforce.) The company had estimated that a spill of this size could only happen once every 241 years, and Alyeska Pipeline Service Company, the consortium of oil companies including Exxon that owns Alaska's North Slope oil, had laid off its oil-spill response team back in 1981. The U.S. Coast Guard had downgraded its tracking operation in Prince William Sound in 1984.

Needless to say, the cleanup was less than perfect; at times, crews resorted to prayers. Exxon's chairman, Lawrence Rawl, claimed that up to half the spill could have been cleaned up if the company had been allowed to use chemical dispersants, and that Alaska's government had prevented this. However, state records showed that the company had been given permission in advance to use chemicals. In *Fortune* magazine, Rawl conceded that "if you want the area to look pristine when we're done, we probably can't restore it. If you accept a reasonable compromise, we'd go ahead." Four months after the spill, with about one-third of the work done, Exxon's notion of compromise became clear. The company hedged on whether it would come back to finish the cleanup job in 1990. At first, it said it would not continue in the spring but would simply survey the area, then it agreed to continue if forced by U.S. Coast Guard officials. As the cleanup cost climbed toward $2 billion, the company also announced that it would pursue another compromise—a financial one. It would claim $400 million in tax deductions to which it was entitled under U.S. law. Legislators took steps to block this when it became known, but the company apparently felt its move was consistent with what Rawl had told *Fortune*: "We're going to demonstrate that Exxon is trustworthy. We're going to do everything possible to mitigate the effects on the environmental situation up there." The company later said that on account of the spill, it earned 10 percent, or $300 million, less than its expected profit for 1989: $3.51 billion.

For all the mess the disaster caused, in a way the *Exxon Valdez* was one of the best things to happen to the environment—politically. It shattered illusions about corporate responsibility for pollution, and any that remained about all the promises that had been made about the environment since the 1970s, even the most recent ones. In the May 1989 issue of *Alaska* magazine, *after* the Exxon spill, an ad paid for by the Alaska Oil and Gas Association read: "After 20 years of activity on the North Slope, the oil industry has proven it can operate without harming the environment." The dead birds and shivering otter were better proof of how promises are kept.

—— **III** ——

In the United States, the political effects of the *Exxon Valdez* spill were substantial, as legislators scrambled to show their concern by holding hearings and passing new environmental laws. But in Canada, the political effects were minimal. This was part of a long tradition in the way Canada deals with oil spills. Before the Valdez accident, in February 1971, Randolph Harding, a British Columbia MP, rose in the House of Commons to ask a question of the external affairs minister, Mitchell Sharp: "I ask the Secretary of State for External Affairs whether he has made direct representations to the United States government in an endeavour to halt oil shipments over the route from Valdez, Alaska, to Cherry Point, Washington?" Sharp told him that once the shipping route opened, Canada would be ready: "We have the situation under very close examination and at the appropriate time we will make representations. We do not think this is the time."

In 1974, Dave Barrett, then premier of British Columbia, complained to Prime Minister Pierre Trudeau that "there is apparently no specific strategy" for oil spills. Trudeau wrote Barrett, assuring him that there was indeed a plan. But environmental groups at the time complained that it was inadequate.

Around the same time, Gary Gallon, later senior policy adviser to the government of Ontario, was an environmental activist in British Columbia. He prepared a brief on the issue for the federal environment minister of the day, Jeanne Sauvé (later Canada's governor-general), "The federal government is not prepared to handle large oil spills on the British Columbia West Coast." "During your October, 1974 visit to British Columbia," Gallon wrote, "you indicated that the federal government had an adequate program to control oil spills on the British Columbia West Coast. We cannot concur with this statement." The coastal waters "lie bare and unprotected, at the mercy of any large ocean oil spill."

Sauvé wrote back in February 1975 with a soothing explanation of the government's position. "We have been continually increasing the capability to respond in containment and cleanup operations," she said. "You may be sure that we are painfully aware of the limitations and deficiencies of the world-wide 'state of preparedness' to handle oil spills. But, we are directing much time, effort, manpower and money toward extending those limits and reducing or eliminating those deficiencies.

"This is not a static situation."

It took until June 1989—following the *Exxon Valdez* spill—for another Canadian government to order a review of tanker safety. The federal government also prepared an internal report containing background information on marine traffic, spills and responses on the West Coast, and a list of all oil spills in Canada during the previous five years. But when the hearings opened, the government would not let the public see this report. Three prominent experts who had headed previous public inquiries denounced the review as "a waste of time." The critics included Tom Berger, the former judge who ran the Mackenzie Valley Pipeline Inquiry in the 1970s, perhaps the most comprehensive study of the effects of oil exploration on the delicate northern environment. The 1989 hearings were conducted in an atmosphere of obscurity, with the public barely, if at all, aware of what was being heard and decided. The panel was due to report in 1990. Meanwhile, the Canadian oil industry assured the public that there were adequate safeguards in place—and that it, too, was conducting a review.

Three days before Christmas 1989, a barge loaded with oil ran into high seas off the coast of Washington State, about 150 kilometres south of Seattle. The barge collided with its tug, leaving a gash that enabled heavy, greasy bunker oil to leak into the water. It was only about 875,000 litres, or 190,000 gallons—less than 20 percent of what the *Exxon Valdez* spilled three months later. But in the week after the barge collision, the heavy, tarry crude oil was buffeted by the Pacific waves, and it broke down from big blobs into millions of smaller slicks. By the beginning of January, ten days after the first leakage, the currents had pushed the slimy globs all the way to Vancouver Island, fouling crab traps and caking up the beaches of Pacific Rim National Park. Most of the west coast of the island was smeared with grease. On the morning of January 3, the ugly blobs reached Tofino, B.C., a town of one thousand inhabitants.

There was no warning. "We didn't know until it was on our beaches," said one resident. The townspeople spent half the next month cleaning globs of sticky bunker oil off the beach. Valerie Langer, a resident of Tofino who works in the bakery, went out to help, and this is when she really became appalled. "It's pure manual labour," she says. "There's nothing else to be done except bend over, pick it up with your hands, or a shovel, put it in a garbage bag and then lug it up above the high tide line." This was just the messy part. The heartbreaking part was cleaning the birds.

A seabird caked with oil is delicate, so it must be handled with care, Langer says. To survive, the birds must remain wet, but the oil hardens their feathers, rearranging them so that moisture cannot get through. At one point, she and some neighbours came across about thirty damp, shivering birds that were clinging precariously to life. The towns-people did what they could: "You take soap and water and you wash the birds several times. It takes a long time because they have to preen their feathers back. The oils have to be completely off. So we'd have to wash them and then keep them in a warm place, then wash them again."

Taking care of the birds was time-consuming. "It took a week for some of them to recover, some of them two weeks. Some of them were getting anaemic because they were ingesting oil. We had to try and flush them out." Most of these thirty birds survived and were released on the other side of Vancouver Island. "There were loons, grebes, auklets, ducks and seagulls." What bothered Langer was that there were also as many as twenty-five hundred sea birds that died after being soaked with oil. "Those are the birds that we found. They say if you find one there are ten others that you don't find. It's pretty devastating to us. Perhaps in some scientists' eyes that's an insignificant amount. But when you talk about an oil spill and all its effects and how the effects move along the food chain, there must be some significance."

As news of the spill spread, volunteers arrived to help, coming from elsewhere on the island and in some cases, across the country. Langer and other residents put them up and fed them. But they were getting next to no help, financially or otherwise, from the authorities. Langer and others who had house guests thought it reasonable to ask the province to give them food vouchers, worth fourteen dollars a day, to help pay the cost.

"You know what it took to get those food vouchers?" Langer asks. "I had gone out on the beach to clean oil, and after a week and half, it was as bad as the first day. And I thought, you know, why am I doing this? So we just hopped into the car and drove to Victoria and took our oily birds that we had and left our oily clothes on." She and a friend made the arduous five-hour drive and went directly to the provincial legislature and Premier William Vander Zalm's office. They didn't get to see the premier, but they left a message—four armfuls of oil-soaked, dead seabirds. As the black, stiffened birds oozed pools of oil onto the floor of the premier's office, Langer told one of Vander Zalm's staff: "This is what we've had to deal with every day. We're feeding people, and we're housing them. Get us some money. Get us some people."

They also had another message. "We just went in and said: This is what we're dealing with. It's not our jurisdiction to clean up oil. And you guys are all saying it's not yours. Well, who the hell's is it?"

As usual, this was a question no one seemed able to answer. Tofino residents and, indeed, people elsewhere in Canada assumed there would be some kind of emergency plan, but the authorities gave conflicting answers to the calls for help. At first, provincial and federal officials argued that the oil wasn't a serious problem. When Environment Canada officials were asked to clean up, they replied that they wanted to see where the oil was coming from first. A nearby army base actually did have contingency plans to send seventy-five men to an oil spill within six hours, but they never received an official request. "There was chaos in the early days," says Vicky Husband, a British Columbia activist who also volunteered for the cleanup. No one in authority seemed to know what to do.

Some government help did arrive, and eventually, more than two weeks into the cleanup, federal Environment Minister Lucien Bouchard arrived to tour the area. Despite pleas from the local residents, he declined to call in the army, but he did secure more money. The same day, British Columbia's environment minister, Bruce Strachan, paid his first visit, too. Nearly a month after the oil began leaking from the barge, Premier Vander Zalm generously offered the volunteers certificates of appreciation, but the local member of the provincial legislature declined to hand them out—he said the volunteers would roll him in tar if he tried.

As a former federal official, Jim Kingham thinks it's amazing the way every time there's a spill, oil manages to seep through cracks in the regulatory and response system. The British Columbia spill "is a very interesting and useful illustration of the failure of the systems approach to solving pollution problems," he says. In his opinion, somebody made a decision that could only result in the polluting of Canadian beaches. "It was an active, conscious decision. That somebody happened to be the U.S. Coast Guard official in charge of oil spill countermeasures on the West Coast."

Kingham explains that when the spill occurred "the vessel was heading toward a certain harbour in Washington State. The Coast Guard official said: This will damage the harbour. Let us tow this vessel out to sea. The result of the decision was to pollute the Canadian shoreline. He said, we never thought it would happen. Well, it did.

"Why shouldn't people feel concerned? Why shouldn't Canadians feel concerned? Why shouldn't North Americans, for that matter, feel concerned that somebody can actively take a decision that results in serious harm? They had trust in the system."

Kingham's account is consistent with what Vicky

Husband was told by Canadian officials. "They told me [the Americans] were worried about it spilling into one harbour. They thought there would be less damage if the vessel were towed out farther. They thought that if they towed it out to sea the oil would just disperse. Is that what we always do with our garbage?"

CHAPTER EIGHT

SMOKE OF A FURNACE

The sun has never visited that city,
For it dissolveth in the daylight fair.
        —James Thomson, *The City of Dreadful Night*

Spills don't only happen in the water. In 1979, a tanker car derailed in Mississauga, Ontario, spewing a cloud of deadly chlorine into the air and forcing 250,000 people to flee their homes until the gas dissipated. The shiploads of PCBs that caused rioting in Baie Comeau were the blackened remains of 159,110 litres of contaminated oil that caught fire in 1988 while stored in a Saint-Basile-le-Grand, Quebec, warehouse that was supposed to accommodate only 4,500 litres. This fire sent a dark, ugly plume of toxic smoke billowing into the sky, casting a shadow over the town's 3,000 residents, who will spend years wondering how their health has been affected.

These kinds of accidents, which now seem to occur almost regularly in North America, inflict a quick and dirty toxic shock on the continent's environment and its inhabitants. But they're only symptoms. Just as oil spills contribute only a small portion to the pollution of the seas, the real threat to the air is not so much these sudden disastrous jolts of pollution, but the everyday, continuous fouling of the skies.

Our air is filled with increasing levels of smoke, carbon dioxide, sulphur, ozone and other chemical compounds. Every breath contains a little whiff of disaster.

—— I ——

To stand in downtown Toronto in July 1988 was to feel as if you had been licked by a big, sweaty dog. By the end of a day – virtually any day that month – just being outdoors in the city could make your skin crawl, your insides burn. Each of the hottest days would start optimistically. The sun would come up brightly, the sky would be clearer and the air would be a bit fresher than it was the previous afternoon. The end of such days, though, had a depressing similarity: you couldn't see and the city reeked. For physical as well as emotional reasons, it made your heart pound and your breath come up short. It felt like downtown Sodom and Gomorrah, where, according to the Bible, "the smoke of the land went up as the smoke of a furnace."

While the days were quite hot, the most oppressive aspect was not the temperature, or even the humidity – it was the air itself, harsh, full of grit. Each day from about ten in the morning, the air had a faint, yet distinctly sour smell, which you could also taste. It would be exaggerating a bit to say the sky was brown that week, but it wasn't exactly bright blue. It wouldn't be exaggerating to say that the air was thick, and it wasn't exactly air. If you had even mild allergies, your eyes would be red, swollen, itchy and watery – much worse than anything that pollen, hay or ragweed could cause. A deep breath would catch the back of your throat. It was like sniffing burning oven cleaner. It seemed to be searing the insides of your lungs.

It was.

At fifteen metres above street level on July 6, 1988, there were 159 parts of ozone for every billion parts of air – enough ozone to ensure that the air itself could burn holes in plants and shrubs, as well as the soft, pulpy tissue of frail human lungs. High ground-level ozone is only one among a group of environmental problems scientists call the Long Range Transport of Atmospheric Pollutants. In simple terms, these are the chemicals that travel in the airborne section of the toxic cycle. The problem is worst in the summer, because many of the harmful substances are formed when chemicals react in sunlight and heat.

A cross-section of Toronto's air that day would have revealed ozone, nitrogen oxides, and various crude pollutants such as sulphur dioxide and lead. The name "ozone" was coined in 1840 from the Greek word *ozein*, which means "to smell." Ozone is a molecule made of three oxygen atoms, one more than the oxygen, or O_2, that we breathe. When new substances are added to the air—smoke, car exhaust and the like—a delicate balance is upset, and the amount of ozone in the atmosphere can change. There can be either more or less ozone, depending in large part on where the changes occur.

High in the atmosphere, beginning at about ten kilometres above the ground, ozone offers protection from the sun's harmful ultraviolet rays, which can cause skin cancer. But at close range, in high concentrations, ozone is poisonous. The ozone at ground level originates largely in cities and built-up industrial areas, but some of the highest pollution readings have been taken in the countryside. In Ontario, the highest yearly average ozone levels are not in sour-smelling downtown Toronto, or industrial Hamilton, but in an otherwise pleasant little place called Tiverton, on Lake Huron. "The high ozone levels in Tiverton were caused by the long-range transport of pollutants, primarily from U.S. sources," Ontario's Environment Ministry says. These sources are responsible "for more than half of the ozone in Ontario."

On the other hand, local sources matter, too: in 1987, the highest ozone levels measured over a one-hour period were in a park in Sarnia, just a few minutes from the belching towers of Chemical Valley. In some cities, such as Los Angeles and Vancouver, geography counts; ozone tends to be trapped by mountains and the weather patterns they generate. In others, its difficult to say how much of the pollution is local and how much comes from far away. Virtually everyone accepts the fact that Toronto is breathing the ozone that comes from the exhuast of too many cars in the city, but residents are also receiving toxic air pollution from the United States. Ontario's pollution in turn blows into Quebec.

While the levels of ozone that climbed to record highs during the summer of 1988 are considered only mildly toxic, they were high enough to make people with chronic bronchitis or other respiratory ailments feel terrible, especially the elderly or children. Such levels are also well past the point where it becomes difficult to ride a bike or jog. Until recently, it was thought that such trouble begins at around 120 parts per billion of ozone—well below what it was in Toronto on July 6, 1988. But more recent studies have suggested that the damage is caused at much lower levels. For example, *Newsweek* reported a study done for the U. S. Environmental Protection Agency, in which healthy men breathed ozone at 120 parts per billion for nearly an hour while riding exercise bikes. "After several sessions, their lung function had declined 12 percent and it hurt to breathe deeply." Worse, "the damage does not go away when clean air blows in." In July 1988, Toronto's ozone was some 30 percent higher than this. Similar levels were reached in 1989, even though that summer was not extraordinarily hot.

Ozone causes smog, which is also formed by compounds called nitrogen oxides—among the main components of acid rain. A chemical reaction takes place when sunlight strikes nitrogen oxides and hydrocarbons which are produced by gasoline vapours and emitted by factory smokestacks and tailpipes. Collectively, the end products of such reactions are called photochemical oxidants, a term that captures their essence: sunlight, poison and rust. Even when these reactions don't turn the sky into a stinging, whisky-coloured mess, the air is still so contaminated that scientists talk about a "chemical soup." When it's dry outside, the ingredients drift to earth; scientists call this toxic fallout. When we get precipitation, we don't just get acid rain—we get toxic rain.

Studies suggest that we eat more pollution than we drink or breathe, but damage from breathing it can be more direct. Breathing bad air can easily land you on a hospital stretcher with a pain in your chest. The contaminants are harmful, numerous and they enter the air in enormous quantities. In 1985, a U.S. congressman from Los Angeles, Democrat Henry Waxman, estimated that 80 million pounds of toxic chemicals, about 36 million kilograms, were emitted into the air over the United States each year. This led to the passing of a law by Congress requiring companies to disclose their toxic air pollution. The companies called Waxman hysterical and accused him of exaggerating, but when they reported under the law, it turned out they were spewing out thirty-four times as much as he had thought—2 billion pounds, or nearly a billion kilograms, of poison a year.

A survey by the U. S. Environmental Protection Agency identified 328 of the worst toxic air pollutants among these 2 billion pounds; 60 of them were linked to cancer. This is the same study that estimated that one hundred million Americans are breathing air that fails to meet government standards for pollutants. Canada doesn't have national standards, but people living in most urban areas are breathing the same bad air. And as usual, Canada is doing little about it. When asked in 1989 if Ottawa was contemplating a U.S.-style list of the nation's air polluters, an environment department official told *Maclean's* magazine that "companies would not really appreciate that."

—— II ——

Bad air is one of the most extensively and historically well-documented forms of pollution. And we continually create and discover newer, more sophisticated forms of it. Early observers identified the problem simply as smoke, something the Industrial Revolution produced plenty of but which had always existed. Some of the first pollution legislation was aimed at controlling it. In 1661, a tract on air pollution was published in London, England, entitled *Fumifugium: or the Inconvenience of the Aer and Smoake of London Dissipated*. Its author, John Evelyn, suggested that London's bad air could be cured by "sweet-smelling trees." Much later, in 1819 and then in 1843, the British Parliament set up committees to study smoke-polluted air and dirty water, and even passed a few rudimentary pollution control laws.

In Canada, people were concerned as long ago as the early 1900s. In June 1932, the *Toronto Daily Star* reported about a meeting of an organization called the Smoke Prevention Association at the Royal York Hotel. The hotel, now a grand old landmark, was then only five years old, but the smoke preventers had been meeting for twenty-six years. When they gathered in 1932, they heard how doctors found that "a definite relationship between cancer deaths and smoke from chimneys exists, more such deaths occurring where a large volume of smoke is found than anywhere else."

The delegates were also told that factory smoke—it was not yet popularly called air pollution—was doing $5 million a year in damage to Toronto, a lot of money at a time when a solid brick house cost about $3,000. No one had ever calculated the amount of "dirt," as the pollution was also termed, that poured over the city, but the experts figured it had to be at least 112 tons a month per square mile. Spread over the city's 37.4 square miles (there were no suburbs then), this would mean 4,195 tons a month. The experts felt this was a conservative estimate; in one city where the "dirt" was measured, Chicago, about twice that much fell each month.

By then, it was understood that the threat was more than just too much smoke in proportion to the air. The *Star* reported that "belching furnaces" were emitting "invisible sulphuric acid" that "rots away shirts" and "eats big buildings." A Toronto expert named J. W. Bell explained that "any housewife will tell you curtains in the country last far longer than in the city." The conditions "are much the same as in other American cities," added Bell.

The smoke also included fly ash, which was described as tiny particles of jagged glass formed as a byproduct of burning coal. Employing the slang of the 1930s, the man who offered this description said that "it has been known to get in the lungs and drill a hole that gives a swell break to pneumonia germs in not very strong people." He also described even more ominous health research: "Rickets in children is caused by defraction [sic] of sunlight, with its vitamin D, by foreign matter, such as smoke in the air. It causes bow-legged children and other things."

The smoke preventers were told that "the only solution is equipment of smoke washing apparatus for every plant," and that the problem could be fixed for $4 million – a heavy cost at the time, but $1 million less than the damage the pollution was causing. Indeed, some cities had already taken action. A visiting inspector from Springfield, Massachusetts, explained that in his city "we have succeeded in licking the tar out of black smoke." (One hopes this was just a figure of speech.) But Toronto's smoke inspector, William Tait, pointed out that there was an obstacle in Canada that made it difficult to achieve the same results: the political system. The city would like to do more, but its pollution law "was a provincial ruling, which allows six minutes of smoke per hour from factory smokestacks. This ruling was said by various organizations not to be highly satisfactory and movements were underway to provide more stringent control."

However, at least one place, Pittsburgh, showed that a city could be cleaned up, and the difference was like night and day.

On Pittsburgh's main streets during the 1940s, the lights from the storefronts would shine, brightening small patches of asphalt beneath a blackened sky. The sidewalks were busy; the slick, dark pavement was crowded with traffic. This was urban prosperity. People moved purposefully, heads down, past a clock on the corner that read eleven. It was eleven – in the morning. The sky was so dark that it may well have been midnight.

"I remember waking in the mornings in those fall days of

1946," says Robert Pease, "my upper lip black just from breathing Pittsburgh's air." Pease has been executive director of the Allegheny Conference, a community development organization that was set up by Pittsburgh's major companies after the war, to clean up. For him, it was obvious why one writer chose to describe Pittsburgh as "Hell with the lid taken off."

The problem was extreme, yet the city was able to clean up in short order, mostly by enforcing a strict smoke-control law requiring coal-burning homes to switch to natural gas. The municipal law was also imposed on the steel and related industries in Pittsburgh. They were required to put "precipitating devices" on their smokestacks – the kinds of scrubbers that today would help cut the acid rain falling over Canada. Unlike so many other regulatory situations, the industries co-operated, spending what was then the large sum of a million dollars each to control the emissions from their major smokestacks.

The journey from darkness to light was a rapid one. "The winter of 1947–8 was the last black smoky winter in Pittsburgh," Pease says. The improvement was so dramatic that residents felt "that a city that could rid itself of such black smoke could accomplish anything." Huge sections of the downtown business district have been rebuilt since then, and Pittsburgh has transformed itself successfully from a brawny industrial town to what the British newsmagazine the *Economist* calls a "brainbox" – a centre for regional banks, computer software companies, high-tech research and airlines. Even today, Pittsburgh refers to its postwar cleanup as a "renaissance."

Thanks to market pressures, the area's steel industry has disappeared. Fewer than 4,000 Pittsburgh residents work for the industry, down from 120,000 in 1950. And aside from the city's football team, there are no more Pittsburgh steelers – no steel is produced any more within the city limits. But the job losses were partly offset by 28,000 new high-tech and service jobs created between 1985 and 1989, and while unemployment soared in the early 1980s, it is now a tolerable 5.4 percent. The downtown gleams with skyscrapers built as banking and company headquarters; its local nickname is the Golden Triangle. It's a good place for companies to locate because it's clean. "The successful smoke elimination program was probably the most important single event leading to the reconstruction of Pittsburgh," Pease says.

By the 1950s the "smoke" and "dirt" that worried the Smoke Prevention Association had a new name, which came from combining the words *smoke* and *fog*: smog. The term is today linked inextricably with Los Angeles, but it originated in London, where in December 1952 a cloud of smoky air became trapped over the city, creating one of the most lethal air pollution problems that has ever been seen, before or since. The city's chimneys filled the sky with deadly gas that hung overhead for five days when a mass of warm air moved in above it, stilling the winds. At noon the streets were dark as night, and when the cloud moved away at the end of the week, four thousand people had died from it – more deaths than during London's great cholera epidemic of 1866. Yet, as British author Fred Pearce notes in his book, *Acid Rain*, not everyone made the connection between cause and effect: "*The Times* [of London] recorded only one death from the smog: a bull."

In fact, as the title of Pearce's book suggests, London's killer pollutant was not the same stuff we now consider to be smog; it was a highly concentrated form of acid rain. However, within two years, Londoners figured out that they had suffered from a pollution epidemic, and that coal was the culprit, so they brought in a cleanup program. Interestingly, the program was much like Halifax's longer sewage pipes solution; it consisted largely of requiring industries to build taller smokestacks that merely sent London's pollution to Scandinavia, where it damages the landscape even now.

Smog itself arrived with the advent of the motor car. More than any other place on earth, North America is the land of the automobile. We go to work in cars, spend our leisure time driving, shop by car, eat in them, make phone calls, listen to music and even make love in the back seat – we're auto-erotic. We devote huge proportions of our homes to

garage space, and even larger proportions of our cities to
make room for cars. Nearly half of all our urban space is set
aside for roads or parking. The American planning expert,
William H. Whyte, delivers a slide show on cities that
includes a picture of some buildings surrounded by acres of
grey asphalt. It's downtown Houston, Texas. "There's more
parking in Houston than there is Houston," he says.

Cars are for driving, of course, and we do this a lot; on a
per-person basis, each Canadian motorist drives an average
forty-five kilometres a day. But while we used to be a happy
motoring land, since the early 1970s driving has become
more of a pain. It's increasingly expensive and less
glamorous. The real heyday of the automobile ended around
1965, when manufacturers finally stopped trying to outdo
each other with chrome and tailfins and pseudo-technology
like pushbutton transmissions. It's no accident that the end
of the auto-loving era coincided with the rise of the Great
Green Wave. Cars poison the air more than anything else.
Despite being equipped with pollution controls, vehicles
account for the largest percentage of cancer-causing
hydrocarbons and they create an increasingly large proportion of nitrogen oxides. In other words, the more cars, the
more smog.

—— **III** ——

Some of the most specific air pollution regulation was aimed
at cars and the twin threat they offered: smog and lead
poisoning. At the beginning of the green wave, there was
pressure on car manufacturers to do something about
tailpipe emissions. They resisted regulations (and still do),
but in the early 1970s, Canada and the United States began
requiring new cars to come equipped with catalytic
converters that limit smog-producing nitrogen oxides. These
converters reduce nitrogen oxides to nitrogen—a harmless
gas that is the most prevalent element in unpolluted air—and
then add oxygen to carbon monoxide and unburned fuel to
turn them into non-polluting products. Unfortunately, they

don't prevent the release of carbon dioxide from tail-pipes—not a pollutant, but a cause of the greenhouse effect. Even with converter-equipped cars, smog has grown worse in most cities, because there are more cars on the road each year.

Ironically, the most positive result of the rule requiring converters has been a side-effect. Cars equipped with these pollution controls need unleaded gas. Lead is a powerful poison that causes brain and nervous system damage and is linked directly to lower IQs among children. Lead was first added to gasoline in the 1920s, under the trade name Ethyl. Researchers from General Motors and Du Pont discovered that it helps regulate the explosion in an internal combustion engine, so that the pistons move up and down in time, the engine doesn't knock and the car doesn't jerk back and forth and go off like a cannon when you hit the gas. Even then, however, there were concerns about lead as a pollutant; five workers died of lead poisoning in the lab where leaded gas was being tested. The U.S. government did a health study at the time, but it also made an agreement with a subsidiary of General Motors to suppress the data and give the company the right to approve the research. Not surprisingly, leaded gas was found to be safe—and just to soothe any lingering fears about lead poisoning, the Ethyl trade name was chosen.

The result of this deal to approve leaded gas was that between the 1930s and the 1970s, the amount of lead in the atmosphere grew by twenty times. The worst year for Canada was 1973, just after unleaded fuel was introduced but when most most of the cars still took leaded gas and service stations were still putting in their new pumps. After the anti-smog regulations of the 1970s came in, there was a dramatic improvement. By 1984, lead emissions were slightly less than half the 1973 peak in Canada, and in the United States, doctors found that the average level of lead in people's bloodstreams declined by 37 percent between 1976 and 1980.

Still, this was not enough. Health experts said lead was still at dangerous levels; when teachers in the United States were asked to rate their pupils' attention spans and behaviour, the results corresponded to the levels of lead in the children's blood. In Toronto and Windsor, up to 65 percent of children tested had lead in their bloodstreams at levels known to cause hyperactive behaviour and short attention spans.

In the United States, the political response was an order by the U. S. Environmental Protection Agency to phase out lead in gasoline by 1990, beginning with a drastic cut in lead content in 1986. The health data were so overwhelming that even the anti-regulatory Reagan administration offered little opposition. But in Canada, through most of the 1980s the legal amount of lead in gas was ten times higher than that in American fuel, and the federal government proposed to wait until 1993 to eliminate the pollutant. In place of a tough regulation, Prime Minister Brian Mulroney's government worked out an arrangement with an industry lobby group, the Petroleum Association for the Conservation of the Canadian Environment, which complained that a short deadline to get rid of lead couldn't be met and would cost too much money. The plan was for a publicity campaign to warn people against using the wrong fuel in their cars – something that was already illegal and which at worst, fewer than 15 pecent of Canadians were doing anyway. "We want to deal with it largely through public information," Environment Minister Tom McMillan said when the plan was announced in 1986. A representative of the Learning Disabilities Assocation of Canada, Barbara McElgunn, had a clearer assessment. "He's condemning children to another six years of brain damage," she said.

Then in September 1988, the government changed its mind, and announced it would get rid of leaded gas by the end of 1990 after all. The industry suddenly discovered it could meet the deadline, and some companies, such as Shell, began advertising the good things they were about to do for the environment. McMillan said privately that the government changed its mind because the first time, "we made a mistake."

Now other measures are being taken. In the summer of

1989, Ontario announced it would require oil companies to change their gasoline formulas with the seasons—a measure that helps decrease the amount of hydrocarbons in the atmosphere. And in the fall, Jim Bradley and Quebec's environment minister, Pierre Paradis, managed to persuade the new federal minister, Lucien Bouchard, to follow suit, and to tighten the emission control standards for cars, so that they match rules coming into place in California.

This incident offers an interesting sidelight on the way personalities affect politics. At first Bouchard resisted the new standards, instead announcing a complicated, lengthy series of hearings on the subject—even though no one disputed that Canada's emission rules were as much as 150 percent less stringent than the California rules. Bradley hinted that Ontario would act unilaterally if Ottawa did not—a move that would make shipping new vehicles between provinces more complicated and, more important- ly, would make the federal government look unconcerned about pollution. Then Bradley, Paradis and the other provincial environment ministers met with Bouchard. There was a hitch; the relationship between Bradley and Bouchard was stiff and testy. And the federal minister was an unabashed Quebec nationalist, who would not want to be perceived as being pushed around by an Ontario cabinet minister. So just before the meeting, Bradley began working on Paradis, chatting him up in the elevator, trading stories, and quietly reminding him that with public concerns about the environment at an all time high, tougher car emission rules would be politically popular. He won him over, and during the closed meeting, the Ontario and Quebec ministers both outlined the case for tougher emission controls. In a sudden move, without having consulted his cabinet colleagues, Bouchard said he would tighten the rules. "I agree with the Quebec position," he said.

—— **IV** ——

The increasingly tighter regulation of car emissions is reflected in other areas of air pollution control. In Ontario, provincial laws have became stricter. The laws measure the actual pollution content of the air in parts per million, and no longer merely estimate the amount emitted over time, as they did when the smoke preventers met. They measure more pollutants than they did before. There's an index of a handful of nasty chemicals that are monitored, and factories are asked to cut back production when the pollution climbs too high and ordered to do so if it climbs even higher. The law also says that factories can be shut down temporarily by the environment minister "when air pollution levels which may be injurious to health occur." The minister relies on the pollution "index" of chemicals, and in practice, factories have been shut—this happened frequently during the summers of 1988 and 1989.

However, former Ontario Environment Minister Jim Bradley himself has complained that the law he administers is twenty years out of date. For example, the province has a provincial "criterion" for ozone of eighty parts per billion, but this is just a guideline, so nobody is required to enforce it. In 1984, the province's own records show that this criterion was consistently broken in Ontario, at least once at thirty-one of thirty-six monitoring stations across the province. "As stiffer automobile and industrial emission standards take effect, ambient ozone levels should improve," the ministry says, but air quality has grown worse during the 1980s.

Recognizing that there was a problem, in late 1986 Bradley announced that he would overhaul the province's air pollution monitoring and control system, which had not been changed significantly since it was created in 1968. But well into 1990, the new system was still being written. At the end of 1989, of the hundreds of threatening compounds in the chemical soup, Ontario was measuring seven.

Ontario is the province with the strictest environmental laws. Lawyers and scientists consider the principal federal legislation, the Canadian Environmental Protection Act, ineffective; it will be years before standards are established for airborne toxic chemicals, if ever, and by the time this happens, we'll probably discover new ones that endanger our health. Whatever laws do exist tend to be chronically weak. A 1986 report issued jointly by the Canadian Environmental Law Association and the Washington-based Environmental Law Institute noted that while "hundreds of different toxic substances are being emitted into the environment . . . very few of these, in most parts of Canada, have been the subject of emission standards or ambient objectives."

In the United States, if the 120 parts per billion level is reached, factories can be told to close. In Chicago, one summer day in 1988, thirty-four industries were told to cut back operations. This is called a "yellow alert." As usual, U.S. rules are stronger than Canada's, but in 1988, more than seventy-five U.S. cities had similar ozone readings to Toronto's. The head of the U. S. Environmental Protection Agency said that urban air was the worst anyone had seen in the ten years that data had been collected, and the agency predicts that if present trends continue, the air will deteriorate even more in the 1990s.

—— V ——

Pittsburgh's experience shows that air pollution can be cleaned up if there's a will, and that cleaning up pays off. In annual surveys, Pittsburgh is consistently voted one of the most desirable places to live in the United States.

But this is a lesson other cities have yet to learn, both in North America and around the world. As vile as the air over North America may be, it's not nearly as bad as the air over cities in poorer countries. Near Cairo, a brown haze is eating away at the Pyramids; imagine what this does to people's lungs. And Mexico City, the world's largest city, is already a mega-version of Rachel Carson's silent little town. Each year there, 4.5 million tonnes of chemicals and suspended particles are spewed into the air; in 1986, birds flying to the north of the city began to drop out of the sky, landing with a thud on people's front yards, where they remained, twitching in agony until they died. In effect, the pollution reached up into the sky and pulled them down. The scale of pollution is now so large and its nature so complex that the toxic cycle has engulfed the planet and extends right up to the heavens.

CHAPTER NINE

SILENT EARTH

The sight of immense masses of timber passing my windows every morning constantly suggests to my mind the absolute necessity of looking at the future of this great trade.

—Sir John A. Macdonald, 1871

Everywhere civilization is making inroads on the wilderness, but few things illustrate better what human beings can do to the environment than a patch of land that once had trees but is now clear-cut. Many environmental conquests, such as cities, are more sophisticated. Some are more grand, such as huge hydroelectric dams. But clear-cuts are the most absolute. In no time at all, whole mountains full of green life that stood when the civilized world was young can be reduced to the geological equivalent of a shaved-off beard. The delicate interplay of sounds—rustling leaves, flapping birds, rubbing branches and the like—is overpowered by the whine of the chainsaw and the arrogant roar of the bulldozer. Then all that's left is the faint whistle of the wind—over nothing. A clear-cut forest really becomes a piece of silent earth.

The environment appears to have reached the point where our survival depends on trees. Ideally, trees help sustain the balance of gases that form the air we breathe, by giving off both oxygen and carbon dioxide. But we have perverted the process by setting fire to forests, and by bombarding the trees with acid rain and smog. If the present rate of forest destruction continues, an area the size of India will be denuded, turned into a desert, within thirty years. Killing trees also kills wildlife, reducing the biological diversity of the planet and robbing our children of genetic material that may some day hold the key to curing diseases and making new, non-hazardous products. We're already losing two species a day, and scientists say that, if our forest destruction continues, by the year 2000 as many as one species an hour may become extinct.

The destruction of forests and wilderness is widespread. Only the means differ from country to country—logging, creating ranchland, urban sprawl or plain, old pollution. Yet if the methods vary, the reasons are depressingly similar around the world, and so are the implications. The *New York Times* once criticized a government for allowing the destruction of its forests, arguing that it "pleads economic necessity; yet its projects are inherently uneconomic. It ignores alternative approaches that would provide income while preserving the forests. It encourages a desolation that will, unless the next government is wiser, become an enduring monument to the limits of human wisdom." The government it was criticizing was Brazil's, but it could have been talking about any of dozens of nations, including the United States and Canada.

There's also an intangible, but equally damaging toll: killing the forests makes the world a harsher, uglier place. Few things in the world are more pleasant than trees; few places are more degrading to the human spirit and capable of inspiring more outrage than clear-cut forests. A few years ago in British Columbia, a group called the Western Canada Wilderness Committee printed a poster with a picture that shows a clear-cut hillside. The sky is white, the twisted, dead branches of the clear-cut trees are strewn about the barren slope. In the middle of the picture is a stump, with a message above it, a quotation from Shakespeare's *Julius Caesar*: "O!

pardon me, thou bleeding piece of earth,/That I am meek and gentle with these butchers."

The trees that tower over misty islands or northern lakes have a mystical aspect that is precious. They are eternity; we are transient. They are part of an intricate web of life on earth; we have become a threat to that web. Science can unravel much of the mystery of the trees—how they grew, what they thrive on, the strength of their wood and the depth of their roots. But there's a part that may ultimately remain unknowable. Science can't explain why we care about them. In the modern world, this unknowable aspect, this feeling, may be our last direct connection to the natural world.

It is a connection we are losing, day by day, hour by hour. In *Our Common Future*, the United Nations environment commission recommended that each country should set aside 12 percent of its area for conservation purposes, warning that "our failure to do so will not be forgiven by future generations." In Canada, as the World Wildlife Fund Canadian president, Monte Hummel, points out, less wilderness is protected in terms of area than in either the United States or Australia, both of which are smaller countries. In terms of percentage protected, Canada fares even worse. Hummel says: "If we added up all national and provincial parks, wildlife areas and ecological reserves in Canada, the area represents 6.3 percent of our country. If we don't count areas where logging, mining or sport hunting are permitted, that 6.3 percent shrinks to 2.6. We have a big job ahead of us." And if, ideally, a national park system should include representative examples of all the natural regions of Canada, the present Canadian park system is only 50 percent complete. There are already 183 endangered species in Canada, waiting for their habitats to be protected before they disappear.

— I —

Canada is one of the great logging nations. It's easy for Canadian city-dwellers to forget that the forest industry helped found Canada and still keeps much of it alive. Urban Canada now has a sophisticated mixed economy, but most of the cities grew because people were needed to do something with the country's raw materials and to co-ordinate all the digging and tree cutting. The Toronto Stock Exchange grew on a diet of penny mine stocks and pulp and paper companies. Brian Mulroney's home town, Baie Comeau, was built by the *Chicago Tribune*, which got its newsprint from a pulp mill there. Even today, forestry employs about a tenth of the Canadian workforce, directly or indirectly, and in 1986, forest-product shipments made up more than 14 percent of all Canada's manufactured goods. The country is dotted with small towns built around pulp mills: the smell of them may bear a resemblance to the odour of vomit, but for 10 percent of the country, this is the smell of money.

In the past, when the forests seemed limitless, the wholesale cutting of trees was tolerated because of the wealth it produced, but concerns arose very early on. When Sir John A. Macdonald complained about the timber rolling down the river by his window, he was really just originating a tradition. He even came up with some suggestions. "It occurs to me that the subject should be looked in the face and some efforts be made for the preservation of our timber," he said. He proposed investigations "as to the best means of cutting the timber after some regulated plan, as in Norway and the Baltic; as to replanting so as to keep up the supply, as in Germany and Norway; as to the best way of protecting the woods from fire." But as many politicians would do later, when Macdonald looked the issue in the face, what stared back at him was a constitutional excuse for not conducting these investigations. The federal government, he said, "has no direct interest in this subject, but it seems to me that it should be very good for the two governments of Ontario and Quebec to issue a joint commission to examine the whole subject and to report."

In a book called *Heritage Lost*, author Donald MacKay relates how, back in 1882, experts were urging the forest industry to stop acting as if the trees would last forever. A

Montreal-based lumber exporter named James Little accused other lumbermen of "an inexcusable ignorance of the timber question, or an astonishing lack of foresight": "I know the idea prevails on the American side of the line that the area of timberland in Canada is so great that supplies are practically exhaustless, but this idea, I regret to say, is not borne out by the facts. . . . There is one thing sure, that our magnificent forests of pine are about all gone. . . . In point of fact, we are following the United States very closely in our efforts to get rid of forests." Little noted how in Glasgow, a journal remarked that "Canada and the United States are busy sawing from under them the high-reaching, fortune-making branch on which, like conquerors, they are sitting and overlooking the world."

With varying interest, successive governments have tried to preserve the forests or at least replant for future profits. In Canada, the forests used by lumber companies are publicly owned (usually by provinces), and governments charge the logging companies a "stumpage fee," or royalty, for the privilege of cutting the trees. This is supposed to ensure that the resource is treated as a public trust, and that the government can make sure the companies using it maintain it and replenish it. However, what it has really ensured is a brushwood tangle of rules.

The bureaucracy of forestry is perhaps more confusing than that of any other part of government in Canada. It's a maze of agencies, overseers and review procedures that appear to have been developed by happenstance. In Ontario, for example, a mid-1980s report by University of New Brunswick forestry school dean Gordon Baskerville accused the Ontario Ministry of Natural Resources of "Betty Crocker forestry," complaining that decisions on where to cut and plant were made from recipes that had little resemblance to actual conditions in the forests. Ontario's forests—about 70 percent of the province, an area the size of California—were divided into management units, which the ministry was to oversee. But many of the ministry's overseers had no idea who was responsible for which unit, Baskerville said. Basic planning to maintain a balance between logging and other uses, such as canoeing, "would be better described as creative writing." The ministry was also supposed to keep statistics on the abundance of trees in individual stands of forests. But the numbers were "substantially misused," the dean said, which "has resulted in considerable confusion." This put it mildly.

As the 1990s began, planning was still as confused. When Don Huff, an activist, met with officials from Ontario's Natural Resources Ministry to discuss which of one area's trees were to be logged and which were not, he was shown a map that was supposed to answer his questions. "Parts of the map were purple. I asked them what this meant and they said these areas had been in the plan to be cut but didn't get cut in the proper time period, so they were allocated for the new interim timber management plan. That meant they would be cut. There was another spot in a different colour, which on earlier maps was the same. They said these trees had been taken out of the plan, and then were put back in, so they were in a different category. But they were the same as the others. They were going to be cut."

Huff notes that under Ontario's Crown Timber Act, it's an offence to leave a cut log behind – as MacMillan Bloedel has done in British Columbia. In Ontario, "if you leave a piece of wood, you get a two-dollar fine." The trouble is that there's a worse offence: not cutting a tree in an area that is marked for clear-cutting. "If you leave a tree standing that was scheduled to be cut, you know what the fine is? Five dollars." The byzantine logic isn't limited to Ontario. According to Huff, in British Columbia, forest companies don't have to pay stumpage for trees that are cleared to build logging roads. Nor do they have to pay for trees that fall on the road. The wood is free. "So what happens is that they build the roads to run through the best trees. And you can cut them so they fall into the roadway."

Under these circumstances, it's nearly impossible to tell whether even the simplest promises are being kept. For example, in 1972 the Science Council of Canada complained of "instances of clear cutting over large areas, for which natural regeneration is inadequate and in which planting programs are falling behind cutting rates. Each year at present, an average of about 500,000 acres [about 200,000 hectares] of potentially productive cut-over and burned-over forest land is not reforested." In the late 1970s, after further complaints, Premier William Davis pledged that two new trees would be planted for every one cut, which seemed straightforward enough, but it took the ministry more than half a dozen tries and nearly twelve years before it was even able to come up with a document explaining how it proposed to do this.

—— **II** ——

One of Canada's ugliest wilderness versus forestry battles has been in a part of northeastern Ontario named Temagami. The battle has been waged since the early 1970s, but its roots go back much farther. Nearly a hundred years ago, the poet Archibald Lampman described the area as:

> Set with a thousand islands,
> crowned with pines
> . . . .
> Wild with the tramping of the
> giant moose
> And the weird magic of old
> Indian tales.

In 1907, it became home to Grey Owl, the Englishman who adopted an Indian identity and became one of Canada's best-loved wilderness writers.

In one of his books, called *Men of the Last Frontier*, Grey Owl told a story of two men — a white and a native — standing at the peak of a hill, looking to the south and to the north.

To the south they saw a valley of farms, at the end of which are "half-cleared fields, in which lay piles of burning roots and prostrate tree-trunks." They heard "the ring of axes and the crash of falling timber, as an antlike swarm hewed at the face of the forest, eating into it, as a rising flood eats into a wall of sand." Beyond this noise was "a mighty city, its tall buildings rising in huge piles of masonry heaped up against the skyline, whilst from its bowels rose the dull roar and whirr of massed machinery, and a confused hum as of a myriad bees within a gigantic hive. Towering smokestacks belched forth heavy clouds of rolling black smoke, which hung over the city like a dark canopy. . . ."

This contrasted sharply with what was to the north—"an endless forest, the tree-covered hills rolling . . . until they merged into the dimness of the horizon." The two men stood and watched the scene for a while, until finally the Indian tapped the white man on the shoulder: "The sun is setting, my ears are filled with the sound of falling trees; it is enough. See! the shadows lengthen; let us go." They walked away, to the north. "And the dark masses of the forest seemed to roll up behind those who had already gone before, to recede like the outgoing waves of an ebbing tide, as though, defeated at last, they retired before the juggernaut that was now upon them, fleeing in the face of the doom that had threatened them for three hundred years."

Ironically, the threat to Grey Owl's Temagami home became worse at a time when concern about the environment grew stronger, during the rise of the green wave in the 1970s and its resurgence in the late 1980s. Temagami had long been a mixed-use area, supporting logging, mining, hunting, fishing, cottages and summer camps for children and teenagers. But it became too crowded. There was pressure to develop the area, to build a ski resort, to expand logging. The area's natives, the Teme-augama Anishnabai, or Deep Water People, said they had never signed a treaty with anyone, so they claimed the entire area, using a legal device called a caution. This was a warning registered with land office officials, which told anyone who purchased property in the area that they might not own what they bought because the claims weren't settled. The natives' claim filtered through Ontario's court system for a decade and was rejected every time, but in 1989, the Supreme Court of Canada agreed to hear their final appeal. While the court battle was being fought, the local lumber industry ran into financial difficulty. It said it needed more trees to survive.

"No one goes there anyway," Premier David Peterson said one day, arguing the loggers' side. With some courage, one of his officials snapped back that "Temagami is a place where people go in their minds." By this time, the area had become extremely popular in real life with canoeists; in 1983 the province had turned one of its more scenic rivers, the Lady Evelyn, into a provincial park. It was a park in theory only: it had no gates, no staff, and logging was still allowed. A local outfitter, Hap Wilson, worked for the provincial Natural Resources Ministry when it drew up the boundaries: "They made no sense. They didn't follow the terrain. It was like working with a bunch of kids holding crayons."

As the lumber industry became more desperate, the provincial government tried to help by planning the construction of a fifteen-kilometre road through the woods, financed with some $3.5 million in taxpayers' money, so that the companies could get at remote areas. This road would effectively strangle the park; canoeists seeking solace in the wilderness would be faced with acres of clear-cut hills and the rumble of huge trucks. The situation attracted the attention of several Canadian celebrities, such as artist Robert Bateman and author Margaret Atwood. "People won't go to an area if you make it ugly, smelly and noisy," Atwood said. She marshalled support for protecting the area with some clever, understated publicity stunts. For example, she let it be known that she was writing the premier about her concern; the idea of a world-famous novelist sitting down to pen a concerned citizen's letter heightened people's interest in the issue. And then she announced that she would spend her vacation time along the Lady Evelyn on a canoe trip.

The issue did attract attention. The future of the wilderness looked so grim that in 1986, the park was placed on an endangered list by a conservation organization in Geneva, the International Union for the Conservation of Nature and Natural Resources. Only about two dozen sites in the world made this list; others include a park in the Soviet

Union near the deadly Chernobyl nuclear plant and an
African area where poachers have been hacking rhinos to
death for their horns. Ontario's minister of natural resources
was outraged that the province was on the list—his
complaint to the Swiss-based group was that he hadn't been
consulted.

In spite of the attention, the taxpayer-funded road went
ahead and was virtually complete by 1990. And as it was
built, the situation grew ugly. People like Margaret Atwood
were detested by local residents as meddlesome outsiders.
"She'd be all right after she's raped by a bull moose," said the
head of the chamber of commerce in one town in the area,
Elk Lake.

In 1988, the Deep Water People set up a blockade in the
area, which drew widespread publicity and halted road
construction for a while. The next summer, a small protest
group called the Temagami Wilderness Society joined the
natives, its members chaining themselves to the road-
building equipment and getting themselves arrested all
through the fall. They argued that Temagami contained
some of North America's last "old-growth" pine forests—trees not planted by foresters, but wilderness-grown.
None of this stopped the road. As one government insider
sympathetic to the protesters put it, some members of the
provincial cabinet couldn't be happy "unless they feel the
hum of a chainsaw between their legs." Only when the road
was nearly complete, and after arresting more than 370
demonstrators, did the province offer to save a small portion
of the old-growth forest.

Unfortunately, this pointless solution—the building of a
taxpayer-funded road for a logging company that will
eventually close—is the model for the handling of wilderness
issues in Canada. The situation seems remarkably similar in
two areas in British Columbia, the 1,088-square-kilometre
Stein Valley near Vancouver and the 6,370-hectare Carmanah Valley on the southwest coast of Vancouver Island. The
latter area contains a Sitka spruce tree that is more than
thirty storeys high and is believed to be the tallest in the
world.

According to officials from MacMillan Bloedel Ltd., the immensely profitable forestry company that holds the tree-cutting licence in the Carmanah, it's like the Domino Theory. Once those preservationists—the derogatory term foresters use for environmentalists—get one concession, they'll demand more and more, until there's nowhere left for the loggers. Considering the reluctance of governments to act, this isn't likely. In some cases like the Carmanah, the federal government generally steers clear of the whole affair, since the provinces have the legal authority to allow the trees to be cut or to stop it. Meanwhile, the provinces usually make a deal with the forest industry to preserve a small portion of the area, but cut the rest. And the natives watch uneasily, siding temporarily with the environmentalists, but not really trusting them. "The government wants to turn the land into a desert," said Gary Potts, chief of the Teme-augama Anishnabai in Ontario. "The environmentalists want to turn it into a zoo."

III

The intangible benefits of saving forests and wilderness makes it a hard cause for environmentalists to pursue successfully. When it comes to trees, the forest industry's argument is that the bleeding-earth metaphor is nonsense: it isn't drawing any kind of blood from the earth. After all, as Ronald Reagan said, "How many more do you need to look at?" And besides, the industry is replanting the trees. True, clear-cutting looks hideous, but when combined with modern reforestation techniques, it's really not much different from harvesting corn. Adam Zimmerman, the chairman of one of the country's biggest forestry companies, Noranda Forest Inc., contends that "a big modern pulp mill replants all the wood it uses and thus maintains a sustained yield forest."

Even if Adam Zimmerman is right that the modern forest industry is clean, lean and efficient, he'd find it awfully hard to point to evidence that this is so. In the late 1980s, a government-commissioned waste auditor found that British Columbia's forest companies consistently left up to twice as much good timber in heaps on the ground as the regulations allowed. In one instance alone, it was reported that MacMillan Bloedel Ltd. left enough wood behind to build a large suburb—2,600 homes. There have been other discrepancies. The British Columbia government identified a "backlog" of 738,000 hectares of cut land where the soil is good enough to support new trees, but a five-year forest agreement that the province entered into with the industry in 1985 aimed to reforest less than 20 percent of this. It did nothing at all to address the problem of the clear-cut areas that can't be reforested in any case, because the soil has washed away.

Today, Canada is surpassing the United States in its forest-clearing efforts. American lumber companies generally own the land where they cut, so they have an incentive to replant. In Canada, governments are more anxious to please the forest industry than to regulate it. As Adam Zimmerman describes it, in their dealings with forest companies, Canadian governments usually "kiss them on both cheeks and give them grants."

A federal-provincial tree-planting program was started in the 1980s, but, as the 1990s approached, the Auditor General of Canada reported that things were not exactly working as planned. Of 24 million hectares of forest that had been cut—an area about the size of West Germany—470,000 hectares had been replanted, leaving a vastly larger area unplanted than the Science Council had complained about in 1972. Federal and provincial governments spent more than one billion dollars on reforestation and forest management during the 1980s, but the federal government's forestry service still had no say over how much timber would be cut and where. Students hired as tree-planters in the summer would return with stories about dumping saplings in ditches, or planting them upside down, doing anything just to get rid of them. Anything left behind was counted as a new tree.

Some provinces seem bent on giving away their trees. Over

a period of sixteen months ending in December 1988, the province of Alberta leased public lands the size of Great Britain to a dozen pulp firms. To two Japanese firms alone, they gave rights to 15 percent of the entire province. The deal would mean a $3.5-billion investment of private capital and could create about 12,000 jobs, but it could also create health problems: four of seven new pulp mills would use the much-criticized bleached kraft process that uses chlorine and releases dioxins and furans into the water. William Fuller, who helped found an Albertan environmental group called Friends of the Athabaska, told the *Globe and Mail*'s *Report on Business* magazine, "We are going to murder a forest before we even know what's in there." An Alberta farmer called one planned mill "the *Exxon Valdez* of the pulp industry."

LeRoy Fjordbotten, Alberta's forestry minister, remained unworried. A year after the deals were done, he said he was *considering* putting in a clause requiring the forest companies to make sure that they would actually regrow trees, now just toss seedlings in the ground. "We're all environmentalists here," he said. Eventually a provincially appointed review panel expressed strong reservations about much of the proposal, and the Alberta plan attracted such notoriety that the federal government threatened to step in. Much to the annoyance of Albertan officials who complained of federal interference, Environment Minister Lucien Bouchard said he would not allow an environmentally damaging proposal to go ahead. Then the review panel recommended that the project be delayed, because the environmental effects hadn't been properly studied. Even so, the proposal may not be dead – federal and provincial officials are still fighting over it, and it has powerful proponents.

There are signs that the present Canadian government is at least beginning to notice that something is wrong. Bouchard said in a 1989 letter to the World Wildlife Fund that he will expand Canada's parkland by the year 2000. But, in comparison to other environmental issues and in view of the danger, little is still being done to save the trees and the wilderness. In 1986, a federal task force warned that "future land use options are being foreclosed on a massive scale in this generation." It recommended a $75-million program to expand the national park system, and offered a grim alternative. If Canadians do not preserve their wilderness, "Canada will squander, bit by bit, its priceless heritage. . . . By the year 2000 the possibility of dedicating wilderness lands will have all but vanished."

CHAPTER TEN

THE SKY'S BITTER TEARS

A tree's a tree. How many more do you need to look at?
— Ronald Reagan, 1966

It was the fish that bothered Harold Harvey. Or rather, the lack of fish. In early 1966, Harvey, a University of Toronto biologist, had introduced four thousand pink salmon into Lumsden Lake, a small body of water in Ontario's Killarney Park. The park is a remote, austerely beautiful area of the Canadian Shield near Georgian Bay, popular with canoeists, artists and, at that time, anglers. Much of its scenery has been immortalized in oils in the 1920s by the Group of Seven; one of the lakes in Killarney is called OSA Lake, after the Ontario Society of Artists. Their striking, rugged impressions of the wildly undulating land, the colours almost hallucinogenic, were not all that different from what was actually there.

The content of the water was different, though. The lakes were no longer as they looked, or as Harvey had expected them to be. Killarney's waters have long been known for their crystalline clarity. You could often see right to the bottom in places where the water was as deep as the height of a three-storey building. Lumsden Lake was like that: cold, clean, clear and sixty feet deep. Harvey chose to introduce his four thousand pink salmon there because, in theory, the water was the kind where his little fingerlings would thrive.

What disturbed Harvey was that when he came back a year later to check on the fish, he could not find a single one.

For the next three years, until 1971, he went on a great salmon hunt through Killarney, looking all through the park for traces of his lost salmon. Not only had his salmon disappeared, so had virtually every other species: perch, herring, brook trout, rainbow trout. All he could find was the odd handful of white suckers, tiny and deformed, their heads strangely flattened and their spines bent out of shape. The other fish had always been there before, so where had they gone? The question, as many politicians would say later, required more study.

Unlike the politicians, however, Harvey came to his conclusions rather quickly. As part of his diagnostic research, he and his assistants recorded the level of acidity in the water, so they could compare it with earlier records. They found that in ten years, between 1961 and 1971, the water had become one hundred times more acidic.

Most fresh water is slightly acidic. Acidity is measured by examining the activity of hydrogen ions in a substance, so the measurement scale is called pH, which stands for potential hydrogen. The pH scale goes from 0 to 14, with the lowest numbers signifying the most acidity, the highest, the most alkalinity. Lime is 12.4, battery acid is around 1, distilled water is 7 or neutral, and pure, uncontaminated rain—if it can be found—is 5.6.

The scale is logarithmic, so a reading of 4 is ten times as acidic as 5, and so on. Harvey's salmon fingerlings would have no trouble in water at the 5.6 pH level, but his measurements showed the lake was heading down toward 3 pH (the level 2 is the same as vinegar). As a biologist, he knew that when the acidity increases, several things make it hard for fish to survive. The acidity of the water destroys their eggs and many of the young hatchlings, so the average age of the fish population gets older and older; then, when the old fish die off, there are no young to replace them. In addition, acidity disrupts the spawning behaviour of certain species, and in some cases it damages their reproductive systems. The acidity doesn't have to change much: lake trout, for example, stop reproducing at 5.3 pH.

It didn't take Harvey long to figure out what was making the water so acidic. In 1883, in the Sudbury area just north of Killarney, a huge body of nickel and copper ore was discovered. The original mining companies extracted their nickel by roasting heaps of ore on open wood fires. The sulphur in the ore would ignite and burn off, freeing the metal from the rock. The sulphur would mix with oxygen to form sulphur dioxide, which smells like rotten eggs.

By 1900, there were more than eighty of these open roasting beds, and their relationship to the environment was clear. Right near them, the trees and plants died from the sulphur smoke. Farther away, but still relatively nearby, the sensitive mosses also died off, robbing the area's delicate soil of its protection against erosion. Whole forests began to disappear; the rain would wash away the soil, mix with sulphur deposits left by the roasting beds, leach nutrients from the ground and evaporate. In addition to the sulphur the water picked up on the ground, the evaporated water also mixed with sulphur dioxide in the clouds. It was a local toxic cycle.

A significant aspect of this for Harvey was that the washed-away soil also made its way into streams, rivers and lakes, acidifying the water. The ducks, loons and mammals that fed on the fish then disappeared, while on land, the owls, hawks, falcons, moose and deer found less and less to eat. There were still farmers in the Sudbury area in the early 1900s, but the smoke was killing their crops as well. In 1916, a group of them asked Ontario's courts for compensation and they appealed for help from the district's board of trade. Instead, the provincial government declared twelve townships unfit for human settlement or farming. The farmers drifted away, their enterprises shrivelling beneath the onslaught of the sour air, and the land changed. At the time, most people could only picture outer space from the tales of Jules Verne or from nursery rhymes, but they started saying that the area around Sudbury looked as barren as the moon.

By 1918, mining was big business, and the nickel companies secured special legislation from the province which let them purchase "smoke easements" from the farmers. In return for money from the mining companies, landowners had to give up the right to sue for damages from pollution or to demand a cleanup. But the damage had spread beyond Sudbury, and so quickly that, in 1921, the province passed another law, called the Damages by Fumes Arbitration Act, which gave a government-appointed arbitrator the power to award money to landowners whose property had been harmed by the pollution. Sudbury's mining industry had changed by this time: instead of dozens of small companies it was dominated by Falconbridge Ltd. and the International Nickel Company, or Inco Ltd. The technology had also changed: the ore was now crushed and melted in enclosed facilities by a process called smelting. The sulphurous smoke went up smokestacks, which typically stood between three and five hundred feet high. These smokestacks spread the smoke over an even larger area.

Harvey understood that it was likely his little fish had been killed by this pollution, falling as acid rain. The term had been coined in 1872 by a British chemist, Robert Angus Smith, in a six-hundred-page work that analyzed the connection between the filthy skies of industrial age—Manchester and the bitter precipitation that fell over its area. It was a hundred years since the pollution had been named, but Harvey had a hard time getting anyone to listen.

He and a colleague wrote an article about their lost fish: "We sent it to *Maclean's* and they sent back a note saying their advertising department didn't really like it. The *Star Weekly* told us, 'If acid rain is a problem we'd have had a story about it already.' And the *Weekend* magazine [a now defunct weekend supplement for Canadian newspapers] told us it couldn't be true because 'one of our guys in the office was up there and he caught a fish.' "

Most people weren't too worried about the pollution at

the time, because the Sudbury area was actually getting cleaner. During the 1950s and '60s, Inco and Falconbridge had improved their technology further, opening "acid plants" to recover some of the sulphur and convert it to sulphuric acid that they would then sell. They also closed down some of the dirtier smelters, and, in 1972, Inco commissioned a new "superstack"—a smokestack 366 metres high, which would send the sulphur emissions far away into the sky, where, the theory was, they would disperse and be diluted by the air. In 1978, this smokestack of Inco's was licensed by the Ontario government to pour out 3,600 tons of pollution a day, 1.3 million tons a year—a daily amount that is double the quantity that flew out of the Mount St Helen's volcano in Washington State at its worst. It is now the largest single source of acid rain pollution in North America.

The superstack was only being planned when Harold Harvey went on his unsuccessful search for the lost fish, but he knew there were other sources of acid pollution in Killarney. In fact, it was virtually impossible to determine exactly which source of pollution did the damage to a particular lake or area, "and that's the part that breaks my heart," Harvey said. By the time all the connections are demonstrated, he explained, "it will be too late." He made this comment in 1986 at a conference in Chicago, twenty years after he had sent his baby salmon to their doom. North Americans are tracing the connections, but what they have discovered during those two decades is that acid rain is everywhere, and it doesn't only kill fish.

—— I ——

It is largely because of Harvey's studies that people became concerned about acid rain in North America—environmental activists now call him the Father of Acid Rain. Within a few years his message that the lakes were dying spread, and measurements were taken elsewhere. They showed that the rain and snow all through eastern North America was as acidic as tomato juice, sometimes as vinegary as the water of Killarney. Worse, it wasn't only sulphur dioxide that caused the problem. Nitric acid, as opposed to sulphuric, was also being formed from nitrogen oxides, the same ingredient that causes smog. Both acids don't just come down with the rain but are contained in snow and "dry deposition"—dust—as well. Acid snow can damage the wilderness the most, because when the snow melts, lakes and trees can be "shocked" by the high concentrations of acidic water. Research also established that the sources went well beyond Sudbury and its smelters. Coal-burning power plants and the tailpipes of cars were also affecting large parts of the continent. By the mid-1980s, more than 14,000 Canadian lakes were found to have "died," becoming clear and devoid of fish. By 1990, 19,000 lakes in Ontario alone had been damaged, and across Eastern Canada as many as 300,000 more were considered in danger.

Then there were the trees. Acid rain causes a mysterious, complex malady called "dieback," which in Europe, has affected as many as two-thirds of the trees. In Canada, it has already cost more than $100 million in lost maple syrup production. About 85 percent of the world's maple syrup comes from Canada (with most of the rest coming from neighbouring New England), and a McGill University professor, Archie Jones, calls the rapid death of the sugarbush "a catastrophe in the making." A University of Toronto botanist, Tom Hutchinson, has an even more depressingly graphic description. He calls it "the AIDS of trees," because the immune systems of trees affected by the pollution seem to be weakened and the trees are unable to fight off disease and pests. Their green leaves turn to fall colours in June and July instead of October. Whole stands wither away.

The pollution also endangers crops, bridges and cars: by the early 1980s, Canada was suffering damage estimated to be at least $250 million a year. Acid rain is literally eating away at the Parliament Buildings, as well as the maple leaf. Perhaps Canada should consider a new flag, featuring a spindly maple leaf full of holes. As more and more evidence suggests, acid rain also endangers human health. Environment Canada documents show that scientists suspected a health threat as long ago as 1980, though it was not until 1986 that David Bates, a Vancouver research physician, told a parliamentary committee that "a considerable body of evidence . . . indicates that the precursors of acid rain have an adverse effect on health." A long-term research project by Dr Bonnie Stern of the Canadian Health and Welfare Department found that "large numbers of humans are potentially at risk." Over several years, she compared children in Tillsonburg, a city located in an area of Ontario affected by acid rain, with children in Portage La Prairie, which is in an area of Manitoba that is not strongly affected. Stern found a statistically significant higher number of children with lung problems in the Ontario community, as well as more children suffering from coughs, colds, stuffy noses and allergies. In U.S. Senate committee hearings, Dr Philip Landrigan of New York's Mount Sinai School of Medicine testified that "acid rain is probably third after active and passive smoking as a cause of lung disease."

The pain of a wheezing lung, or the emotional agony of comforting a weakened child with a chronic cough is bad enough, but there's also the financial cost. In 1990, a consultant named James S. Cannon prepared a paper for the American Lung Association, in which he looked at other economic studies of pollution and tried to put a price tag on the cost of acid rain to health. He found that although it was impossible to come up with exact numbers, "nevertheless, in three studies where direct comparison of the various economic effects was possible, health costs appeared as the most significant or among the most significant of the adverse economic repercussions of air pollution." A study of the pollution "from a hypothetical coal-fired power plant, for example, attributed 95 to 97 percent of the total expected economic costs from all sources to health costs from pollution-induced illnesses or premature deaths."

Concern about acid rain is still not universal. Some people point at areas where the rain falls, but lakes don't die, forests thrive and many people don't get sick. But this proves only that there are always exceptions. "It's like a person who has a cold," explains Judy Keith, who administers a research centre for the Ontario government. "Certain people are able to recover. Others get pneumonia and die."

—— II ——

Acid rain became Canada's national obsession, and politicians were willing enough to speak out against it. In 1977, the federal environment minister, Roméo LeBlanc, called acid rain an "environmental time bomb." But combating it was something else. Studies showed that pollution blows both ways across the border. In Canada, about 50 percent of the problem is caused by American sources, mostly older coal-burning electric plants in the Ohio River Valley. In some sensitive areas, such as Ontario's Muskoka cottage country and the Laurentians in Quebec, as much as 75 percent of the damage can be blamed on U.S. sources. In turn, Ontario's and Quebec's coal plants and smelters poison certain parts of the United States, such as the Adirondack Mountains and the maple syrup sugarbush areas of Vermont. This meant joint Canadian-U.S. action had to be contemplated, with all the accompanying problems that the Great Lakes Agreements had so thoroughly illustrated. And before that, everyone had to be educated in the reality of the problem.

A key figure was Michael Perley, who, at this point, began organizing an international conference on acid rain. Perley was an environmental researcher who had drifted toward the environmental movement after helping an author prepare a book about mercury pollution. The conference only had one goal—to educate the public about acid rain. Because its purpose was well defined, it was successful. The meeting was given widespread coverage in both countries, but particularly in Canada. Soon every Canadian, including the politicians, knew that poison was blowing across the border.

Perley followed up the conference by co-writing a book with Ross Howard. In it, Harold Harvey is quoted as complaining that whenever you talk to federal officials about taking action to clean up, "all you get is a large sucking sound." The major polluters had argued, apparently successfully, that controls were too expensive, or not feasible, or not needed. Perley and Howard concluded by warning that "acid rain is an environmental crisis with sweeping financial implications, but its solution is political. In the U.S. the politicians are making laws and finding ways around them; in Canada they still seek to avoid making laws concerning acid rain."

Some politicians tried to make progress. On October 22, 1979, John Fraser, the federal environment minister during the brief Progressive Conservative government headed by Joe Clark, rose in Parliament and instantly made acid rain an official Canadian political issue. "The time bomb is much bigger than anything envisaged in 1977," he announced. "The precise extent of the damage being done is difficult to determine but the continually emerging evidence indicates ever more serious concerns. . . . While some of the potential damage cannot be irrefutably proven at present, by the time it has manifested itself the damage could be irreversible."

Fraser then outlined what the government was prepared to do about acid rain. More studies. The *Toronto Star* advised its readers in an editorial to "cheer up" about the pollution, because "something is being done. An extensive research program has been under way for several years and it is being stepped up." However, Fraser did promise to do more than investigate. He said Ottawa would work with the provinces to come up with a plan to control the pollution, and "I was assured that a similar effort will be made in the United States." As a matter of top priority, Canada would raise the idea of a cross-border agreement to control the pollution with U.S. President Jimmy Carter, who was scheduled to visit Ottawa within weeks.

Carter never came: the U.S. hostage crisis in Iran erupted right when his trip was planned. But this didn't matter, because relations were good between the two countries, and their officials had been quietly laying the groundwork for an agreement since 1978. The talks continued even after the

Progressive Conservatives lost the 1980 election and were replaced by Pierre Trudeau's Liberals. By August 1980, Canada had actually secured a deal, a "memorandum of intent" on air pollution modelled on the Great Lakes agreements of 1972 and 1978:

> The Government of Canada and the Government of the United States of America.
>
> Share a concern about actual and potential damage resulting from transboundary air pollution, (which is the short and long range transport of air pollutants between their countries), including the already serious problem of acid rain;
>
> . . . Are concerned that environmental stress could be increased if action is not taken to reduce transboundary air pollution;
>
> Are convinced that the best means to protect the environment from the effects of transboundary air pollution is through the achievement of necessary reductions in pollutant loadings;
>
> Are convinced also that this common problem requires co-operative action by both countries;
>
> Intend to increase bilateral co-operative action to deal effectively with transboundary air pollution, including acid rain.
>
> In particular, the Government of Canada and the Government of the United States intend:
>
> 1. to develop a bilateral agreement which will reflect and further the development of effective domestic control programs and other measures to combat transboundary air pollution;

2. to facilitate the conclusion of such an agreement as soon as possible;
and,

3. pending conclusion of such an agreement, to take interim actions available under current authority to combat transboundary air pollution.

The memorandum was signed by the new Liberal environment minister, John Roberts, and by U.S. Secretary of State Edmund Muskie. Talks on an actual agreement were to begin by mid-1981. Once again, like a long shadow falling across environmental issues, Ronald Reagan's election interrupted hopes for a cleanup, less than three months after the memorandum was signed.

Reagan never made any secret of his general antipathy toward environmental rules, and he made his opposition to acid rain controls expressly clear. Twice during the 1980 election campaign, he uttered his famous comments about trees causing more pollution than cars (leading one reporter to suggest he try spending twenty-four hours in a locked room with a tree and then the same time locked up with a running car, to see which is worse). The new president claimed, too, that the Mount St Helen's volcano in Washington State had produced more acid rain than ten years of car exhaust. (In reality, cars produced nearly twenty-five times as much acid pollution.) As a result, throughout the 1980s, the White House spent its time calling for more research into acid rain. The more than five thousand studies tended to confirm Harold Harvey's worst fears, and scientists were constantly coming up with more and more evidence of just how damaging acid rain was, but the link was never conclusive enough for some American officials. It was like smoking and cancer—not absolutely provable, just painfully obvious.

In 1982, Canadian negotiators walked out of talks aimed at preparing a cross-border cleanup agreement to follow up the memorandum, and, around this time, the U.S. State Department officially designated two Canadian National

Film Board documentaries about acid rain as foreign propaganda. Meanwhile, the environment suffered. During the six years before Reagan took office, U.S. sulphur dioxide emissions had gone down 19 percent; during the Reagan years, they remained the same.

Yet, while the setbacks were largely due to Reagan, they were also partly Canada's fault. Canadian emissions actually went up during part of the 1980s, and during the first half of the decade, both federal and provincial governments claimed they could not regulate the pollution unless the Americans were willing to do the same. As with the Great Lakes agreements, Americans could legitimately point out that their standards were more stringent – which was the case for automobile emissions and U.S. coal-burning power plants. American utilities had installed pollution-scrubbing equipment at more than 140 coal-burning generating stations, while even in 1990 Canada's utilities had none.

To make matters worse, provincially owned Ontario Hydro, whose coal plants collectively caused more acid rain than any other company, lobbied the federal government for permission to put a transmission line across the bottom of Lake Erie, from Ontario to Ohio. To many Americans, Canada's fight against acid rain looked like little more than a sleazy plot to hobble the Ohio utilities with costly cleanup programs, so that prices would go up and Hydro could sell its cheaper power through this line. Given Canada's record, the remaining scrubberless plants in the United States could wait a little longer to be cleaned up, the Americans said. The acid-producing midwestern states were already hurting economically, and they feared being saddled with a cleanup bill that could cost up to five billion dollars – all to clean up a problem which, if it was real, affected another country, anyway. Reagan's remarks on trees, however strange, reassured them that this would not happen. They were consistent with his approach to many issues: he would say something incorrect and then act on the basis of what he said.

Throughout the 1980s, many Canadian politicians, with

equal consistency, misread the president, seeming to believe that he just needed a little education and persuasion about acid rain. As it turned out, Reagan knew all he needed to know—and the Canadian politicans had a lot to learn about how cross-border environmental politics work. One Canadian who did understand, however, was John Fraser. Shortly after he left the environment minister's post in 1980, it was he who quietly approached Michael Perley and suggested that he set up what was for Canada a new kind of environmental organization: a lobby group to be based in Washington, called the Canadian Coalition on Acid Rain.

Perley and his fellow activist, Adele Hurley, were—and are—very influential, and it was due to them that in 1984 Brian Mulroney promised to cut acid rain, if elected. He would bring in a program to cut acid rain pollution in half by 1994, and would back the plan with financial assistance to industries that required help in cleaning up. He kept his word, announcing on March 6, 1985, that the cleanup would go ahead.

Under his plan, acid emissions coming from Canada east of the Manitoba-Saskatchewan border would be rolled back to no more than 2.3 million tonnes a year by 1994. The figure was arrived at by scientists, who calculated how much "wet sulfate"—acid pollution—could still fall without doing serious harm. They came up with a figure of 20 kilograms of wet sulphate for every hectare that was endangered by acid rain. Since roughly 250 million hectares (more than a million square miles) were endangered, it was believed that this cutback would effectively "stop" the acid rain created in Canada.

Mulroney also promised to tighten Canada's weak automobile exhaust emission standards—which were tightened in 1987 and again in 1990. In addition, he offered up to $150 million in federal funds for polluters who couldn't afford to pay. The provinces promised to co-operate with the cleanup program. People who had been lobbying for action were encouraged. So far, so good. But this was only half the solution, and to achieve the other half Mulroney had another idea: he would talk to Ronald Reagan about it.

On March 17, 1985, Reagan came to Quebec City for a twenty-four-hour meeting with Prime Minister Mulroney. Playing up the fact that it was St Patrick's Day, as well as their Irish ancestry, the White House and the Prime Minister's Office encouraged the nickname for the meeting that the media quickly adopted: the Shamrock Summit. As *Time* magazine reported in a cover story a few days later, "the meeting was as carefully choreographed as a ballet. Pure stagecraft prevailed. . . . There was a moment of pure hokum as the two leaders, joined by their wives, left their flower-bedecked box at Quebec City's Grand Theatre during a Sunday-evening gala and joined contralto Maureen Forrester and other entertainers in a rousing chorus of *When Irish Eyes Are Smiling*." The net result, as far as acid rain was concerned, was a decision by the two men to appoint "special envoys," who would each be paid a dollar a year and would look for a solution to the Canada-U.S. acid rain dispute. Reagan picked his former transportation secretary, Drew Lewis, while Mulroney chose former Ontario Premier William Davis. It has never been entirely clear who talked whom into the idea of special envoys, although it was established in court that a former presidential adviser, Michael Deaver, was paid $105,000 by Canada to lobby the White House on acid rain, in violation of U.S. law. (Deaver was later convicted of perjury, but the conviction was overturned.)

Whatever Canada's efforts had been, they were in vain. The "breakthrough" damaged Canada's hopes for progress for several reasons, the first one being the choice of Davis as the Canadian representative. His time as Ontario's premier, from 1971–84, coincided almost exactly with the rising concern in the province about acid rain, yet he had done next to nothing—or worse. At the beginning of the 1970s, a stringent pollution control order had been imposed on Inco at Sudbury; when the company couldn't meet it, Davis allowed the order to be rewritten. He said in 1981 that Ontario's approach was to move "in a balanced way"—a code phrase for "let's not do anything unless we're forced." Davis had no credibility as an environmental advocate. Not that it mattered, because there was a problem with the process: it was pointless.

Reagan had said in his 1984 State of the Union address that his administration would "study" acid rain but not control it. As Reagan's chief of staff, Donald Regan, later testified at Deaver's trial, the White House considered appointing Davis and Lewis to be a cheap, painless way to appease Canada's hard feelings. According to people involved in the envoys' research, Lewis took his job seriously. He aimed to come up with a recommendation that would offer some hope to Canada, but could also be accepted by the president. But Davis was said to be detached and uninterested, frequently declining to speak to concerned groups about the work, saying he had "scheduling problems."

Canada-U.S. summits were an annual event during the 1980s, and by the time the next summit rolled around, Davis and Lewis had presented a report calling acid rain a "serious" problem in both countries and a "serious transboundary problem." They also recommended a $5-billion, five-year study program, to search for ways of burning coal more cleanly. Davis admitted at the time the report was released that the recommendations were tailored more to please the White House than to address Canadians' concerns.

Mulroney praised the report. It had no deadlines or timetable for stopping acid rain, but this didn't seem to worry him. Polluters could take the research money to modernize their equipment, whether it reduced pollution or not; if it didn't, they could say they needed more research. A subsequent study by Environment Canada found that only about $1.7 billion of the money to be spent on the program—less than 30 percent—would actually do anything significant to reduce acid rain. Eventually, years later, Ottawa acknowledged that the whole program was more or less a sham.

Not surprisingly, the main acid polluters in the United States agreed with Mulroney that the report was a good one. It was lauded by the American utilities and the U.S.

National Coal Association, whose president called environmental activists "the Abu-Nidals of the environmental fringe." (Abu-Nidal was a prominent Palestinian terrorist.) But one of Mulroney's own senior advisers admitted that praising this acid rain plan was "like trying to make a chicken salad out of chickenshit." An adviser to the U.S. Senate's Environment Committee was even more critical—of Canada: "Your government is getting sold out by its socks. And the sad thing is, it doesn't even know it."

The result of Mulroney's summitry was that while Canada was moving ahead on its own to clean up acid rain, its negotiating position with the United States grew worse. It became embarrassing. At the very beginning of 1987, the *Toronto Star* reported that the United States was about to sign its first acid rain cleanup agreement with a foreign country—Mexico. Americans in Arizona on the receiving end of acid emissions acted quickly to push the issue with Mexico; ironically, a Canadian engineering firm got the contract to install the pollution controls.

With problems over trade negotiations compounding the humiliation of Canada by the Mexican agreement, Reagan sent Vice-President George Bush to Ottawa in early 1987 to mollify the Prime Minister. Mulroney and Bush met in a building at the governor-general's residence, Rideau Hall. The vice-president brought along the U.S. treasury secretary, James Baker, and the prime minister had with him several people, including Environment Minister Tom McMillan. One of the Canadians presented a letter from a U.S. official, outlining the American position on acid rain. As Mulroney listened, his face drew into an expression of cold fury.

"I haven't seen that," he said. "Let me see that." He was handed the letter and he read it. It seemed to push back the U.S. position on acid rain even farther from where it had been. According to McMillan, Mulroney then lectured Bush, explaining that Canadians had to have some sign that the United States was actually listening to their concern, if not addressing it yet. When they emerged, Bush stood outside in the Ottawa cold next to Mulroney, who maintained the fierce, glaring pose he had struck inside when he had asked for the letter. Bush, ever the polite visitor, told reporters that he had been given "an earful" by Mulroney on acid rain and promised to take the message back to Washington. About three months later, on April 6, 1987, Ronald Reagan visited Ottawa and addressed a joint session of Parliament. He had met with Mulroney earlier in the day. In a brief departure from his prepared text, Reagan added a sentence: "The prime minister and I agreed to consider the prime minister's proposal for a bilateral accord on acid rain."

The Canadian government made much of this remark, but of course in actual terms it conceded nothing. Within a day, the White House was backpedalling, explaining that "the details and the mechanism" of what Reagan promised were not clear. Within a few months, a Canadian assistant-deputy environment minister, Robert Slater, was describing the current talks as "preliminary," nearly ten years after Canadians had started discussing acid rain with American officials. As Michael Perley said, Canada's environmental bureaucrats "seem to feel that these processes exist to be managed into the future indefinitely."

It took until June 12, 1989, with Reagan out of office, and amid fears of another summer of environmental horror, for President George Bush to say the words that mattered more to Canada than any bilateral agreement: "We will make the 1990s the era for clean air." Speaking from the White House, Bush said, "Too many Americans continue to breathe dirty air, and political paralysis has plagued further progress against air pollution. We have to break this log jam." From dead fingerlings in a small Canadian lake to international negotiations, acid rain has finally become recognized as an American and therefore a North American problem. It doesn't mean that the air will be clean soon, or even that it will be clean at all. But it was more than anyone in North America might have hoped for before: the president of the United States was saying that his role is to preside over the politics of our survival.

CHAPTER ELEVEN

CONGREGATION OF VAPOURS

. . . this goodly frame, the earth, seems to me a sterile promontory; this most excellent canopy, the air, look you, this brave o'erhanging firmament, this majestical roof fretted with golden fire—why, it appeareth no other thing to me than a foul and pestilent congregation of vapours.
— William Shakespeare, *Hamlet,* Act II, Scene 2

In the winter of 1990, wild winds whipped Britain, France and Germany, flooding towns and killing nearly one hundred people. In the summer of 1988, North Americans roasted and endured a costly and damaging drought. The weather in 1989 was less unusual—unless you were in northern Manitoba, where forest fires licked through the trees toward the edges of towns, under rainless skies. The five warmest years of the past century were 1981, 1983, 1987, 1988 and 1989.

Our scientific analysis of all this is still rough and incomplete, offering several possible interpretations, but it points to certain trends: the materials we put into the toxic cycle are altering the weather in two separate but related ways. Some of the compounds are destroying the ozone layer in the upper stratosphere, which protects us from the harmful radiation of the sun. Others are turning the atmosphere into a heat trap, which we call the greenhouse effect.

In a cold country like Canada, it's tempting to see this latter development as for the better. "Good weather is just around the corner!" a *Toronto Star* article said during a cold snap in 1988. "Within 50 years— and maybe even 30—our climate will be so much milder that ice in the harbor and snow on the roads will be almost unheard of. Home heating costs will be down 30 to 45 per cent." But research conducted by the federal environment department suggests that dreams of palm trees in the backyard may turn into nightmares.

On the East Coast, for example, warmer temperatures would reduce ice and extend the fishing season, but this invites overfishing, which has already devastated the region's economy, and the circulation of currents could change the whole makeup of the fishery. The seas would also rise about a metre, putting large parts of most Maritime cities underwater, as well as much of Prince Edward Island. In Charlottetown alone, as many as 225 buildings could be flooded.

And while balmier winters may become more common in Ontario and Quebec, so would economic loss. Quebec's ski industry, which brings in more than $200 million in revenue, could decline by as much as 70 percent. Lake Ontario would drop by thirty to eighty-three centimetres (approximately one to three feet), and Lake Erie would decline as well, making shipping more difficult, reducing hydroelectric power generation and requiring costly changes to port facilities and those fancy harbourside condominium projects with docking space for yachts. Farmers' growing seasons would be longer, but there would likely be less rain; Ontario agriculture alone stands to lose as much as $100 million a year because of global warming. It would be worse in the Prairies, where farming is more important to the economy. In Saskatchewan, an increasing number of severe droughts similar to the one in 1988 could cut productivity by as much as 75 percent in some years. Unfortunately, the warmer temperatures don't mean that farming can move farther north on the Prairies, because the soil is not particularly good. Even the rainy West Coast forests might be damaged, becoming more prone to disease, insect damage and fire.

In central Canada's cities, there will be a social as well as an economic cost: people will have to sweat through more temper-snapping days like those of the summer of 1988. A week-long heat wave in a normal summer tends to make people crabby and angry; police report more beatings and stabbings, for example. A week in a greenhouse summer could drive nearly all of us crazy. According to Environment Canada's predictions, every year there would be two heat waves with three days or more above 31 degrees Celsius (88 degrees Fahrenheit); until recently, these came only about once every three years and never lasted more than five days in a row. In a greenhouse world, we can expect them to last for as long as twelve days. And this is in Canada: the temperature would go routinely above 100 Fahrenheit in most U.S. cities, where people have guns.

—— I ——

The question of whether humanity is engineering its own meltdown is still very much in dispute. Some experts say we are already far down the road toward this hot, nasty world. For example, James Hansen of the U.S. National Aeronautics and Space Administration (NASA) says the crazy weather swings of recent years don't simply mean the greenhouse effect is coming, but that "it is already happening now." Two days into the summer of 1988, he told the U.S. Senate's Energy and Natural Resources Committee that "we can ascribe with a high degree of confidence a cause and effect relationship between the greenhouse effect and observed warming." He said he was "99 percent confident" that the greenhouse effect has arrived.

All that year, Hansen watched the weather get stranger, and, when he compared it to historical records, he found it was not strange at all: it was part of a long-term, worldwide pattern. From January to May at his lab in Manhattan, he recorded temperatures from monitoring stations around the world and compared them with a base period from 1950 to 1980. He also looked at measurements beginning in the late eighteenth century. He found that from 1780 to 1880 the world's average temperature had gone up about half a degree; the earth heated up at an even faster rate in the early twentieth century. But the most striking aspect of the pattern was the change that has come in recent years.

Hansen found that during the first five months of 1988 alone the average world temperature had gone up about four-tenths of a degree Fahrenheit–nearly as much as it had risen in the entire nineteenth century. And this was before the unbearable heat wave drove North American temperatures consistently above 30 degrees Celsius. On the basis of these first five months alone, Hansen predicted that "1988 will be the warmest year on record"– which it was. The next year's weather, although cooler, was not out of sync with the long-term pattern; it is this slow, but clear, trend toward higher temperatures that makes the greenhouse effect more than a theory, if not yet an absolute fact.

Not everyone agrees with Hansen's weather forecast. A week after Hansen's Senate testimony, John Maddox, editor of the authoritative journal *Nature*, wrote that "people who should know better have been talking as if they know the greenhouse effect has begun." And Reid Bryson, a geologist from the University of Wisconsin at Madison, called the testimony "a phenomenal snow job" and "a triumph of sociology over science."

The sceptics offer various reasons for their doubts. Some have come up with differing measurements; for example, three American climatologists who studied U.S. records, as opposed to world temperatures, found that there was no significant change in the weather between 1895 and 1987. Others contend that the historical records used to compare the past and present are unreliable. In December 1989, the *Economist* explained that the old records were filed by sea captains, who measured water temperatures by collecting buckets of water: "Before the 1940s the buckets used to collect sea-water were made of canvas, which could be warmed or cooled by the elements as the buckets were brought up on ship."

Just as there are disagreements over the past, there are alternative theories about what is going to happen in the future. One idea is that temperatures vary according to a twenty-two-year cycle controlled by the sun's magnetic field. Another expert, geologist Frank Koucky of the College of Wooster in Ohio, told the weekly business magazine *Barron's* that "the earth is going to cool noticeably over the next 50 years, by my calculations."

Many of these arguments are thought-provoking, but Hansen's numbers are consistent with a long line of mathematical models and predictions that indicate that the weather will gradually get hotter. The first suggestion that there might be a greenhouse effect was made by a French mathematician named Jean-Baptiste Joseph Fourier, who was born in 1768. After the French Revolution he became an artillery officer, and in 1798 he joined Napoleon's expedition to Egypt, where he served as governor for the next four years. It was during this period, in 1799, that Napoleon's soldiers discovered the Rosetta Stone, which made it possible to decipher the hieroglyphics of ancient Egypt. Fourier became one of the first experts on Egyptian archaeology, and, like the sunworshipping people of the Pharaohs, he wondered about the earth's relationship to the solar system.

By Fourier's day, it was understood that space was a void, that earth had an atmosphere, and that beyond the atmosphere the temperatures were probably too extreme for life to survive. So Fourier wondered, how is it that the rest of space is either too cold or too hot, but the earth is mild and warm enough to support life?

He had an idea. What if the atmosphere let in the heat that radiated from the sun, but prevented the warmth from getting out? It's the same effect that you notice on a sunny but cold day if you stand indoors by a window: you feel warmed. Fourier reasoned that this was also how plants grew indoors, and he decided the earth was much like a big hothouse. He was only partly right. For one thing, a hothouse, or greenhouse, works differently. The glass keeps the warm air inside from mixing with cold air outside; in the case of our planet, no such mixing occurs because there is no air outside the atmosphere. For another, most of the earth's atmosphere is made up of nitrogen and oxygen, and it did not take scientists long to discover that neither of these elements absorbs heat. What does are the tiny amounts of water and carbon dioxide in the atmosphere. Carbon dioxide is exhaled by every living thing, and in the natural atmosphere there are about 315 molecules of carbon dioxide for every 1 million molecules of air.

In later years, Fourier's interests took him on a strange tangent. He became fascinated with heat. He wore layers and layers of clothing, and kept the fires going in his home so that the rooms were like roasting ovens. One day he was killed in a tumble down the stairs, and the greenhouse effect was all but forgotten for the next six decades.

But, near the end of the last century, the earth's heat-trapping ability intrigued a Swedish chemist, Svante Arrhenius, who later won the Nobel Prize in 1903 for his analysis of how solutions conduct electricity. He was interested in Fourier's problem of why the earth stays warm. By this time, the sun's heat was understood to be a form of radiation, and the intensity of this radiation could be measured using calculations taken from the full moon. Arrhenius turned these data to good use, publishing a paper called "On the influence of carbonic acid in the air upon the temperature of the ground." He figured that although there were only trace amounts of water and carbon dioxide in the atmosphere, their molecules absorbed enough of the sun's radiation to warm the earth by about 15 degrees Celsius, or 60 degrees Fahrenheit. Without these molecules, the planet would be ice-bound; with them it was warm enough to support ten million different species.

Arrhenius was right about this. Each square metre of the earth emits an average 390 watts—about the power of six light bulbs—but only 237 watts, about four bulbs, leave the atmosphere. Two or so light bulbs worth of heat stays in the air to keep us warm and alive.

Arrhenius took his ideas further. He wondered how the world was changing. There had been great transformations between Fourier's death and the end of the nineteenth century, most of them as a result of the Industrial Revolution. Theorists from Mill to Marx had analyzed the political effects of industry, writers like Dickens gave voice to the cultural tensions the revolution caused. The machine had changed everyone's life. But Arrhenius was intrigued by what fuelled the Machine Age: coal. He commented that the civilized world was "evaporating our coal mines into the air." The burning of coal and the other fuels—oil, natural gas, wood and peat—was pumping the atmosphere full of carbon dioxide. He wondered what would happen if people kept burning these fuels in the twentieth century: what happens to the weather, for example, if the amount of carbon dioxide in the air is doubled, or tripled? He wrote: "If the carbon dioxide is increased 2.5 to 3 times its present value, the temperature in the Arctic regions must rise 8 to 9 degrees Celsius and produce a climate as mild as that of the Eocene period."

The Eocene period, about 55 million years ago, was marked by cataclysmic changes. The great mountain ranges formed—the Rockies, Andes, Alps and Himalayas—and primitive horses, apes and elephants began to appear. More significantly, temperatures were warmer than in modern times, and the seas rose and flooded the edges of the continents. Arrhenius's ideas were obviously provocative: they suggested that the planet's weather could shift to that of 55 million years ago and do so in less than two hundred years, that the shift may have started before the twentieth century began and that whatever was happening was caused by human behaviour. Yet, for four decades after Arrhenius published his paper, hardly anyone paid attention. Finally, in 1938, a British engineer named G. R. Callendar compared increases of carbon dioxide with temperature records from two hundred weather stations, proving the accuracy of the Swedish scientist's predictions.

Callendar's research was not intended as a warning. Actually, he thought burning huge amounts of fossil fuels to warm the earth would likely "prove beneficial to mankind in several ways," especially in places at "the northern margin of civilization" like Canada. He was neither the first nor the last scientist to suggest that we could tamper with the planet and come out ahead.

There wasn't much serious interest in global warming until two more decades passed. In 1957, scientists around the world decided to co-ordinate their research on a common subject, and through the United Nations, a special year of study was proclaimed: International Geophysical Year. It was a time of important psychological shifts in our understanding of the earth. The Space Age began in this year, with the launch of the first Soviet Sputnik satellite, and around this time Rachel Carson was pondering the ideas that she put into *Silent Spring*, which came out five years later. During the Geophysical Year, scientists started measuring trace gases in the atmosphere from the top of Mauna Loa in Hawaii. From then on, an accurate record of carbon dioxide was kept.

It took until the mid-1980s for there to be enough data to make a judgment. An American chemist named William Moomaw describes this record as "the most striking set of natural data ever recorded." Writing in the *Orion Nature Quarterly*, he said that "it displays the remarkable interplay between ecology and economics." Depicted on a graph with the advancing years across the bottom, the carbon dioxide levels in the atmosphere look like the profit line for a booming business. A closer inspection shows that the levels actually fluctuate every year, dipping in spring and summer and rising when the weather gets colder. Nonetheless, at the end of each year there's a bit more carbon dioxide in the air than the year before. The fluctuation is ecology: trees and plants convert more carbon dioxide to sugar and cellulose in the summer, so the air receives less, but when they lose their leaves in fall and winter, more carbon dioxide enters the atmosphere. The increase is human activity: "The burning of fossil fuels," Moomaw says, "is responsible for most of the carbon entering the atmosphere, some 5.9 billion tons each year, or one ton for each person living on the planet."

If the data from Hawaii are extended into the past, Moomaw estimates "that we have seen a 25 percent increase in atmospheric carbon dioxide since the beginning of the Industrial Revolution." More than half this increase has taken place since 1958. "If current trends continue ... pre-industrial levels will have doubled before 2075." At the moment, carbon dioxide in the atmosphere seems to be increasing by about 4 percent a decade—and even if that percentage remains constant, it's 4 percent of an already high level of CO_2. Many scientists now think the growth in greenhouse gases from all these sources means that carbon dioxide in the atmosphere will be double its natural level as early as 2030, when the children of the 1990s reach middle age.

Proponents of the greenhouse effect theory don't point to the burning of fossil fuels alone. Another major source of carbon dioxide is deforestation. The relentless removal of trees, especially in the tropics, is believed to add about one-fifth to the yearly increase. This happens for two reasons. First, in many cases the trees are burned, which has the same effect as burning fuel. And then, fewer trees also mean fewer leaves to absorb the carbon dioxide. It is estimated that an acre of rainforest, or nearly half a hectare, is now destroyed every second.

There is also the addition of methane to the atmosphere, a gas that smells like rotten eggs and has heat-trapping attributes. It comes from rice paddies, coal mines, garbage dumps—and, worse, the burps of an estimated 250 *billion* termites that infest deforested areas, and the flatulence of animals, including the worldwide herd of some 3.3 billion cattle, sheep, goats, buffalo and camels, which feeds and works for human beings and keeps growing along with the human population. In Margaret Atwood's novel, *Cat's Eye*, one of the characters remarks, "If we don't get burped to death by the cows we'll end up like the Sahara Desert." It is estimated that between 385 million and 612 million tonnes of methane enters the atmosphere each year and that it is increasing by 1 percent a year—which means that burping and flatulence are responsible for much of the greenhouse effect—one-quarter of which is caused by methane gas.

Worst of all is the effect caused by chlorofluorocarbons, or CFCs. These are the chemicals that are destroying the ozone layer, which protects us from cancer-causing ultraviolet rays at the same time that it keeps some of the sun's heat from reaching the earth. Scientists say that CFCs have a double effect: they destroy ozone and they trap heat the way CO_2 does. According to two experts in the United States, Verabhadran Ramanathan and Ralph Cicerone, each chlorofluorocarbon molecule wafting skyward has a warming effect roughly ten thousand times that of a single carbon dioxide molecule, and the spread of chlorofluorocarbons is increasing at ten times the rate of carbon dioxide. It is ironic that, while CFCs are eliminating the ozone we need in the stratosphere, smog is producing ozone at ground level that we don't want—and both processes are causing global warming.

—— II ——

The damaging effect of CFCs is one aspect of atmospheric pollution on which scientists do generally agree, and, while political action against the greenhouse effect is only just beginning, legislation to control ozone destruction started to appear in the 1970s. The roots of the CFC hazard go back to 1928, when a team of chemists at General Motors invented chlorofluorocarbons. (The team's leader, Thomas Midgley, may have done more harm to the environment than any other individual; he also developed brain-damaging tetraethyl lead as an additive for gasoline.) General Motors developed chlorofluorocarbons for refrigerators, since at the time the company owned Frigidaire and wanted to fix a flaw in the design of its early fridge models: the gases they used to cool food and drinks were ammonia, which is toxic, or sulphur dioxide, and both of these stank. The replacement Midgley's team came up with was called chlorofluorocarbon because it was based on a molecule made up of oxygen, chlorine and fluorine atoms.

Scientists soon came up with different variations of these atoms, and, as with leaded gas, the Du Pont Company got involved, in this case by buying GM's CFC-manufacturing facilities and assigning numbers to the different varieties of chlorofluorocarbons. The most important ones were CFC-11, 12, 113, 114 and 115, and the compounds were marketed under a trade name, Freon. Almost as soon as they hit the marketplace, CFCs were viewed as a miracle product—fireproof, corrosion-proof, explosion-proof, indestructible. They were just perfect.

Manufacturers of all sorts quickly realized that CFCs were useful for more than cooling beer in the fridge. You could also cool a room with them, which meant you could air condition buildings, even cars. They were good solvents, leaving even the tiniest surface clean and dry—a quality that would prove invaluable to the computer industry years later. CFCs were also useful as blowing agents for companies making foam insulation, for buildings, appliances and food packages. All kinds of products that had never existed were now possible—everything from comfy seat cushions made with CFC-blown foam to disposable cups that kept your coffee warm.

Also, you could use CFCs to spray things out of cans. They would not alter the materials to be sprayed, such as paint or fragrances—or insecticides. In the late 1940s, an American named Robert Abplanalp invented a leakproof valve, and aerosol sprays began to appear on store shelves. By 1973, the average American bought about fourteen spray cans a year. Abplanalp became both wealthy and a close friend of U.S. President Richard Nixon, and around the time Nixon was assailed in the Watergate scandal, the president's friend also became embattled—because of his spray cans. Researchers in the early 1970s began to question whether the CFCs that shot the deodorant out of the cans were really as harmless as had been thought. The spray-can inventor shot back that CFCs "would not make the sky fall in"—an unfortunate phrase.

One of the main initiators of the concern was a man named Sherwood Rowland, who was chairman of the chemistry department at the University of California at Irvine, in Orange County, south of Los Angeles. In 1972, he was at a conference where he heard a presentation by James Lovelock, the British scientist who had come up with the *Gaia* concept of the earth as one big living system. Lovelock had invented a sophisticated device that could detect tiny traces of different gases in the air. Using this device, he noticed that CFC-11 and CFC-12 were in the atmosphere in concentrations equal to about a drop in a big swimming pool; Lovelock thought these CFCs presented "no conceivable hazard," but could be used as tracers to advance his *Gaia* concept, by showing how the air moved through the living system. But Rowland wondered about the idea of all these man-made chemicals floating around for a different reason: if CFCs are so stable and indestructible, where do they go?

In October 1973, he began to investigate, working with a graduate student then in his twenties named Mario Molina. By December of that year, their research was done. "I just came home one night and told my wife: 'The work is going very well,' " Rowland said. " 'But it looks like the end of the world.' "

In June 1974, Rowland and Molina published their findings in *Nature*. Increasing amounts of CFCs are being sprayed and blown into the atmosphere, they said (at the time, the United States alone was producing 850 million pounds of the stuff each year – today, nearly 1 million *tons* per year are released worldwide), and the only place for these indestructible compounds to go is up. The article went on to say that, over the decades, the compounds have been drifting to the stratosphere, between ten and fifty kilometres above the ground. (Mount Everest is less than nine kilometres above sea level.) When the CFCs reach there they are finally vulnerable; the sun's ultraviolet radiation is strong enough to decompose them, releasing chlorine.

In contrast to the stable chlorofluorocarbons, the upper atmosphere is a wild chemical anarchy. The sun's powerful ultraviolet rays strike the two-atom oxygen molecule in this thin air, releasing an atom that quickly finds another two-atom oxygen molecule, forming three-atomed ozone. But the sun also hits the three-atom ozone structure, breaking away the third oxygen atom, which then looks for a single partner to form more oxygen. The whole process repeats infinitely, but, each time it happens, some of the energy from the light is absorbed by the ozone. This weakens the solar rays that reach us; it keeps us from burning, much in the way a good sunscreen, a window, even a shirt, protects us. Ultraviolet rays, known as UV-B, are the same ones that cause sunburns, and for people who get too much exposure, skin cancer and eye damage. In some animals, overexposure to UV-B rays can also harm the immune system, and high concentrations of this light will damage the food chain at the very bottom, by killing the tiny organisms that fish and other sea creatures eat.

When CFCs get involved, as Rowland and Molina explained, the chlorine atom released by the man-made molecule seeks out the unstable third oxygen atom of an ozone molecule and "eats" it before it can combine with another single oxygen atom. This breaks up the ozone into two new molecules—O_2 and chlorine monoxide—and starts a chain reaction: the chlorine monoxide finds another oxygen atom in an ozone molecule, again frees the chlorine atom, which finds more oxygen, and so on. Each chlorine atom can gobble up thousands of oxygen atoms. If this keeps up, the chemists said, eventually the ozone layer will be destroyed.

It's also just the beginning of the problem. The two scientists pointed out that CFCs aren't the only ozone-eating chemicals; compounds called halons, used in fire extinguishers, are a hundred times more efficient as ozone destroyers than CFCs, and they may account for a quarter of the world's ozone depletion. In addition, all the CFCs ever made have been produced since 1928, and since it takes decades for them to reach the upper atmosphere, the real damage is still to come. CFC-11, 12 and 113 remain in the lower atmosphere for anywhere from 75 to 120 years. As Rowland noted later, even if no more CFCs are ever produced, "a 120-year average lifetime means that . . . [CFCs] will survive in the atmsophere for the next several centuries." At the time he said this, in 1987, about 400,000 tons of CFC-12 alone were being released into the atmosphere every year.

The destruction of the ozone layer by CFC propellants became a popular issue, even making it into a trashy and quickly forgotten horror movie called *Day of the Animals* (starring Canadian Leslie Nielsen) in which the world's beasts go crazy and attack people because of the irresponsible use of spray cans. It was already out of date by the time it was released in 1977, since the United States, Canada and Sweden had begun to phase out aerosols using CFCs (most other countries, in the absence of public outcry, did not).

The political response in North America and Scandinavia was so quick for two reasons: the green wave was still running high when the *Nature* article appeared, and spray-can inventor Robert Abplanalp came up with a new type of spray. His new Aquasol cans used butane, and they were more efficient than the old ones. They delivered a more even mist and required less propellant, leaving more room for the deodorant or hairspray. The threat to the ozone layer appeared to go away, and so for a while most people ceased to worry about it. Anne Burford, Ronald Reagan's head of the U.S. Environmental Protection Agency, wrote, "Remember a few years back when the big news was fluoro-carbons that supposedly threatened the ozone layer?"

The trouble was, despite the phasing out of aerosol sprays in some countries, CFC production kept going up, as the air-conditioned U.S. Sunbelt's population expanded and the personal computer industry, which uses the chemicals, grew in a few years from nothing to become a crucial part of the modern world's economy. By the late 1980s, CFCs were a $110-billion industry. Besides, as Rowland and Molina had said all along, most of the ozone-eating chemicals hadn't made it to the stratosphere yet.

It made sense that when they did, the first place they would have an effect would be in those parts of the stratosphere that hang lowest over the earth, the poles. For-tunately, one of the research stations that had been set up during International Geophysical Year was a small outpost at Halley Bay, Antarctica.

Run by the British, the station measured ozone and traces of other gases, including CFCs, using a device called a Dobson spectrophotometer. Since ozone protects the earth from ultraviolet rays, the machine can measure ozone by recording how much ultraviolet light penetrates to the earth. For twenty-five years, the station sat quietly on its spot near the South Pole—the spectrophotometer's readings didn't indicate anything startling. Then, in 1982, the team's instruments picked up something unusual. There seemed to be about 20 percent less ozone over Antarctica than there was normally. At first, the British scientists thought their equipment was faulty; the government-funded station had a chronic shortage of funds. But when the team looked more closely at the data, they found they were even more striking: the ozone levels had actually begun to slip in 1977. The figures for 1983 showed an even sharper decline, and by 1984, the British survey team had determined that as much as 40 percent of the ozone over Antarctica disappeared during the late winter and early spring of the Southern Hemisphere, from September to October. It looked as though there was a big hole in the sky.

The British announced their findings in May 1985, telling a suddenly concerned world that the ozone hole they had found was as big as the continental United States. They discovered that it was seasonal—the ozone increased by mid-October, as the Southern Hemisphere summer approached and warmer air from the north moved in—but the ozone levels in the 1980s remained consistently lower than those of the 1960s and early '70s. Scientists figured there were three possible reasons. The first, suggested by NASA scientists, was that an eleven-year sunspot cycle had reached its peak in 1980, which might have caused nitrogen oxides to form, eating ozone in a similar way to CFCs. The second was that the ozone wasn't destroyed; it just moved elsewhere due to weather patterns. The third was Rowland and Molina's argument that compounds like CFCs were to blame. "The first two theories have not held up," Rowland wrote. "Only the idea that the hole is caused by chlorine chemistry has held up."

Then in the spring of 1986, another hole was discovered—over Canada's Arctic Circle. It was observed the following spring as well, both times by Environment Canada scientists who launched large research balloons to take measurements. "Scientists feel there is no increased risk to people living over the Arctic," the researchers said, but they warned that the two polar holes could easily turn out to be part of a dangerous pattern. While ordinarily "the ozone layer is at its thickest over the poles and becomes thinner at lower latitudes," the hole over the South Pole had the thinnest ozone anywhere, and it was quite possible that the one over Canada was spreading. At times, the edge of the thin spot came as far south as Saskatoon.

Needless to say, scientists talking about holes in the sky alarmed people, but as late as 1987, U. S. Interior Secretary Donald Hodel was still able to remark that people concerned about the ozone layer could wear "hats, sunglasses and sunscreen lotion." It was a Canadian official, Vic Buxton, who helped break the logjam. After the ozone holes were sighted, countries had begun talking about doing something to control the spread of chlorofluorocarbons, and in 1986, as head of Environment Canada's chemical control division, Buxton, along with two other Canadian officials, Alex Chisholm and John Allen, met with American and European officials. Buxton had spent years trying to get action from his counterparts in countries that were less concerned about the ozone layer than they were about finding new markets for the CFCs their factories made.

Canada, which produces only about 2.5 percent of the world CFC supply, was prepared to go along with a worldwide cut in production of the ozone-eating material, and the Canadians wanted the Europeans to join the ban on aerosol spray cans. However, the Europeans wanted merely to cap existing production levels—the European Economic Community's share of the market for CFCs was 40 percent. Europe also suspected that the North Americans wanted to ban CFCs because their companies had a head start in the search for alternatives. The compromise the three Canadians offered was to drop the demands for immediate measures in return for a promise to consider an international agreement, or protocol, to protect the ozone layer. The protocol would be worked out under the auspices of the United Nations, and, as a reward for the Canadians' efforts, the meeting to hammer out the agreement was to be held in Montreal.

It was a compromise that could have backfired horribly. Promises are cheap, and environmental promises are the cheapest of all. But, by the mid-1980s, even the most phlegmatic bureaucrat could recognize that the need to protect the ozone layer had moved from an abstract concept to a necessary priority. As Buxton points out, the scientific evidence in this case is overwhelming, and the consequences of the damage we have done already are severe. "If we allow this depletion to occur, what will life be like in the year 2050? We could expect routine health advisory notices warning the public of high radiation counts and requesting we stay indoors between the hours of 10 A.M. and 3 P.M. We could expect to see very major increases in suffering from skin cancer. A 1 percent decrease in ozone relates to a 3 percent increase in skin cancer." Measurements over Toronto have already shown a 5 percent decrease in ozone since 1970. In addition, Buxton says, "we can expect to see major increases in the incidence of infectious diseases and a decrease in the effectiveness of vaccination programs."

By the time of the meeting in Montreal, in September 1987, environmental activists were calling for an end to CFCs, and jockeying began between the forty-six countries at the conference to see who could gain the biggest commercial advantage from a ban on CFCs. That depended on the terms. The proposal on the table was to freeze production levels of CFCs at 1986 levels of about one million tonnes, beginning in 1990. Then the use of these substances was to be reduced through the '90s, falling to 50 percent of the freeze level by 1999. The agreement would take effect after it had been ratified by eleven countries that together consume two-thirds of the ozone-eating chemicals. But, although negotiation sessions had been held beforehand, many countries introduced their own agendas, making suggestions that would make the terms more favourable to them or would treat them as exceptions.

The Americans, for example, wanted the agreement to take effect only after countries representing 90 percent of production had signed it. The Americans did change their minds, partly because the stalling tactic was transparent, but also because large chemical firms such as Du Pont were already well on the way to developing safer substitutes for CFCs. The Soviets also wanted the freeze on production delayed, arguing that their (then) centrally planned economy had already drawn up new factories to make CFCs. They won this concession for themselves – the others considered it a price worth paying to get East and West signed up. Developing countries argued that they should be allowed to use more CFCs, arguing that it was unfair for rich countries to use air conditioners and fridges and then deny the poor ones the chance to enjoy such amenities. This would have been a dangerous concession: it would mean more CFCs, and, as had happened with other products like DDT, would allow companies to peddle chemicals banned at home to developing countries.

To get around this dilemma, another compromise was reached: developing countries could use more CFCs each year providing their consumption didn't go over 0.3 kilograms (about three-quarters of a pound) per person. But then there was another snag. The members of the European Economic Community wanted to participate in the agreement both as a single unit and as twelve separate nations, and the United States objected, fearing this would set a precedent for future trade talks. Another compromise was reached, one of those deals that fascinate diplomats and make ordinary people scratch their heads: the Europeans could first sign as twelve countries, then participate as a unit, too. This final problem was one of the most difficult for the negotiators, which demonstrates how much more concerned the countries were about their trade relationships than the environment. Even before the 1987 protocol had been reached, the head of the United Nations Environment

Program worried about "how much had been compromised" to hammer out a deal. "This will still mean a growing incidence of skin cancer and other health hazards," Executive Director Mostafa Tolba said. There was concern, too, that as more data rolled in from remote polar research stations, the ozone problem would turn out to be worse than anticipated. Sure enough, scientists discovered later that the world has already lost as much ozone as the treaty-makers assumed would be destroyed by the year 2050 — the year in which Vic Buxton fears that health warnings will be broadcast daily and widespread disease will be rampant.

Still, the Montreal Protocol proved that countries actually could get together and take the first, tentative steps toward fixing the planet. Mostafa Tolba said that, despite his wish for a stronger agreement, "never before in the history of science and law has the international community agreed to take such radical steps to avert a problem ... before the problem has begun to take its toll." Once there was an international framework for regulation, however inadequate, companies started scrambling to develop substitutes for CFCs. By 1994, for example, most auto manufacturers plan to introduce car air conditioners that don't use ozone-eating coolants, while existing car air conditioners can now be serviced by "vampire" units, which suck out the chlorofluorocarbon so that it can be cleaned and re-used without any of it escaping. This kind of marketplace innovation demonstrates that, for all their complaining about being over-regulated, corporations can benefit from sensible rules, by channelling their research to meet new demands.

Substitutes for CFCs are expected on the market in the early 1990s, but many experts say the ozone chemicals should be phased out completely, not reduced by 50 percent. To his credit, in February 1989, Environment Minister Lucien Bouchard announced that Canada would no longer produce or use the compounds by 1999. The twelve European countries have done the same, and the United States has agreed to discuss a new international agreement that will get everyone else to follow suit. A few days before

Bouchard made his move on CFCs, then Ontario Environment Minister Jim Bradley made the same announcement on behalf of his province. Bouchard's officials were angry and politically embarrassed: it looks as if what Bradley later threatened to do over car exhaust emissions—to take unilateral action to force the federal government's hand—he did over CFCs.

Some municipalities are pushing even harder for action. Toronto has passed a bylaw, for example, that will require all garages that service car air conditioners to have CFC-recovery equipment by 1991. American cities are acting as well: fittingly, the U.S. city that has pioneered tough CFC controls is Irvine, California—where Sherwood Rowland first came up with his theory that the chemicals are a threat.

—— **III** ——

Nine months after the Montreal Protocol was signed in 1987, hundreds of scientists gathered in Toronto to discuss the larger environmental problem, the greenhouse effect, or, as the conference title put it, "The Changing Atmosphere."

The meeting was addressed by Prime Minister Brian Mulroney, who used the occasion to announce his promise to have a national environmental "seal of approval" for products; it also featured a speech by Norway's Gro Harlem Brundtland, who had headed the United Nations environment commission. But the real star of the show was the weather—the conference began just a few days after the searing heat wave of the summer of 1988 started.

The first speaker at the conference was Dr Kenneth Hare, a respected Canadian climatologist who was known among environmental activists for being extremely cautious. Serving on government commissions, he had recommended against removing lead from gasoline and had supported nuclear power. But Hare opened the Toronto conference with a decidedly uncautious zinger: "The human search for necessities such as warmth, industrial energy and food is altering the optical properties of the atmosphere, and thereby threatening the world climate and all living things." No one could be absolutely certain of this, he said, but the prediction was at least as reliable as the ones made by economists about financial matters. "If the decision makers are willing to listen to economists, they should be even readier to listen to us." Unless drastic measures were taken, there would be "a revolutionary change in world climate, of a sort not rivalled in the history of civilization, not since the abrupt end of glacial climates ten thousand years ago." Hare was merely repeating what Svante Arrhenius had said nearly a hundred years before.

As the convening of the conference shows, at last there is considerable political support for this viewpoint. For example, speaking at the United Nations the next year, Environment Minister Lucien Bouchard said that "Canada does not dispute the scientific evidence of global climate change and other issues of ecosystemic crisis. We believe that change is occurring in our air, water and soil—and that, beyond reasonable debate, the causes are man-made and highly dangerous." He later called the greenhouse effect a "silent enemy," and promised to bring in a sweeping new "environmental agenda" that would deal with it. But when the agenda was finally put on public display in March 1990, it turned out to be a "framework for discussion on the environment," a thirty-one-page series of questions about environmental problems, with no specific answers. As one disappointed official said, after watching the plan's specific goals removed by cabinet and senior government advisers in the months before its release, "It's so easy to get governments to not do things. It's so hard to get them to do things."

At the international level, the United States, Japan and the Soviet Union teamed up in late 1989 to scuttle a proposal made by Western European countries to cut carbon dioxide emissions just 20 percent by 2005. They managed to substitute the words "as soon as possible" for a specific goal. And in early 1990, U.S. President George Bush called for an even vaguer goal. He said the world needs "an international bargain, a convergence between global environmental policy and global economic policy, where both perspectives benefit and neither is compromised." That could mean any-thing—and apparently the president likes the ambiguity. He declined even to use the terms "greenhouse effect" or "global warming," preferring to call the problem "climate change."

Provincial and local governments haven't done much better. In 1989, Canada's federal and provincial energy ministers sat down to talk about a greenhouse battle-plan, and all they could agree on was that the issue deserved study. It's ludicrous that in the last weeks of the 1980s, with the greenhouse effect apparently imminent, if you went to the federal energy conservation office in Toronto, you'd meet people packing boxes: the place had been shut down by budget cuts from Ottawa.

While Canada and other countries acknowledge the problem, they haven't been quite prepared to do what is necessary. By early 1990, only one province, Ontario, had come up with a proposal to reduce carbon emissions, but even this called for cutting them by only about 30 percent of what the scientists said was necessary. Cities have also talked about their ideas, which are usually common-sense ones like discouraging drivers and encouraging transit riders and car pools through higher parking charges, instituting special lanes for cars with passengers, closing certain streets to traffic and providing bus lanes. But this talk, while promising, remains mostly talk. Even pollution-conscious Toronto's city council has had difficulty deciding whether to close its trendy Queen Street West area to cars in order to reduce emissions.

Naturally, much of the politicians' reluctance to tackle the greenhouse effect comes from their deference to industries, which object to costly changes to protect the world against what is still unproven. The cost would be high: for example, in Canada, greenhouse gas—spitting coal provides much of the electricity in the Maritimes, as well as more than 90 percent of Alberta's power. The largest coal terminal in the world, the Roberts Bank superport, is just south of

Vancouver, loading 20 million tonnes a year for steel mills and power plants in the Far East and South America. Plans call for increasing this port's coal-loading capacity to as much as 33 million tonnes a year—enough to pump more than 30 million tonnes of carbon dioxide into the air when the coal is burned.

Indeed, one of the only major industries anxious to see new policies is the nuclear industry, which doesn't produce carbon dioxide—it just produces waste that can remain radioactive for as long as 4.5 million years. Their interest, of course, is the promotion of nuclear power as an alternative; however, such a measure would be futile. Nuclear plants take twenty years to design, approve, build and license, and to reduce the greenhouse effect significantly, the world would need to open a new plant every one or two days between 1990 and 2020.

In 1897, an editorial in the *Hartford Courant* commented that "everybody talks about the weather, but nobody does anything about it." It is a line that is taking on new meaning, yet there are measures that could be taken. Experts who accept the greenhouse effect as a real threat say the threat could be minimized if the world cuts its use of fossil fuels drastically in a short time—for example, enough to cut carbon dioxide emissions in half by 2020. Reductions could be achieved by a tax on all fuels, which would encourage people to drive less and turn down the heat; Canadian environmentalists say a tax of 2.5 cents per litre would raise $40 billion in just fifteen years, which could be used to ease the painful economic adjustments that would be needed to wean us off our addiction to gasoline, oil and coal. We wouldn't have to walk everywhere and freeze, either. Rather, fighting the greenhouse effect means replacing coal and oil with natural gas, which produces less carbon dioxide, and restoring many of the energy conservation programs that were started in the 1970s but abandoned in the '80s. The reluctance of governments to act, the resistance and the misleading proposals that come from industries, the continued disbelief in the greenhouse effect are perhaps the most hazardous things of all to our health. The changing weather is the final link in a chain of warning signs, and the balance of scientific data indicates that we should be more worried about it than our efforts to control it show. The scientists at the "Changing Atmosphere" conference released a statement that sums up the situation:

> Humanity is conducting an unintended, uncontrolled, globally pervasive experiment whose ultimate consequences could be second only to a global nuclear war.

If they are right, then the only way to gain control of the situation is to try another experiment—a political one. We have strong reason for action, we have the record on the issues, and we can no longer afford a system where everybody talks about the environment, but nobody does anything about it.

PART THREE

THE BEGINNING
OF SURVIVAL

CHAPTER TWELVE

THE POLITICAL EDIFICE

I suspect that the politicians and businessmen who are jumping on the environment bandwagon don't have the slightest idea what they are getting into.
— Denis Hayes, Earth Day organizer,
addressing a rally, April 22, 1970

Politics is largely the art of manipulating change, and there can be little doubt that the public now wants more than just talk about environmental problems. Contrary to what cynics believe, politicians in a democracy *do* listen to their constituents, since the alternative is to be voted out of office. Today, every politician wants to be clothed in green, and they all sprinkle their speeches with generous doses of the "E-word." George Bush says he's an environmentalist. So do the senators and congressmen who have fought hardest against an acid rain cleanup. In Canada, Prime Minister Brian Mulroney talks about environmental vision, the Liberals say they could better protect the environment, and the New Democrat leader Audrey McLaughlin says she heads "the party of the environment." Which party *isn't*, these days? We seem to be approaching a time predicted by an Indian chief named Seattle, who wrote in the early 1850s

that "it is the end of living and the beginning of
survival."

—— I ——

If, then, the time is ripe for working within the political
system, how do you go about it? The first problem is that in
Canada there isn't really a system, and in the United States,
it's highly influenced by deal-making compromises.

The root of the problem in Canada goes back to
Confederation. When Canada became a nation in 1867, the
Fathers of Confederation meticulously divided jurisdiction
over different matters of state between the federal
government and the provinces, but they didn't give either
level of government legislative authority for the environment. In 1867, no one thought about it. So by default, both
levels of government ended up with the power to make laws
in this field. As a result, Canada has thirteen environment
ministers—one from Ottawa and one from each province
and territory—and the point where the responsibilities of
each begin and end is extremely murky. When sewage pours
into Lake Ontario, for example, and closes Toronto's
beaches, no one agrees on who should pay to clean up. The
federal government, which administers the Boundary
Waters Treaty of 1909 and signed Great Lakes agreements
with the United States? The provincial government, which
funds municipal sewage treatment programs? And which of
the departments or ministries or agencies should help?
Toronto's shoreline is managed by more than thirty federal,
provincial, regional and local bodies or commissions, and
each level, either vertical or lateral, can come up with
arguments for either acting or doing nothing. When it comes
to the highest level, as one provincial minister has said, when
the environment officials meet "the Ontario minister fights
with the federal minister, Quebec asserts its independence,
the Maritimers get drunk and the Westerners go home
early."

Decision-making on environmental issues starts at the

top—or at least it's supposed to. Under the parliamentary system, virtually all major proposals depend on the initiative of cabinet ministers, who introduce most of the bills that eventually get passed. Usually, the government formally promises legislation with a vague reference in the Throne Speech, and then lawyers from the department that will introduce it start writing. Their draft is sent to lawyers from the Justice Department, and it may go to other departments if it affects the subjects they deal with. Changes are often made, and eventually the bill is introduced by the minister in Parliament. Once introduced, a bill can be changed again through parliamentary debate. Some of the changes may be suggested by parliamentary committees such as the Environment Committee, but as the chairman of that committee, David MacDonald, says, "We have a lot of catching up to do. The major limitation is that we have never really encouraged MPs to be professionally engaged [in committee work]. We are at such a superficial level."

In the summer of 1989, MacDonald took a delegation to Washington to compare how U.S. congressional committees operate in the Senate and House of Representatives. MacDonald was a seasoned legislator who had served in cabinet and as ambassador to Ethiopia, but he was amazed at the sophistication of U.S. committees. "One guy asked us how our committee system worked and I explained it to him. He said: 'We used to operate that way, in the middle of the nineteenth century.' He didn't mean to be funny."

MacDonald found that the difference between Canadian and U.S. legislative environmental committees was partly scale—the U.S. committees have far more money for travel and investigation—but the U.S. committees also had better support. The legislators were backed by teams of experienced lawyers and researchers, those behind-the-scenes people who give shape and form to committee hearings. In the United States, a committee's staff starts researching a problem that has come to the attention of a legislator by gathering information and then meeting with lobbyists from environmental groups and industry. After they have heard what issues are being pushed by the interest groups on all sides, they figure out who should be invited to testify. The lawyers help prepare the questions for the senators and representatives to ask, and give immediate advice, as in a trial, but most of all, they and the researchers provide an institutional memory. "Some of them have been working for fifteen or twenty years on the same committee," MacDonald says. So in the United States, if someone like Lucien Bouchard promises a "new agenda," the committee staff can tell if there really is anything new.

MacDonald also notes that in the U.S. system, there is less party discipline than in Canada, so American legislators tend to be more freewheeling in their questioning. Even when the White House comes up with a proposal, the president will have to woo Congress, phoning key legislators, having them over for breakfast or a chat. Canadian legislators know that ultimately, if their party supports the proposal being discussed, they'll have to vote for it whether they like it or not. Perhaps this ultimate lack of decision-making power is the reason for the proliferation of the next layer of the Canadian system: the bureaucracy, which is supposed to implement and administer the rules.

In December 1989, in New York, an American who specializes in analyzing Canada-U.S. issues was discussing how he did some work for the Canadian government on environmental issues. He explained what, through his contacts, he understood Canada's vision to be. Leaning close, he bowed his head with a look of disapproval, peered over his glasses and said: "It's *very* bureaucratic."

Harold Harvey, the father of acid rain, says that in the early 1960s when he worked for Canada's fisheries department "there were three layers of bureaucrats between me and the deputy minister. Since that time, they've added another eleven layers."

In fairness, sometimes even the people paid to handle an environmental issue have trouble figuring out if it's really their responsibility, and if it is, how to exercise that responsibility. There are so many layers of rules, and the rules sometimes contradict each other. Air quality, for example, is measured using both federal and provincial measurement guidelines, some of which are derived from U.S. Environmental Protection Agency measurements, some of which are based on World Health Organization figures, and some of which are home grown. No matter how urgent the issue is, the bureaucrats must consult with all the other departments, consider all these rules and estimate all the external and internal political implications. No wonder the process takes endless time. "I can slam a piece of paper on my desk and say, I want that done now!" explains Ontario Environment Minister Jim Bradley. "If everything is done as quickly as possible, it will be back on my desk for me to sign in a month. And that's considered fast."

Under the U.S. system, proposals for new legislation come from the White House or either level of Congress, the Senate or the House of Representatives. When proposals come from more than one of these sources, each congressional house can pass its own version of the legislation, and then conferences take place between representatives, senators and sometimes White House officials to merge the separate proposals into one, which is then passed by both houses. This system encourages genuine debate among legislators and competition to improve proposed new laws, but it also encourages deal making, and this is a serious drawback.

Unlike Canada, where most trade-offs are made in cabinet before legislation is introduced, American politicians make their trades openly on the floor of Congress and the statehouses, and they must negotiate with one another for support on various issues. In a situation like this, it is easy for an environmental issue to be bartered away, particularly if it comes up against a "pork-barrel" issue. Each legislator has a handful of these issues that could help tip the balance in an election and so are too important to be traded off. There are a few legislators who consider the environment their top priority, but, although their numbers are increasing, they are still a small minority. Deal making is such an integral part of the congressional system that it even affects the way laws are written; many bills are "omnibus" pieces of draughtsman-ship, with sections that have nothing to do with one another but are added to gain key congressional votes. So a pollution law, for example, may be part of a totally unrelated tax or spending bill.

If the idea for a new pollution control comes from Congress, it can easily fall by the wayside. The legislator who proposes it may be satisfied if it results in committee hearings, where experts explain the problem. Snippets of hearings are often shown on TV news. They can make the legislator look good, and, if he or she is really concerned about the issue, they can help marshal public opinion in favour of action. However, because committees are more significant in the U.S. than in Canada, they tend to be used more for grandstanding and posturing. To study the farm crisis, one committee had actresses such as Jessica Lange testify, on the grounds that they had starred in movies about farms. Sometimes new laws get blocked by committees, for example when legislators have old scores to settle. One of the reasons Congress could not pass acid rain legislation for nearly a decade was because no bill could get past the Energy and Commerce Committee headed by John Dingell. It wasn't simply that he opposed such laws; he hated their main advocate, a fellow Democrat named Henry Waxman. They were opposites: Dingell tall, Waxman short; Dingell representing a lunch-bucket Michigan district where cars are made, Waxman representing trendy Los Angeles, where cars make smog. After years of antagonism, it got so that anything Waxman liked, Dingell hated. When the two made peace in 1989, it took only a few weeks for them to co-sponsor a plan to curb acid rain. As in Canada, the environment is often not just at the mercy of cold economics, but also hot-blooded personalities.

Sometimes a major initiative in the United States affecting the environment doesn't require a new law at all. The reason leaded gasoline was banned so quickly was that it wasn't done by legislation, but by the Environmental Protection Agency using its power under existing laws to come up with a new regulation. This took effect after a short period allowed for interested parties to comment on the move. Canada's government agencies have similar powers, but as Canada's slower move to get rid of leaded gas shows,

Canadian regulators are afraid to defy the industries they regulate. In the United States, it's more a matter of conflicting pressures, but generally, an arm of government such as the EPA will take years to gather evidence and make its case that a particular type of pollution is bad enough to require stricter controls.

The chief difference between the American rule-making process and the Canadian is that, in the United States, the places where pressure can be applied on both legislators and agencies are all institutionalized: hearings, public opinion forums, lobbyists who are required to register their activities. In Canada, the process that creates environmental rules is less confusing—cabinet discusses, ministers introduce, Parliament passes—but it's more haphazard and arbitrary, since it depends even more on personal loyalties and favours than the American system does. Until 1989, for example, lobbyists weren't even required to register in Canada, so no one could tell who was bending whose ear to weaken proposed laws.

In both Canada and the United States, the environment has a paradoxical position in the political structure. It's more noticeable than in many other countries as a political issue, because there's so much talk about it, but it's less significant—the political results have neither been as dramatic as those in Europe nor as comprehensive as those in places like Japan. It may be that we need a complete overhaul of the system, and we may come to realize this the next time we have a big environmental disaster. We already have examples of how environmental issues can change the political structure. It's not entirely a coincidence that the political makeup of the Soviet Union shifted the minute the Chernobyl nuclear fire sent its hellish flames into the sky. And late in 1989, when Eastern Europe's Communist governments fell, some of the earliest protests were started by environmental groups.

In other countries, political action has come from outside the established structure, forcing the mainstream politicians to accomodate environmental demands. The Green Movement, those political parties whose platforms focus on environmental issues, had a strong influence on West Germany's politics during the 1980s – and indirectly, on all of Europe's – resulting in some of the most stringent environmental controls in the world. Greens are also influential in Britain, and they have captured seats in the European Parliament. In still other countries, such as Japan, strict environmental regulations have resulted from consensus. Japan protects its trees and tightly controls its industries' smokestack emissions, even while its whaling ships ply the seas and its companies hack down the rainforests in Malaysia and Indonesia. However, for the moment, in Canada we are working with what we have.

Looking at the people in the system, what exactly do we have?

—— **II** ——

In both the Canadian and American systems of government, the most important person as a force for environmental action is the one who is sometimes most difficult to budge: the prime minister or the president. This is particularly true in the United States, where a president exerting negative influence can do a lot of damage, as Ronald Reagan did. It is difficult to tell what will happen with George Bush. Judging by his first year in power, he is not as strong an environmentalist as he claims to be, but not as weak on the issues as his toughest critics would have it. He has backed new clean air legislation – even if it is not the tough proposal most experts believe is needed – and U.S. polluters are now paying record fines. On the other hand, the Bush administration is reluctant to take action against the greenhouse effect, and the White House was notoriously slow and inept in dealing with the *Exxon Valdez* oil spill.

In Canada, Brian Mulroney's Progressive Conservative government has suffered from a persistent inability to figure out how to deal with environmental issues – specifically, whether his government should protect the environment or protect those who are doing bad things to the environment.

Mulroney's first environment minister, Suzanne Blais-Grenier, was a newcomer to politics who was clearly unsympathetic to the aims of her department. She was hampered by the fact that just two months after the September 1984 election, Mulroney hacked $46 million out of Environment Canada's budget, cancelling programs like Doug Hallett's study of dioxin in the Great Lakes. But she did defend the budget cuts zealously, and, a year after her appointment, she suggested that it would be okay to allow logging and mining in Canada's national parks. When given several opportunities to back away from her statement (she had never said it directly), she declined to do so. Mulroney defended her, and her statement, too, but in 1985 he demoted her and replaced her with Tom McMillan.

Under McMillan, the department continued to implement Mulroney's first budget cut (in later years, Environment Canada's budgets were increased, to the point where they almost kept up with inflation). The department also began moving away from its stated role as an advocate of a healthy environment. The move was never announced openly, but it was signalled in a report on the environment department's activities that was commissioned in 1985 by then-Deputy Prime Minister Erik Nielsen. The report was a secret follow-up to an earlier study that was done as part of a government-wide task force review of all departments. Nielsen – never an advocate of environmental protection – was said to be unhappy with the first review, which recommended "a stronger commitment of the federal government to environmental issues." The second study called for a "major shift from recent practices." It suggested "moving away from the 'advocacy' approach" toward a more "balanced" approach – less finger-pointing. "The sooner the 'advocacy' approach is replaced," it said, the better the chance for officials "to make their critical judgments in a timely manner."

Traditionally, calling for a "balanced" approach when it comes to the environment is a euphemism that means listening less to environmentalists and more to industries that don't want to be regulated. Just before the secret report was completed in early 1986, its message was reinforced at a meeting of senior environmental officials, who were told in no uncertain terms that they were no longer to advocate a clean environment, but would act as referees in disputes between companies and people complaining about pollution. The secret report's contents were revealed publicly in 1986, through a leak, and a few months later, the government relented and released the entire review.

McMillan says the secret report was never adopted by his department, because "it didn't have all its facts straight." The latter point may be true, but in fact, many of the things the secret report called for—the hands-off approach to problems, more emphasis on provincial responsibilities, a reluctance to regulate—have been followed almost to a fault.

McMillan himself has been given mixed reviews by environmentalists: some were happy with him for creating new national parks in British Columbia, the Arctic and Ontario's Bruce Peninsula, but most dismissed him as a weak minister with a shallow understanding of the issues. Now that he has been replaced, his record has proved him to be more complex than either his supporters or critics understood him to be—a minister who could utter some of the most meaningless environmental rhetoric, yet who, at the same time, compiled a list of achievements that is more accomplished than any predecessor's. This may say more about how weak his predecessors were than it does about him.

If the first problem Prime Minister Mulroney's government is having with the environment is in deciding which side it is on, the second is in deciding whether or not to take the matter seriously. As Canadians know, a preference for style over substance has persistently plagued the prime minister, and this caused serious embarrassment when it spilled over into the environment department in 1986. After cutting its budget twice in two years, the department spent $1 million on a publicity campaign to promote National Environment Week. This was a substantial increase from the

$40,000 the government had spent on Environment Week the year before.

As much as $650,000 went to a Montreal advertising agency, which prepared a song and video, featuring celebrities such as Carole Pope and Kim Mitchell, along with a few bored-looking athletes. The song's chorus was "Wasting away, wasting away." A photo of McMillan at the video session appeared in *Le Journal de Montréal*; he had flown up just for the picture in a government jet, interrupting talks in Washington about a plan to clean up the Niagara River. Proceeds from record sales were supposed to go to some sort of environmental fund, but sales were dismal, and Canada's Auditor General wondered, if there were proceeds, where the money ended up; perhaps the only ones who know are those who have some in their pockets.

Just before this Environment Week, in a tense phone call to a reporter (myself) one afternoon, McMillan warned that "if this gets pissed over . . . I'll walk away from it." But it was difficult for the media to take it seriously, when, in a bit of unintended symbolism, the week was kicked off with the launch of two hot-air balloons on Parliament Hill. "If I were an irresponsible journalist," McMillan said, "I could have a field day with this."

The campaign was a familiar political tactic. The federal government spends more money—taxpayers' money—on advertising than any corporation in order to sell unpopular policies such as free trade or the Goods and Services Tax. Here, it was unclear even what they were trying to sell: after the budget cuts, they had nothing. But instead of filling this gap, the government has gone on to focus on getting its publicity campaigns to work better. In 1987, as election time approached, officials from Environment Canada and the Prime Minister's Office began to work out a strategy: the government would abandon any remaining pretence of going all-out to protect the environment and would stress what it was doing on a few high-profile environmental issues, such as pollution in the Great Lakes and the St Lawrence, and especially, parks. One official involved at the time remembers that "they were interested in parks in particular. The discussions were always around making the government look good, with the election in mind."

Meanwhile, Mulroney went on the radio in Quebec, proclaiming: "We need a collective commitment . . . to give ourselves, as citizens, the best environment that could exist. It is a kind of national vision that I am looking at, a collective commitment of the Canadian nation in favour of this great question of environmental protection."

After the 1988 election, McMillan, who had lost his seat in Prince Edward Island, was replaced by Lucien Bouchard as environment minister. A former Canadian ambassador to France and an ardent Quebec nationalist, he resigned suddenly in May 1990 in a dispute over the government's constitutional proposals. Before that, Bouchard's strongest asset was one he played up incessantly: he was a good friend of the prime minister. He was said to have been the one who taught Mulroney to speak French. The point was obvious; the environment would be better protected with Bouchard as minister because, in cabinet, Mulroney would listen to his friend and no one else would dare ignore him. Such is the Canadian system.

In the fall of 1989, Bouchard testified to Parliament's Environment Committee that "we are working very closely on the definition of new policies. What we are doing is something that is coming out of the reorganization of the government decision process system." He explained that the federal cabinet's Planning and Priorities Committee had "made a very, very important decision here in Ottawa in the quiet days at the end of the summer while some of you were taking a very deserved vacation. There were no media around. It was a lengthy meeting at Meech Lake." This committee decided that there would be a new cabinet committee, the Environment Committee (not to be confused with the parliamentary Environment Committee, made up of non-cabinet MPs from all three parties). With almost Biblical cadence, Bouchard went on: "And this was not an empty word, this was reality. You will begin more and more to see the realization of this concept and this structure."

The government had already appointed a National

Round Table on the Environment and the Economy, to advise the prime minister. What Canada would begin to see now was how the cabinet Planning and Priorities Committee had "made the decision to mandate my environment committee to prepare an agenda for environment for Canada for the next five years, a wide-ranging agenda touching all departments whether related to the environment or not to the environment." This followed on a promise made in the government's Throne Speech that opened Parliament in April 1989. It had pledged that the government would "deal more effectively with environmental concerns and their relationship to the challenges of economic growth."

The measures Bouchard promised were to include the opening of an international centre, located in Winnipeg, to promote the prescriptions for "sustainable development" (economic growth compatible with environmental protection); a tax on fuels that emit carbon dioxide (virtually all of them) to minimize the greenhouse effect; extensive reforestation; and new powers to review major government economic proposals, such as new building projects or transportation plans, to see whether they will affect the environment.

Within five months of Bouchard's testimony before the parliamentary committee, it became clear that he was unable to deliver even a remotely significant part of what he had promised. One by one, his proposals were either watered down or eliminated; then, after many of them had been restored to the overall plan, the plan itself was downgraded to a non-binding "discussion paper" – thirty-one pages of notes for what was not a plan, but a questionnaire for a plan. When it was released in March 1990, it promised, "The views of Canadians on [the] issues raised in this paper will help transform the Government's *Framework for Discussion on the Environment* into *The Green Plan: A National Challenge.*" Presumably government officials now wait, pens at the ready, for public response so that they can transform the framework for discussion into a plan, which might then daringly even become the basis for suggestions for new legislation. In any case, Bouchard did not wait; less than two months after releasing his plan, he was gone, having crossed the House of Commons floor to sit as an independent.

There are several possible reasons for Bouchard's failure to deliver an actual plan. One is that within cabinet, policy differences won out over friendship with the prime minister, and other ministers were persuaded that Bouchard's plan would cost too much (he had suggested spending as much as two billion dollars). Another is that some ministers didn't like the idea of regulating industries more tightly, and industries, which are influential in Conservative circles, didn't like it, either. Bouchard's deputy minister, Len Good, was said to have been raked over the coals by more senior cabinet officials for failing to clear some of the environment minister's ideas with other departments. A third possible reason is that, while Bouchard had the prime minister's ear, the prime minister also had Bouchard's. Whatever the ultimate reason, the government's decision to release a discussion paper is somehow fitting. On the evidence so far, when it comes to its influence over environmental change in Canada, the federal environment department is now little more than a discussion group. A member of Parliament, Charles Caccia, who was environment minister under the Liberals, has asked the pertinent question of the day: "How can you go on like this?"

—— **III** ——

Since both Canada and the United States are democracies, the workings of the system can be speeded up by public pressure. Governments are sensitive to this even when elections are a long time away. They take frequent polls, and contrary to a commonly held belief, governments regard angry letters from concerned citizens seriously. It *does* help to write. The general political rule is that each letter represents one hundred voters who are also upset about the same issue but were too busy, shy or lazy to compose a letter. Handwritten or typed letters are taken most seriously;

mail-in postcards that are part of an organized campaign less so. (They require less effort, suggesting less public concern.) Legislators try to send replies to letters: word gets around that an MP or minister actually answers the mail – or does not. If the polls are negative, or if enough letters about a particular law or policy are critical, and if the critics zero in on a particular aspect of it, the government can be persuaded to change its plans.

Organized and direct pressure is more effective, of course, and this is where lobbyists and environmental groups are supposed to play an important role. In the United States, the major groups are so influential that politicans can no longer afford to ignore them. In the wake of the *Exxon Valdez* disaster, for example, U.S. groups quickly pressured Congress to shelve a plan to expand oil drilling in Alaska. They did this by figuring out which legislators had not yet decided how to vote on the issue, and then writing to them, phoning them and talking to their aides. But in Canada, this kind of pressure would be difficult to apply: most governments consider environmentalists less as power brokers than as pests.

Part of this results from the difference in the systems; unlike their American counterparts, for example, Canadian environmentalists can't go to court as easily to enforce the law. But part of this is also the fault of the Canadian environmental movement. As environmentalists go, Canada's are among the most poorly organized and fuzzy in their thinking of any in the Western world. Canadian groups are tiny compared to their American counterparts, some of which boast as many as 500,000 members. With a few exceptions, the Canadian organizations are also relatively poor and, as a consequence, often easily manipulated. With only a few exceptions, they depend for survival on handouts from the governments they criticize. For a while during the late 1980s, the federal environment minister even had a special fund to dole out to the activists, and a special adviser, Elizabeth May, who was responsible for giving out the money. The fund was worth $150,000 a year; in Canada, an environmentalist can be bought pretty cheaply.

The money doesn't directly buy an activist's silence or
co-operation. Most of Canada's environmentalists are more
honourable than that. What it does buy, however, is
dependency; government funding is the environmental
movement's drug. Activists in remote parts of the country
know, for example, that if Ottawa is going to consult them on
a proposed new policy, it will send them plane tickets and
pay their long-distance phone bills. Some groups, most
notably Greenpeace, refuse to take money from the
government; most others don't, though, and it shows in the
quality of their criticism: our governments get away with a
large number of merely cosmetic measures to protect the
environment.

The Canadian environmental movement has also been
hampered by intense internal rivalries and feuds, which
unfortunately are not necessarily battles of great principle.
From 1986 to 1988, for example, it seemed as if the biggest
division among Canadian activists was between those who
liked Elizabeth May and those who did not. At one point
when she was a government adviser, May showed up at an
activist meeting, and to this day a dispute rages among
environmentalists as to whether she was invited or whether
she crashed the party. The bad effect of all this bickering is
most noticeable by how well things work when it stops: when
May joined forces with all the other environmentalists to
fight to preserve British Columbia's South Moresby area as
parkland, the area was saved.

Environmental groups bicker in the United States, too,
but the arguments there tend to be more over tactics. On one
side, there are the "suits"—lobbyists who write briefs, meet
with congressional aides and dine with legislators, playing
the traditional political game. On the other side, there is the
"deep ecology" movement—people who find such conventional methods disgustingly inadequate. For deep ecologists,
the end, protecting the environment, justifies the
means—any means. The most ardent advocates of this
anything-goes approach belong to a group called Earth
First! founded in 1980. They were inspired by *The Monkey
Wrench Gang*, a 1975 novel by the late Edward Abbey, which

centred on a plot to blow up Arizona's Glen Canyon Dam. In one of its first protests, Earth First! members unrolled a plastic "crack" down this dam to protest the way it changed the surrounding area. Then, borrowing from the novel's title, they started "monkeywrenching" – their term for activities that included putting large spikes in trees to break chainsaws and disabling road-building and logging equipment. Earth First! has a small following in Canada – mostly subscribers to its magazine – and a few minor law-breaking incidents have been reported. The closest most Canadian environmentalists come to monkeywrenching tactics is to engage in civil disobedience. The actual ranks of the deep ecologists in the United States are few, but their uncompromising attitudes find widespread sympathy. Many of the slickest "suits" privately express grudging admiration for the monkey-wrenchers, figuring that they not only gain attention for environmental causes, but also make the moderate lobbyists appear more reasonable.

—— IV ——

Given this political system and its options, what *does* work? In all cases, obviously nothing, very well – otherwise, the political system would protect the environment and people would no longer worry that the end is near. But as environmental problems grow more serious, public concerns expressed in philosophy, polls and votes, conventional lobbying and outright militancy are all becoming more influential. It can depend on the issue. When activists began chaining themselves to bulldozers in Temagami, for example, the Ontario government became nervous about its forestry policies. On the other hand, the most successful activists in Canada, perhaps in all of North America, are a group of consummate political lobbyists: the Canadian Coalition on Acid Rain.

CHAPTER THIRTEEN

SUCCESS STORIES

They shall be as thorns in your sides.
                              —The Book of Judges 2:3

A thunderstorm was threatening Toronto on June 12, 1989, but Adele Hurley and Michael Perley had reason to feel sunny.

They had organized a dinner party for that evening, a banquet for eight hundred at the Royal York Hotel. It was quite unlike the traditional gathering of people concerned about the environment. For one thing, the guests were hardly the outsider-types so often associated with environmental groups. There were no backpacks, no jeans, no flannel shirts from the outfitter's store. Instead, these were corporate Canada's leaders; many companies had bought whole tables and sent their senior executives to represent them. Ontario Premier David Peterson and the leaders of the two provincial opposition parties were there. Hurley and Perley's mentor, Speaker of Parliament John Fraser, was there, and so was the newest federal environment minister, Lucien Bouchard. Ontario's environment minister, Jim Bradley, was there, as were top officials from Quebec.

This was a dress-for-success evening. The women wore sleek evening clothes that radiated understated, but high-priced, good taste. Hundreds of men filed into the hotel's immense banquet hall in well-tailored suits, their brightly coloured silk ties like tiny boats in a sea of double-breasted blue and grey. There were no tuxedos, but that was only because the invitations called for business attire. This was misleading. The ostensible purpose of Hurley and Perley's dinner party was to raise funds for the Canadian Coalition on Acid Rain, which they run, and the dinner at $150 a plate would net about $80,000. It was not to be business as usual that night. For once, it looked as though there would be something to celebrate about the environment.

A few hours before, President George Bush had announced that he would end a decade of White House resistance and support a new law to stop acid rain. He made the announcement at the White House. "First," he said, "we will cut the sulphur dioxide emissions that cause acid rain by almost half, by 10 million tons. And we will cut nitrogen oxide emissions by two million tons – both by the year 2000. We have set absolute goals for reductions and have emphasized early gains. And that means five million tons will be cut by 1995 and the degradation caused by acid rain will stop by the end of the century.

"Second, this federal proposal will cut the emissions that cause urban ozone – smog – virtually in half. . . . We propose bold new initiatives to reconcile the automobile to the environment. . . . We'll accomplish this through alternative fuels and clean-fueled vehicles. We propose to put up to a million clean-fueled vehicles on the road by 1997.

"The third leg of this proposal is designed to cut all categories of airborne toxic chemicals by three-quarters within this decade. . . . The bill I'm proposing today will set a schedule for regulating sources of air toxics . . . and it will make state-of-the-art technology an everyday fact of doing business. . . . This initiative should eliminate about three-quarters of the needless deaths from cancer that have been caused by toxic industrial air emissions."

For Perley and Hurley, the announcement was a reward for the work and bitter struggle for survival that has gone into their organization, the first of its kind and the most effective environmental action group in Canada. It also brought them one step closer to their ultimate goal for the Canadian Coalition on Acid Rain. They dreamed—and still dream—about holding another party. It will take place when acid rain has been beaten. "We'll rent out Casa Loma [a fake medieval castle in Toronto built by an eccentric million-aire]," says Hurley. "We'll invite all our friends to the castle and then we'll tell them: the coalition is going out of business."

—— I ——

People often ask how one becomes an activist. If Perley and Hurley are models, then the answer is, don't try, just let it happen. Both of them more or less stumbled into the field. Perley has a degree in French literature, and, as a student, Hurley didn't even know what environmentalism was. "I wasn't particularly interested in it, except I had to take this course in the last year of university," she says. "I was going to go to law school. But to finish third year, I had to take this option, and it was natural science. So I took this course and it had this incredible reading list. It was the first time I would go to the library carrel and instead of just doing the required readings, I'd say, hey, maybe I'll have a look at this extra stuff. This was when Earth Day and the Green Movement was starting. I had a very good grade." At the end of her third year, in the early 1970s, Hurley went to her professor to ask about graduate work. "To be honest, he was a fairly dry individual. He wore grey suits and then wore grey shirts and grey ties to match. But his reading list was excellent. So I asked him, What do they call this, if I were to do this at the graduate level? Like, is it science? What is it? He said, they call it a masters of environmental science." She figured it was worth a try.

After getting her environmental science degree, Hurley did a stint at Pollution Probe, where she learned what affects the environment most: politics. She often supplied opposition politicians from the Ontario Legislature with data, and eventually, the New Democrats offered her a job. "There were about eight people in the room and I didn't know what the hell they were talking about. They were asking about all this socialist stuff, and I did environment. What did I know? I'd say, Well, I don't really have a view on that – and you could see they were not happy." After her job interview, however, as she was leaving the Ontario Legislature building she was approached by the Liberals, who invited her to become a researcher. "I said, look, I guess I could do this." She did, but when the Canadian Coalition on Acid Rain opened, she went to Washington to lobby for clean air.

Perley also drifted toward the acid rain issue along an indirect path, having worked at a Bay Street brokerage and lived in the Yukon and Africa before becoming an environmental researcher in Toronto. The former environment minister, John Fraser, urged him to stick with the issue after Perley organized the first major acid rain conference in 1979 and co-authored *Acid Rain: The North American Forecast* with then-*Toronto Star* reporter Ross Howard.

Outside of work, Hurley and Perley maintain a certain distance; contrary to a common misunderstanding, they are not married to each other, living together, involved in a relationship or even particularly close beyond the office door. But at work, they are like two halves of one individual: their skills complement each other as clearly as their names rhyme. Hurley is the tough, almost cutthroat, behind-the-scenes manipulator, while Perley is the soothing diplomat.

Hurley's political instincts are said to be so sharp that she can figure out what lawmakers and bureaucrats are going to do before they've thought matters through themselves. When she believes officials aren't trying to deal with acid rain, she has two approaches: if the officials are important she attacks them, if not she ignores them. But unlike many environmentalists, she also looks for heroes. After Ontario Environment Minister Jim Bradley ordered a crackdown on pollution in the province, Hurley organized a secret dinner for him, inviting dozens of environmentalists, many of whom she personally did not like. "When Bradley's sitting in his office at midnight, wondering why he knocks himself out, I want him to know there are people who will thank him," she explained.

Hurley also quietly courted local and state officials in Pennsylvania, going to banquets in small towns, speaking to service clubs, making friends. Her reasoning was that the state was both a cause of acid rain—it has coal mines—and a victim, because its lakes and trees are harmed. If Pennsylvanians could be persuaded that stopping acid rain is worthwhile, then maybe Washington could, too, she figured.

"Adele has got balls," said one Ontario official—one of her strongest admirers. At one point, there was talk about asking Hurley to become deputy environment minister. (She let it be known she wasn't interested.)

Perley is the one whom Canadian TV viewers most often see explaining the issues whenever there is a political development involving acid rain. Despite his conciliatory image, however, he is hardline, too, and is as fed up with goverments as Hurley is—particularly with his own. In Canada, "you get a lot of verbiage and nonsense," he says. "They never tell you what they're doing. They find it offensive that you even expect to be told." In the United States, on the other hand, "they just tell you what they're doing," good or bad.

Other Canadian environmentalists generally do not mix with Hurley and Perley. They don't sign the same open letters, prepare joint submissions to commissions or hold press conferences together. They grumble quietly that the acid rain fighters "are not team players." This generally suits the two just fine; they consider many environmental groups too ineffective, and tainted by the 1960s "brown-rice-eaters" image. "Don't call us environmentalists, we're lobbyists," Hurley says.

Indeed, the two are plainly different. Even their office in Toronto distinguishes them—no cardboard boxes piled up, no makeshift filing cabinets made of bricks and boards. It's all salmon-and-grey decor, accented by expensive-looking polished wood furniture, attractive wildlife art and subdued lighting, like a lawyer's office, or a small private company. In fact, it is a company; in 1986, the pair incorporated as Hurley and Perley Ltd., a consulting firm, and they contract their services, with their main client being the Canadian Coalition on Acid Rain. They call it a business arrangement, but it's also a statement: We're not like the others.

One of the things that makes Hurley and Perley stand out from Canada's other environmental groups is money. They care about money. Fighting acid rain hasn't been cheap. Since 1981, the group has spent about $3.6 million trying to persuade Canadians that something ought to be done, and trying to inform Americans that they too have a problem. The coal companies and utilities in the United States—the companies that cause much of the acid rain—spent this much in less than three years lobbying congressmen, telling them not to crack down too hard, or at all. About a third of Hurley and Perley's money comes from the Canadian and Ontario governments, but the rest comes from individuals and from more than fifty groups that belong to the coalition: cottagers' associations, churches, unions. Hurley and Perley don't turn away government money, but they don't want it to compromise them. They worry about the question that hovers constantly over any interest group backed by government funds: What if the government pulls the plug on us?

Indeed, in 1988, the federal environment department tried to cut off the group's funding, probably because Hurley and Perley were effective critics of Prime Minister Brian Mulroney's environmental record. The cutoff, engineered by senior federal environment officials, was stopped at the last minute, but events like the Toronto dinner are designed to ensure that Hurley and Perley are ready for the next time. For them, the important thing is to make sure they don't need to depend on the government to survive.

It is perhaps a measure of Adele Hurley's and Michael Perley's abilities as lobbyists that many government officials and environmentalists agree on one thing: they hate their guts. The officials don't like them because their questions, their letters and their testimony at hearings point to inadequate work by many bureaucrats; the environmentalists don't like them because of their lone-wolf image and because, unlike so many other activists, they win.

One highly placed federal official flat out called Hurley "a cold-hearted bitch." Cabinet ministers are terrified of them, and their relationships with many opposition politicians are equally testy. Hurley and Perley can recall a fierce argument, in an elevator, with the former Liberal environment minister, Charles Caccia, who was sensitive to their criticism of his acid rain program as weak. They often criticize the New Democratic Party as well, for offering empty environmental promises. "People accuse us of being Conservatives," Perley says. "They also say we're Liberal hacks and they say we're tight with the New Democratic Party. That's just fine with us." It's not that Hurley and Perley want enemies; they just don't care to have false friends. Hurley loves to recite the old political aphorism: "There are no permanent friends or enemies, just permanent interests."

Hurley and Perley's tactics have always boiled down to a simple formula: Get the facts out. This means using different methods for different audiences. American tourists visiting Muskoka, for example, could turn on the radio during certain summers and hear public service ads placed by the coalition urging them to "Get Mad About Acid Rain," and listing the bills before Congress that they should ask their representatives to support. Hurley laboured for months to persuade the Ontario government to hand out information about acid rain when people buy fishing licences. (The government was at first afraid that this would scare away would-be fishermen, but then relented when it realized that anglers would support acid rain controls.) Different industries, such as maple syrup producers or tourist operators, have been told how acid rain is threatening their business. Sympathetic members of Parliament get the latest scientific reports, or poll results, or gossip about what the bureaucrats have been up to behind their backs.

With U.S. politicians, they had two points to get across: how much the issue matters to all Canadians, but also, more importantly, how acid rain hurts Americans, too. U.S. opponents of acid rain controls often considered environmentalists élitists, and, to dispel this image, on one occasion Hurley brought a delegation of Muskoka tourist operators to Washington. "Congressmen saw they wore plaid jackets and had crewcuts and they realized: Hey, they're just like us!"

The Canadian Coalition on Acid Rain is both a Toronto organization and an officially registered foreign lobby group in Washington. This registration marked the beginning of the group's success, but Hurley's first experience was that it's never easy for Canadians to be noticed in Washington, let alone Canadian issues. When she arrived there in 1981, she deliberately kept a low profile. She hated the place; she was lonely and scared. "I remember one time just making it home after being followed by a scary guy, clicking the lock on the door and hearing him fiddling with the handle on the other side," she says. Gradually, she figured out that in order to get congressmen to talk about acid rain, she should feed information to their lowly aides. Within a year of her arrival, a congressional committee decided to discuss acid rain, and she became known as the resident expert in the U.S. capital. She got the issue onto national TV and into the American newspapers.

In Canada, it was a bit easier because, by the mid-1980s, they had a willing accomplice: Ontario's environment minister, Jim Bradley, a self-effacing former teacher and a Sudbury native who had a lingering resentment of the company that dominates that city, Inco, as well as an instinct for the political jugular. Hurley and Perley helped put together Ontario's cleanup plan; it was the linchpin of their strategy to get North America to stop acid rain. They understood that other jurisdictions would only clean up once they saw the part of Canada most harmed by acid rain doing so.

When the Liberals came to power in Ontario in 1985, Bradley recruited three people for his staff: Gary Gallon, a former American draft-dodger who had been active as an environmentalist on Canada's West Coast; David Oved, the

former reporter who coined the phrase "Iron Ring Disease";
and Mark Rudolph, who had been an assistant to Caccia
in Ottawa, but more importantly, was an old friend of
Hurley's. It had bothered Rudolph that while he was
working for Caccia the Liberals had no national program to
fight acid rain. "I always felt that somehow I had let Adele
and Michael down," he said, and he decided to make up for it.

Rudolph held extensive talks with Perley and Hurley.
Within days of the Liberals' coming to power in Ontario, he
came up with a formula that would force the province's four
main polluters, Inco, Ontario Hydro, Falconbridge Ltd. and
Algoma Steel, to cut their acid pollution to less than
one-third of what was allowed in 1980. He had to work fast;
the aim was to get the provincial cabinet to approve the plan
before it understood what a radical change it represented,
and before the government's environmental officials, who
had resisted change for years, could organize their
resistance. The plan represented a radical departure from
the past practice of letting polluters do as they pleased. As
Bradley said later, the proposal to slash acid emissions came
at a time "when much of the zeal for environmental reform
had not permeated through governments."

Just how radical a change the acid rain plan was became
apparent when Rudolph and Oved went to brief the head of
Inco at the time, Charles Baird, on their plan. They
deliberately dressed down—sportshirts with little polo
players on the chest—and explained that, by 1994, Inco
would have to cut the acid pollution from its huge
smokestack to 265,000 tonnes a year, two-thirds less than
what they were allowed to pollute in 1980. One person
familiar with the encounter says that "Baird hit the roof"
when he heard this.

Bradley remembers that Baird phoned him the next day,
and demanded, " 'Who were those young radicals in the pink
polo shirts asking the impertinent questions?' I still smile
when I look back on that. Inco wasn't used to being asked
questions of the kind we were asking, such as, How much
money are you making in Ontario, sir? It was used to calling
its own tune."

Slapping new regulations on Inco gave Bradley special pleasure. While he says that his experience growing up in the company's shadow in Sudbury wasn't "the primary motivation" for cracking down, he recalls how "my father worked in a machine shop which produced diamond drill bits for Inco. Inco subsequently bought the place. They had a labour dispute, and Inco ended up closing the company, giving as I recall at most a week's notice, perhaps no notice. My father had worked there for twenty-two years, he was forty-nine years old, and it was a year of recession, 1957. The 'thank you for your service' was non-existent."

Inco continued to resist the new controls right through the 1980s, but it became increasingly difficult to maintain that they could not afford the expense: the company began enjoying record profits, and, indeed, to avoid a takeover, it declared a special dividend of one billion dollars so that the shareholders wouldn't sell. By the end of the decade, unable to claim that they could not afford stringent pollution controls, the company took another approach, publicly at least, taking credit for the cleanup plan as if it had wanted to do it all along. In a full-colour advertisement inserted into Toronto newspapers, the company's executive vice-president, Roy Aitken, announced, "It's time to stop talking—and take action." The company took different action elsewhere, though—testifying before a legislative committee that the program was too onerous, and writing privately to Bradley that the cleanup plan didn't fit in with Inco's concept of "sustainable development," the phrase used by the United Nations commission on the environment. Fortunately, Ontario's regulation is written so that it is non-appealable.

Around the same time that Ontario began cracking down on its acid rain polluters, Perley and Hurley also made headway in Quebec, which launched an ambitious program with deadlines even shorter than Ontario's. Although some of the other provinces, most notably Nova Scotia and New Brunswick, persistently resisted (and in some aspects, still resist) coming up with cleanup plans, having the two biggest provinces committed to cleaning up was most important. It did make it harder for other jurisdictions to justify any delay, and the provinces' co-operation with the federal government showed that, despite constitutional tensions, different levels can work together. While Canada's acid rain diplomacy with the United States has been an embarrassing failure, its domestic cleanup plan is for the most part on track – and cleanup programs promise to actually reduce acid rain, protecting our water, trees and lungs. This is all Hurley and Perley really wanted in the first place.

It has been harder and taken longer for the Canadian Coalition's initiatives to bear fruit in the United States. For anyone concerned about acid rain, Bush's announcement on the day of the Royal York dinner party was cause for pleasure, but barely a month after it, when the White House released a 279-page draft of the kind of legislation it proposed, Perley denounced it. He said it gave corporate polluters "a lot of breaks, which is bad news for our lungs, lakes and forests." Then the House of Representatives and the Senate came up with their own versions of a new clean air law, both of which were considerably stronger than Bush's proposal. Senate Majority Leader George Mitchell insisted that the clean air law be the first item on the legislative agenda in the 1990s.

Early in 1990, Bush wrote to Mitchell, saying, "I want to sign a clean air bill this year, so that the 1990s can be known as the 'Clean Air Decade.' But I will only sign legislation that balances environmental *and* economic progress [his emphasis]." He set a ceiling of $21 billion for the cleanup, and the Senate and the House then decided to advance their legislation toward a final vote, noting but not necessarily listening to Bush's warning about the cost. Early in April 1990, the Senate voted overwhelmingly to approve its version of the acid rain cleanup program, and a few days later, after a forty-eight hour meeting, the House's Energy Committee, which had blocked acid rain controls for thirteen years, sent its cleanup proposal to the floor for a vote. "Michael was waiting outside the committee room for so long," says Hurley, "that at two-thirty in the morning he and the other people in line started baa-ing like sheep." But once he got into the committee room and heard the cleanup plan had been endorsed, Perley switched to a more positive barnyard analogy, calling it "a remarkable exercise in horse-trading with an excellent result."

For Hurley and Perley, the good news on acid rain outweighs the bad, but only slightly. "You always have to watch these people," Perley says. "You can't turn your back for a moment." If there is one thing Perley and Hurley learned as environmental lobbyists, it's that you can win environmental battles, but that doesn't mean you've won the war. Their experience in battling acid rain shows both sides — how difficult the battles can be, but how, with skill and dedication, there can be victories.

—— **II** ——

Not many environmental battles are won by relentless lobbying; there aren't many people like Hurley and Perley. Usually they're achieved by a combination of public pressure and accidental circumstances, as when politicians figure out that doing something good for the environment can help them out of a jam over other issues. It's this combination that led to Canada's other success story of the 1980s — the decision to preserve British Columbia's South Moresby area as national parkland.

South Moresby is an archipelago of 138 islands that together form a pattern shaped roughly like a knife. The area makes up about 15 percent of a region called the Queen Charlotte Islands, a temperate, rainy zone where the weather is something like Vancouver's, only more so. The region's native Haida Indians call the Charlottes Haida Gwaii and they refer to the southern part as Gwaii Haanas. One site, called Ninstints, contains the world's largest collection of totem poles in an original setting and is protected as a United Nations World Heritage Cultural site, just like Egypt's Pyramids.

Only twenty-five hundred people live in the archipelago, but the Charlottes are also home to some of the most remarkable plant and animal species on earth such as giant black bears and deer mice, hairy woodpeckers and tiny saw-whet owls. Beneath the trees, the islands are covered with lush green moss that grows to the depth of the thickest executive boardroom carpet. The cedar trees there are believed to be among the oldest in the world. A big old tree in a Canadian city may have been planted when your great-grandparents were young; a big cedar in the Charlottes may have started its life when Charlemagne ruled Europe or Mohammed was preaching in the Arabian desert.

In 1974, a local logging company applied to cut some of the southern end of the archipelago. It had just finished logging half of one island in a nearby area, clear-cutting it, and the heavy rains that the forest once absorbed cascaded down the bare mountainsides, carrying stumps and rubble into streams where salmon spawned, crushing the eggs. A small group of environmentalists wanted the logging in South Moresby curtailed, arguing that the area contains only one-tenth of one percent of British Columbia's commercial forest land. The industry and provincial government were unimpressed by the argument: if the area were saved as a park, they said, only the rich and a few wilderness freaks would ever see it, anyway.

But, shortly after he became environment minister in 1985, Tom McMillan went to South Moresby and fell in love with the region. When he got out of the helicopter that took him there, the environment minister of Canada sank into the moss and rolled around, laughing with delight. "He was like a little kid," said someone who accompanied him. "I knew then that he was committed to protecting the area."

By then, the small group of environmentalists had nationwide support, and there were ugly confrontations going on in South Moresby. Members of the Haida Nation and their supporters began blockading a logging road and getting themselves arrested. In all, seventy-two people were hauled in, including New Democrat MP Svend Robinson and a sixty-seven-year-old Haida woman named Ethel Jones. The Mountie who arrested her was her nephew, who broke into tears as he took her away. If there are any real heroes among the activists who saved South Moresby, then they are these environmentalists who live in the area and who had been fighting to protect it for years. The skill of a Haida leader named Miles Richardson, for example, also put the battle into a new framework: the natives claim the area, but Richardson helped negotiate a deal where the land would be protected as a park "reserve," with the ultimate issue of who owns it to be settled later. This made the battle one for native justice as well as environmental justice, creating an uneasy but workable alliance that has been duplicated in other wilderness conflicts, such as the one over Temagami in Ontario.

So in the fall of 1985, McMillan pledged to secure South Moresby as a park, along with another wilderness area – Ellesmere Island, the northernmost part of Canada. He was inspired by his visit, but also by the fact that the government's record on environmental issues was being derided from coast to coast. In the spring of 1986, he recruited Elizabeth May as his adviser. A well-known environmentalist, she was passionately in favour of creating more parkland. She took charge of the cause.

May worked in odd ways. Like Hurley and Perley, she is disliked by many activists – but for the opposite reasons. While the acid rain lobbyists are cool, detached and single-minded, May is bubbly, engaged and a bit of a throwback to the days of brown-rice environmentalism. "She's into occult," says someone who has known her for years. She is viewed as both a folk hero and a reviled publicity seeker: her supporters see only one side, her detractors the other. Controversy has swirled around her since she first gained a reputation as an activist in Cape Breton, where her family had moved from Connecticut in 1972. Four years after her arrival in Canada, May, then twenty-two years old, fought a successful battle to prevent aerial spraying of a pesticide in the region. Then, in 1980, she began law school at Dalhousie University in Halifax, and became involved in another battle with the provincial government. May went to court with a coalition of Micmac Indians and environmentalists to fight a plan to spray

herbicides in Nova Scotia's forests. In September 1983 the
coalition lost and had to pay court costs. May's family had to
sell $23,000 worth of property to pay their expenses. They
lost their farm. She wrote a book about her experiences,
called *Budworm Battles*, which was published in 1982.

May applied herself to the South Moresby fight with a
will. Although she worked for a cabinet minister, when talks
opened between Ottawa and the British Columbia government over the area's future she operated more as an activist
than an adviser, quietly passing information to opposition
members of Parliament. It's unclear whether or not this
helped. At the same time, May also arranged to meet with
Dalton Camp, then one of the prime minister's most
important advisers, to persuade him that the whole of South
Moresby was worth saving from the chainsaws. She operated mostly on her own, concerned that McMillan's senior
bureaucrats were recommending a weak compromise that
called for some of the most scenic parts of South Moresby to
be logged.

May applies great significance to her role and the meeting
she arranged with Camp, but the way South Moresby was
settled may have been more prosaic. With national public
opinion behind it, the federal government made a massive
transfer payment to the province of British Columbia.
Essentially, it was a legal bribe, and both its terms and the
negotiation methods set a dangerous precedent for future
negotiations to protect other valuable wilderness areas in
Canada. The British Columbia government, the forest
industry and loggers were understandably concerned about
the loss of some hundreds of jobs if the trees couldn't be cut,
but the trade-off was incredibly out of proportion. Ottawa
agreed to fork over $106 million to British Columbia in
return for a halt to the logging of South Moresby. Of this
money, $31 million was for the logging companies. For all
the talk about lost jobs, only $1 million was earmarked for
their employees.

It is still an environmental achievement, perhaps the
one for which Tom McMillan will be remembered, and
deservedly so. He showed considerable courage in pressing

for the deal. Most of the British Columbia Progressive Conservative caucus and much of cabinet were against it. McMillan gives May credit for her role, but suggests that she alienated as many people in government as she won over. Shortly before the 1988 election, May left the government, loudly accusing it of making an unsavoury deal to get Saskatchewan to preserve French language rights in return for the granting of federal licences to build two environmentally threatening dams, the Rafferty and Alameda. She made an appearance in McMillan's riding, doing a radio interview; he lost by a narrow margin.

McMillan says the South Moresby agreement was given the go-ahead after he placed a rare call to the prime minister at home one evening. Away from his advisers and caucus members who were hostile to environmental protection, Mulroney was quite receptive to the idea of saving the trees, McMillan says, and he could see the obvious political payoff. "Who knows? Maybe Mila [the prime minister's wife] talked him into it."

—— **III** ——

Some of the most notable environmental successes today are being scored not by activists, but by their traditional adversaries—bureaucrats and companies. In Chesapeake Bay, for example, one of the world's richest estuaries and one of the most polluted, the governors and other officials of the states surrounding the basin agreed to co-operate in a cleanup plan. Over three years the states spent about $100 million on improving the water, slapping restrictions on waterfront development, limiting sewage discharges, and coming up with innovative programs to control runoff and erosion, major sources of pesticide pollution. The action came after the U.S. Environmental Protection Agency concluded a seven-year, $27-million study in 1983, finding that the bay was in a pollution-fed decline and that immediate improvements were needed. The basin is still filthy—more than 2,600 plants hold permits to pour wastewater into the bay—but if all the plans now being implemented work out, it may not be dirty forever, and that's more than anyone could have hoped for before.

The most ambitious cleanup proposal, however, is on the other side of the continent, in Los Angeles, where efforts are underway to do what seems impossible: roll back the smog. This is significant not just for the area's residents, but for all of North America, because trends start in L.A. The Los Angeles basin is the continent's most important economic region; if it were treated as a separate country, its gross domestic product would make it the eleventh-wealthiest nation in the world, ahead of Switzerland. It has a population of 12.5 million, and so many people want to live there that it is expected to grow to 18 million by the turn of the century. Because of the region's size and economic clout, and its movie-star glamour, the Los Angeles political scene has national, even worldwide importance.

But the most powerful person in Los Angeles today is not a politician, a movie mogul, actor or even a celebrity. James Lents, the man who thinks he can clean up the L.A. smog, is a bureaucrat.

A six-foot six-inch tall Tennessee native with a background in aerospace engineering, Lents serves as the head of the South Coast Air Quality Management District. This agency is in charge of improving the air in a 21,360-square-kilometre area of southern California—an area larger than nine states. It was formed in 1977 by Governor Jerry Brown, following a five-year battle during which the law to establish it was twice vetoed by Brown's predecessor, Ronald Reagan. In its first decade, the agency was regarded by environmentalists as a toothless pawn of oil companies, utilities, chemical firms and automakers. But since Lents took over in 1987, it has attracted the attention of the entire world. Lents has been called a "Gary Cooperesque figure" by one environmental journal. But compared to Lents, Gary Cooper had it easy.

In *High Noon*, Cooper had to face one outlaw on the main street of town; for Lents, the challenge is on thousands of streets and freeways. He must do something about the pollution caused by eight million cars and trucks—three times as many as in all of India. In this pollution war, every day is high noon (or at least it would be if you could see the sun). "We violate [national] health standards more than 200 days out of 365," Lents says. "Children living here have 15 percent lower lung capacity than children in less polluted areas."

One of the press officers at Lents's agency, Tom Eichhorn, describes Los Angeles as "the Super Bowl of Smog." The amount of pollution that pours into the air every month over the L.A. basin is as much as the 37-million–plus litres of oil that spilled from the *Exxon Valdez*. It takes a day for pure white filters in the agency's air monitors to turn as black as the back of an oil-soaked otter. About two-thirds of this air pollution comes from cars. The basin is the world's largest single market for gasoline. The rest comes from drying paints and solvents, fifteen oil refineries and drying ink from newspapers and other printing presses. Paints alone give off more toxic fumes than the region's huge aerospace industry, among the world's largest.

They put up with "smog alerts" in southern California. There are two kinds, stage one and stage two, and there's a toll-free line to find out which is in effect. During a stage two alert—the more serious kind—"it is highly advisable to limit outdoor activities to arts and crafts, quiet games, or slow walking," the air agency suggests. "When children and teens breathe polluted air deep into their lungs, the chance of lung damage increases." Smog does an estimated $330 million a year in damage to the valuable southern California orange and grape crops, and the state estimates that toxic air may be responsible for thirty thousand cancer deaths.

Like dozens of American cities, Los Angeles is consistently out of compliance with standards set by the U.S. Clean Air Act; the larger Canadian ones would be similarly out of compliance, except that there are no enforceable nationwide standards in Canada. By law, the U.S. cities were supposed to clean up by 1977. They couldn't, and were given an extension until 1982. They didn't meet this one either, and were given until 1987. That deadline passed, too. As it approached, the southern California agency realized drastic measures were needed.

Lents came into this toxic hell with a hatred for pollution that he developed from direct experience in the late 1960s, when he was an aerospace engineer working on rocket fuel for the U.S. Air Force in Chattanooga. "When I was first married we lived in a very sooty area. At first we figured, that's part of life. But then we wondered, Why is it part of life? A lot of the air we breathe is not that much different from smoking."

His irritation led him to design a college course on air pollution for the University of Tennessee. Then Chattanooga asked him to help set up a pollution control program, which he did. He later moved on to Denver, which, like Los Angeles, has chronically bad air. His program encouraging people to leave their cars at home reduced driving by 10 percent. He believes the same thing can happen in Los Angeles. But this, he knows, would not be nearly enough. Los Angeles is not only choking; it's under a court order to clean up.

In 1984, a twenty-five-year-old UCLA environmental studies graduate named Mark Abramowicz got angry that the Clean Air Act wasn't being enforced, and he sued. He was furious because the air pollution agency, before Lents's day, had won approval from the Environmental Protection Agency for a cleanup program that flatly admitted that achieving federal standards was impossible in southern California. "It was very simple, but also very scary," he says. "The aerospace industry went berserk. We had the whole world becoming involved—the electric companies, the utilities, the L.A. Chamber of Commerce. Somebody described it as 'everyone versus Mark Abramowicz.'" For a while he was so broke that he couldn't afford car insurance for his old Volkswagen (licence plates: FGT SMOG). Then something strange happened. He won. The Environmental Protection Agency asked to settle out of court. However, victory was short-lived. The EPA changed its mind, and when the case reached court it was criticized for recalcitrance. The legal issues have become increasingly complicated; Abramowicz has filed more suits and the cases are still piling up.

Meanwhile, around the time of the 1984 Olympics in Los Angeles, the political situation changed. Experts predicted that traffic would be a disaster because of all the tourists, so the region developed a highly efficient traffic plan that worked. When the Olympics went away and traffic got bad again, a burgeoning movement called "no-growth" or "slow-growth" started up. It was a bit like the anti-highrise crusades of Toronto in the early 1970s, when neighbourhoods railed against plans for office towers and apartments. But it is more widespread, and it dealt with more than just buildings. People complain that there are just too many pressures on the area – too many people moving in, too many new buildings, too many cars, too much pollution.

As a full-blown political movement, no-growth is just beginning to take hold, electing a few city councillors, generating debate and so on. But its rise helped create a political climate that favoured action against pollution, so that officials like Lents have the clout to start changing the way people live. Lents, an administrator, has started to sound a lot like Abramowicz, an agitator. "Industries have banded together, put huge amounts of money into trying to undercut our effort. . . . There are some industries that would be better off operating someplace other than in the middle of 12 million people," Lents told the *Amicus Journal*, a quarterly published by the U.S. Natural Resources Defense Council.

An even more important result is that the air pollution agency has come up with the most comprehensive cleanup plan ever contemplated in North America. It has three stages, or "tiers," with 120 separate measures.

The first tier requires that by 1994, paints, varnishes and solvents must be reformulated using less-polluting chemicals. Barbecues that use starter fluid will be outlawed, and so will gas-powered lawn mowers. Dry-cleaners will require extra pollution control equipment and breweries will have to put new filters on the tops of their brew kettles. Aerosol cans will be banned; although most aerosols in North America don't use ozone layer–damaging CFCs, they do use compounds like butane, which are unhealthy to breathe. Even bakeries will have to clean up: they will have to install equipment on their ovens to reduce emissions. All this is expected to cost $2.6 billion but generate a $7-9 billion in health benefits. Smog-causing pollution will be reduced by 58 percent.

The second tier calls for 40 percent of the area's cars, and all buses, to run on "clean" fuels, such as methanol, by 1999. It is expected to reduce emissions by 70 percent. And it has received a surprising degree of support. One oil company, ARCO, announced a plan to replace leaded gasoline in California with a new "designer" fuel that could cut pollution in older cars by 15 percent, and other companies are following their example. As Bill Kelly, a spokesman for Lents's agency, says, "They are seeing the writing on the wall."

The third tier, contemplated for 2009, is the most severe: all cars in southern California will either burn clean fuels or run on electricity. The auto industry maintains that this is an impossible goal, but Lents doesn't care. He figures the deadline will help focus research efforts. And he believes that what is happening in California will spread across the continent. "We're the largest manufacturing region in the United States. We're the showplace, the testing ground." Already, the governors of the six New England states, New York and New Jersey have agreed on a resolution to push for similar plans for the East Coast.

Los Angeles is also the showplace for another idea now in vogue – the notion that market forces, as well as regulation, can best protect the environment. The idea works in a way similar to President Bush's clean air proposal, which would cut pollution through a system of "emission reduction credits" – pollution rights that could be bought and sold. A dirty plant could reduce its pollution beyond the required limits, and the excess reduction would be a marketable commodity, to be sold to another plant that wanted to increase its production. Although the second plant would then pollute more, the total pollution would be cut because of the first one's reductions. Because Los Angeles has such bad air, the system has actually been operating there since 1976 – the federal clean air standards were being violated so badly there that the U. S. Environmental Protection Agency said that every new ton of air pollution had to be offset by a ton of pollution reduction. Trading has become the rule across the United States for new industries emitting one hundred tons a year or more of the six most common pollutants. Bush now wants to extend the principle to more polluters, including those causing acid rain.

—— **IV** ——

The Los Angeles plan is just unfolding, but it's possible to take hope from it already. For example, few of its 120 rules are all that complicated; in many cases, they simply ban things. The point they illustrate is that the best way to stop pollution is to stop it, period, not to play around too much with fancy gizmos. New technologies can ease some of the most severe situations, but they are medicines that ease the pain. They don't cure the disease.

The twenty-first century will begin with some of the greatest scientific minds trying desperately to make electric cars. The direct goal is to minimize pollution from gasoline fumes, and there's a more subtle one, too: saving the private car from oblivion. But why not encourage more mass transit? Why not concentrate more on building communities closer to where people work? These are the lines along which planners in Los Angeles are thinking; the city of freeways is even building its first subway, for example.

Still, even there, few people believe the car will be replaced by less environmentally threatening modes of transportation. And sadly, in smoggy Canadian cities such as Toronto, municipal and provincial officials are slow to pick up cues from the more innovative aspects of L.A.'s plan. Canadian cities boast about their transit systems, but the truth is that they still favour the car, and they're still intent on building more highways. The automobile is firmly entrenched in our society, and there is little sign that it is losing its hold.

In other areas of the environment, significant changes in thinking are taking place, most importantly in the corporate world. Many companies appear to be trying sincerely to figure out what environmentalists want, and some are trying to satisfy their demands. "Corporate polluters rank somewhere between drunk drivers and sexual assaulters" in the public's mind, says Tom D'Aquino, president of Canada's Business Council on National Issues, a corporate lobby group. No business can sustain this kind of image indefinitely without suffering in the marketplace. Cleaning up the environment "is the single most important imperative facing . . . economic leaders," D'Aquino says. "The heaviest responsibility is really on us."

Where goodwill or altruism are not strong enough, there are other incentives for companies to recognize their responsibilities. In the wake of the *Exxon Valdez* spill, the president of the Exxon Corporation recommended naming an environmentalist to the company's board and setting up a special board committee to review the company's impact on the environment. This decision came after pension funds holding about one billion dollars in Exxon stock hinted that they would trigger a sell-off if the company resisted. A similar arrangement was reached with Texaco when that firm was fighting a takeover and seeking protection under U.S. bankruptcy laws.

More and more industries not only want to clean up, but also want to avoid making a mess in the first place. It's starting to hurt the bottom line to be a polluter. In just a few years, the cost of dumping hazardous waste for U.S. firms has gone from twenty dollars a ton to a thousand dollars. And in an American court case, a Maryland bank that foreclosed on a company's loan discovered it also became responsible for cleaning up the company's toxic waste dump. Exxon alone faces some 150 lawsuits because of the *Exxon Valdez* spill. They range from a bartender suing for tips he lost because fishermen could no longer afford to drink to California drivers suing because their gasoline prices went up after the spill. Many banks and insurance companies are now compelling their clients to perform environmental audits before they can get policies or loans.

In September 1989, activists and investors huddled and came up with a set of "environmentally ethical" principles, a guide to companies that want to behave. The concept is modelled on the "Sullivan Principles," which companies such as General Motors have adopted to govern their dealings with South Africa's government, on the recommendation of anti-apartheid activists. The environmental principles are a mixture of vague and potentially costly ideals, but perhaps they will actually work and improve the environment.

On the vague side, they ask companies to pledge to "protect the biosphere" by eliminating pollution, using renewable resources and conserving materials, reducing waste and disposing of it properly, becoming more energy efficient and reducing environmental risks. On the potentially costly side, they ask them to disclose the environmental impact of their operations, promise to repair any environmental damage or human injury they cause, report hazards and protect employees who blow the whistle on bad practices, put recognized environmental experts on their boards and conduct yearly environmental audits, which would be made public. Companies adopting these principles would be recommended by "ethical investment funds" – increasingly popular stock portfolios that include only clean, green corporations. Fittingly, the creators of the ten points call them the Valdez Principles.

A parallel, though not identical, set of principles was drawn up for the Canadian Chamber of Commerce by Tom McMillan. It calls on companies to identify their environmental impact, prepare environmental audits, share expertise and work with governments. In many cases, industries now come up with their own pledges, trumpeting them in newspaper ads. For example, Canada's notoriously dirty pulp and paper industry has been advertising an environmental code of ethics. Some executives think this corporate enthusiasm for marketplace environmentalism means that regulation is no longer necessary. "There is enough already," says Inco's Roy Aitken. "An excess of regulation frequently leads to a negative reaction, to resistance and lack of co-operation."

But if anything, the acid rain, South Moresby and Los Angeles success stories suggest that society needs both the co-operation of polluters and a stick to get them to co-operate. After all, Inco is cleaning up its acid rain because people like Hurley and Perley worked for years to have them regulated, and politicians brought in laws that insist on it.

CONCLUSION

I have nightmares and dreams about the environment.

In one of my worst nightmares, I picture a little girl, anyone's child, maybe five years old, lying in bed as her parents stand quietly by her side. She has no hair; after extended chemotherapy treatments, her wild red tresses began to fall out in clumps, and her head has become as smooth as a glass sphere. A year ago, her skin was pink and her cheeks were chubby; now her face is sallow—she has the colouring of a TV picture where someone has fiddled with the tint button.

She still can manage a wide, innocent smile, but others have trouble smiling in her presence. Her parents take turns grasping her hand, caressing her tiny, bony fingers and murmuring softly that everything will be okay. Every few minutes her mother or her father gives her hand a little squeeze. The thing they dread is the moment when she no longer squeezes back.

In my nightmare, her parents keep wondering: Did we make this happen to our daughter? Did we let her play in the sun too long? Did we feed her the wrong foods? Should we have used a water filter? Were we wrong to live in a polluted city? They know what their tragedy is, but they want to know why. Yet they can't answer, and neither can anyone else.

And this is what my nightmare has to do with the

environment: I want to know who can answer these kinds of questions. To me, this little girl's cruel predicament symbolizes what is ailing the planet: we're living with a debilitating illness, perhaps fatal, and the specialized experts we turn to don't understand the all-encompassing nature of the problem. Many can say what might have caused the girl's symptoms and what might have contributed to them, but none of them can tell us the breaking point in her life. I think there are only two types of specialists who can ease my nightmare: the environmentalist and the politician. But they have to learn how to work together.

One of the biggest points of debate among environmentalists is whether it is better to work within the system or oppose it. But the most effective environmentalists do both. They can galvanize public opinion, or they can walk into a politician's office and ask for a specific environmental improvement, and if necessary, they can offer a timetable. They understand the pressure points of the political system and they use them: they're unwilling to let politicians off the hook. Too often, many of Canada's environmentalists appear to be tough, but they're really just strident. They ask for vague things – and then they get them. There are still too few effective environmentalists and too many ineffective ones, and the environment is too important to leave up to the latter kind.

We're often told that changing society's economic rules to protect the environment is a complicated task, but I don't think it is. It's more a matter of straightening out some of our more twisted ideas of what makes life better. This is what the environmentalist does. We should accept the environmentalist's vision and stop looking for the point of no return for our illness, stop taking as an article of faith that we're too close to it already. Rather than take part in an endless debate over what cause leads to which effect, we should believe inherently that pollution and wastefulness are bad and that the consequences will be worse.

As for the politicians, now that everyone is listening, at least, to what the environmentalists have to say, they can set directions and establish rules so that people gain by helping the environment, not hurting it. The way politicians deal with the environment on our behalf reminds me of the book *God's Little Acre* by Erskine Caldwell, a steamy Depression-era novel in which a poor cotton farmer in Georgia destroys his land by digging holes. "My daddy told me there was gold on this land," the farmer says, so he keeps digging. A religious man, he leaves one acre alone—God's Little Acre. But he keeps moving it to a different site, believing that there just might be gold in the one he has set aside. At the end of the book, he's digging frantically, so deep and so close to his house that the building's foundations need to be propped up with logs. The message is obvious: keep digging and you'll dig your grave.

It's easy to blame the bureaucracy—those thousands of government officials who are supposed to be protecting the environment—but we should understand that part of the problem is the needless complexity of the system, the overlapping of responsibilities, and the fact that there are too few decisions passing through too many hands. The other day a fairly senior federal official came up to me, to lament what had happened to Lucien Bouchard's master plan for the environment—its metamorphosis into a public discussion document, just another piece of paper. This official was mad. Although he was a veteran bureaucrat, he had worked on this plan with the idealism of any young student asked to draw up a program to save the world. But he couldn't even get his minister, or the prime minister, to see what he had done. "I know my minister wants to do it. I think even Mulroney wants to do it. But I can't get it to them." Just then, he exploded in rage. "There's this *layer*!"

But at least there are bureaucrats who care and the situation is improving. Many environmental groups are showing more skill and professionalism than before, and the actions of dedicated individuals continue to be the most effective catalysts for change. In the St Lawrence estuary, the persistence of Leone Pippard did result in a promise by the federal government to spend $110 million to clean up the river and create a marine park (the agreement to establish the park was signed with Quebec in April 1990). Perhaps the most telling sign that we're becoming more interested in protecting our environment than exploiting it is on our money: the pictures of churning chemical factories and logs floating by Parliament Hill have been replaced by birds.

They call the 1990s the Turnaround Decade, when we protect the environment or face doom in the next century. It's a daunting task to have the entire future on your shoulders, but this is the responsibility my generation will have to face. Nobody can predict how it will turn out—challenges don't have schedules—but those most intimately aware of the problems believe the challenge can be met. Gro Harlem Brundtland, whose report on the environment contains such dire warnings, nevertheless says, "There is a new hope, a feeling of common concern and common destiny. We have made progress in our efforts to prevent war . . ." and now for the environment, too, "we must continue to move from confrontation, through dialogue to co-operation."

The actions of individuals have a cumulative effect, just as Rachel Carson and her book did; perhaps the actions people have already taken will make a difference in the decades to come. The international political situation is also helping to pressure individual countries, and the spread of information about worldwide pollution problems is breaking down political stalemates. Instead of wondering who will go first, people are starting to understand that we all have to move together.

In 1992 the world's nations will gather in Brazil to discuss the greenhouse effect, and they will all feel pressure to come up with a plan to reduce fuel use and save the remaining rainforest. In addition, work is underway to develop an international system to stop the wiping out of thousands of plant and animal species each year. Leone Pippard said the problem is that "we are too clever," but it's also the solution: we're going to have to be smart enough to pull back from the brink of doom.

I think we can.

I said I had dreams about the environment as well as nightmares, so it's only fair that I share my dreams, too. As I am writing this, I am on Wickaninnish Island, in British Columbia. From a perch in a cabin about thirty metres above the water, I'm looking out at the Pacific, which is anything but. The waves are crashing furiously against the rocks, and the whistle of the wind has a touch of menace.

Steve Lawson, Suzanne Hare and their three children live on this island in a wooden house they built with their own hands. Lawson is a fisherman; Suzanne is an artist. They live the environmentally pure life most of us only dream about: collecting rainwater for their drinking supplies, heating and cooking with a wood stove, raising a few chickens for eggs, getting the rest of their food through barter, from their garden or from the sea. They re-use their bottles and cans and compost all their waste. They use electricity sparingly; their power comes from a few car batteries and, for big projects, a small generator.

It is harsh, but idyllic. But as I visit with them, it is also tense, for Steve Lawson is wanted by the law. At any moment, a Royal Canadian Mounted Police officer may knock on the door and serve him with a summons, and soon he'll be off to spend a week in jail – not for the first time. This time it's because of a fight Lawson and Hare have been waging to protect a nearby area called Clayquot Sound from logging; they have blocked bulldozers and picketed, and both have already served sentences. "We're completely unrehabilitated," he jokes.

They believe there's a conspiracy – that the CIA, the Canadian government and the corporations are engineering all the pollution to preserve profits for faraway millionaires. I think they're wrong. If there's any conspiracy, it's a conspiracy of dunces and although, in the 1970s, someone like me might have dreamed of living like Steve Lawson and Suzanne Hare – back to the land – I don't think that's realistic now. Certainly they are heroic, dignified people and I admire their determination to live in harmony with nature, but I don't think many people can exist the way they do, collecting water from the sky and dinner from the sea. It's a bit like spending your time in the nineteenth century, and we're about to enter the twenty-first.

So what is my dream?

It is that ultimately my country will no longer need to have fanatics like Steve Lawson and Suzanne Hare—people who will go to any lengths to protect us from environmental folly. My dream is that they will be able to live as they please—"We take only what we need," Suzanne says—and not have to worry about the Mounties, or the trees, or the possibility that the birds will arrive at their shoreline caked with bunker oil. I dream that everyone in Canada will have a little bit of Steve Lawson and Suzanne Hare in them. If we all have a bit of the spirit that says "Enough," our politicians will start understanding exactly what this means. To achieve this, we need to know what *is* enough: society has to reach a consensus that the environment comes first, ahead of every other possible political decision.

This is not an easy dream to achieve, but it's not an impossible one. Remember, the little girl in my nightmare is totally in my imagination, but Suzanne Hare and Steve Lawson are real people. And the thing that keeps me going—the thing that makes me more optimistic than apprehensive for my children—is that in the time I have grown up, more and more people seem to dream the same kind of dream.

Because I write about the environment for a large newspaper, people often ask me what I think about our chances.

I think the story of the trashing of our environment is not how we're going to die, but how we're going to overcome the problem and live.

EPILOGUE

Why does pouring oil on the sea make it clear and calm?

— Plutarch, *Natural Questions IX*

I still think my dream—that we won't turn the world into a Silent Earth—is achievable, but a single, twisted, greasy seabird testifies to how difficult it will be to achieve.

The bird is a Socotra Cormorant, and although the species may not be a household word, this particular bird is quite well-known. It attained a kind of a celebrity status as the ultimate victim of the Gulf War: the environmental casualty. Normally graceful, exotic and elegant, this cormorant was an awkward, blackened, quivering mess, evoking a mixture of pity and guilt. Its image was broadcast and reprinted thousands of times: the sticky, tarry feet, the greasy husk of fused feathers and the oily, brittle gizzard. The worst thing to look at was its head; dripping with black slime, it stared and blinked into the cameras in a way that was somehow both bewildered and accusing.

This cormorant almost certainly died within a few hundred minutes of being photographed, innocent, but tarred and feathered nevertheless. It was caught in the giant oil slick created by the Gulf War, a zone of thick, chocolate-coloured water stretching for more than a hundred miles down the coast of Saudi Arabia and entrapping any living thing it touched. We'll never know what this bird understood about its predicament but we should easily understand the accusation in its gaze: we are the accused.

Yet this bird may be one of the luckier creatures in the Persian Gulf because its suffering was mercifully, relatively short. In many cases, surviving longer means enduring more pain and less certainty. Other species are waking up to habitats that are all but destroyed by the hundreds of oil wells set ablaze in Kuwait. An estimated 1.5 million barrels of oil are being burned every day—more than six times as much as the oil that spilled from the *Exxon Valdez*—and the most experienced oil-well firefighters believe it will take a year to extinguish the flames. Birds flying through the filthy skies drinking the contaminated rainwater may ingest oil and die slowly from haemolytic anemia, a condition that causes a sharp, sudden drop in the number of oxygen-carrying red blood cells, leaving the birds too weak to look for food.

Of the estimated two million birds that migrate to the Arabian Peninsula's mud flats every year, no one knows how many have died or are doomed; according to one early estimate, as many as 20,000 have perished, but an investigation is hampered by the presence of unexploded mines and cluster bombs scattered along the shore.

Other animals are threatened as well: green and hawksbill turtles, schools of dolphins, whales and dugongs (pudgy, walrus-like creatures whose existence in large herds was only discovered in the 1980s). On land, the pollution endangers desert foxes and the few wild cats that still inhabit the region—and, of course, the people.

Due to the Gulf War and its aftermath, the daylight over Kuwait alternates between red, from the glowing oil-well fires, and grey, from the thick sooty clouds. Temperatures have fallen by ten to twenty degrees Celsius, and only one percent of the normal daylight reaches the earth. One doctor has compared conditions in Kuwait to those in Britain during the early Industrial Age, and soon after the war ended, Kuwaiti hospitals reported a sharp increase in cases of respiratory ailments such as asthma, pneumonia and pleurisy. In satellite photos, the smoke, a dangerous, concentrated form of acid and toxic rain, looks like a great black blob covering the top of the Persian Gulf, and on the ground, it can be seen and smelled in Bahrein, 300 miles away, and sometimes as far as Oman, 600 miles away. Because it darkens the sky, the smoke threatens to kill off the sea's phytoplankton, which depends on light to grow and which forms the base of many food chains. A kind of anti-ecology has been created in the Gulf – relations between living organisms and their environment have broken down.

One of the biggest consequences of the 1991 Gulf War is that we now know how quickly and easily we can take a portion of the globe and create a Silent Earth.

—— I ——

The Gulf War of 1991 was only 42 days long. In military terms it was decisive. Politically, for the victors, it was remarkably successful, although the complex diplomatic relationships arising from it will be sorted out for years to come. Environmentally, the consequences of this war will plague the living in ways that we can't even predict at this time. And the war's effect on the politics of pollution will be even more difficult to figure out. The little we know already says a lot about how we are going to cope with the environment in the 1990s – and why we have to find a better way. The politics of pollution did not have a good Gulf War, and the better our understanding of this fact, the better our chance to avoid a botched, polluted peace.

It has become a common complaint that we all received a lot of bad information about this war, from the wildly inaccurate predictions of its outcome by so many analysts to the tightly restricted data handed out by the military. The information about the area's environmental damage was no different. Some predictions were especially alarming. At a conference in London just before the fighting began, experts predicted that the oil fires would burn for a decade and could trigger mass starvation by altering the monsoons that grow Asia's food supplies. Other very credible scientists, such as the astronomer Carl Sagan, predicted that the clouds could encircle the globe. After the war started, a lot of the information reported was quite simply wrong. Authorities described the oil slick as the largest in history and estimated that up to ten million barrels were burning out of control each day—about seven times more than experts later stated. And some newspapers even falsified the sad picture of the cormorant by recycling an old photograph of a bird caught in the *Amoco Cadiz* spill near Brittany in 1979.

But not all the information was inaccurate. The Pentagon was largely justified in accusing the Iraqis of "environmental terrorism" and blaming them for a deliberate spill, although bombing by the U.S.-led allies may also have aggravated the situation. And inaccuracy is not the real problem. As happens in so many cases of environmental disaster, the real problem comes not from what we are told, but what we choose to hear. We appear to be heading toward another eco-panic, and that could send the Turnaround Decade turning in the wrong direction.

Each time there's an environmental disaster—which is more or less every year at this time—panic tends to set in and then leads to a reaction. First we're shocked by the horror, but then our horror fades as we discover that we've survived; after all, we've had environmental problems before and we're all still here. We blame the activists who predicted the problem for scaring us more than the actual damage warranted, and many activists trigger this reaction by concentrating on the most negative aspects of the situation and failing to suggest plausible alternatives to doom. By the end of the whole cycle, we feel bad about the current mess, but we lose interest, and we put our concern on hold until the next disaster.

This eco-panic cycle is happening already in the Gulf. The magnitude of the mess and the sheer amount of wrong or misleading information threaten to derail the latest push toward environmental awareness, spreading confusion where there should be concern. But it doesn't have to be this way. The saving grace is that we can avoid this cycle, if we absorb the right lessons.

There are lots of wrong lessons to distract us. Many reports emphasize that the spill is not history's largest (an offshore blowout in the Gulf of Mexico in 1979 was bigger), and that the damage, while extensive, is essentially limited to the region. Other sources reassure us that the Persian Gulf is a desert in any case, and that the area has been polluted for years by tankers spilling oil. And some people argue that the Gulf pollution is essentially the problem of the Gulf people; while Canadians and others are happy to rush in with clean-up crews and technical help, what happens to the environment in faraway places is ultimately of little consequence to us.

These are exactly the kinds of mistaken understandings that allow our politicians to serve us so poorly on environmental issues. Even if the Persian Gulf's pollution turns out to be a regional rather than a global horror, a horror it is, and by now we ought to recognize that these environmental catastrophes are regular occurrences—only the events that trigger them seem to change. As this decade progresses, there will undoubtedly be new disasters, perhaps not as sudden as what happened in the Gulf, but in many cases just as serious. The right lesson from the Gulf War is that environmental desolation is not something we have caused in one place by a war, but something we are slowly creating all over the earth by what we do every day.

What exactly should the Gulf War teach us? I think it's this: the worst thing is not how we're harming the environment, but how we keep shrugging it off.

Yet it is possible to learn from our mishaps. The Gulf War actually did bring political changes that could improve the way we deal with the environment. The war has shown that several countries can work together in the face of a sudden crisis, even if their interests, while shared, are not identical. It has also demonstrated that people actually are trying to do something about the environmental mess. As far as I'm concerned, the signs that were apparent when I first wrote this book are still evident: getting human beings to change their behaviour is an awesome task, requiring leadership and political skill, but the balance of evidence suggests it can be done. If we can work together on our continual, worldwide environmental crisis, we will avoid Silent Earth.

—— II ——

Unfortunately, in Canada, hope must be tempered by the performance of our politicians, who when it comes to the environment seem more adept than ever at combining cynicism and incompetence. There are exceptions; for example, in its first year, Ontario's New Democratic Party appears at least interested in tackling environmental issues, unlike most provincial governments. Bob Rae is the first Ontario premier to have been arrested for environmental protest; he was hauled in (though later released without trial) for demonstrating against the controversial logging road that his predecessors built in the Temagami region. And there has been an even bigger cause to celebrate—the new U.S. Clean Air Act to control acid rain has become law and in November, 1990, the Canadian Coalition on Acid Rain finally got to throw a party and close down.

But environmental politics in Canada has proved depressingly predictable for the most part, which is to say that nothing has changed except perhaps the ministers. After several delays, Environment Minister Robert de Cotret—Lucien Bouchard's successor, who was later replaced—eventually released the federal Green Plan, but it was met with hoots of derision. The plan called for an impressive $3 billion to be spent on environmental programs over five years, but all of this funding was made subject to cabinet approval—meaning that the entire plan was little more than a speculative exercise that could be swept away by a show of hands and a few signatures. Within months of its release, the money started to disappear: the federal government's budget in early 1991 chopped $600 million from the Green Plan.

Canada also remained more or less idle when the United States released its long-term energy strategy during the middle of the Gulf War. The strategy calls for reducing American reliance on foreign supplies, but does not offer incentives such as higher gasoline taxes or strict requirements that car companies improve their vehicle's fuel efficiency. More significant to Canada, it proposes oil exploration in Alaska's Arctic National Wildlife Refuge, an area that is supposed to be protected and whose development would threaten huge herds of caribou that migrate from the Yukon. To its credit, Canada is on record as opposing this development, but those trusty Canadian senior environmental bureaucrats seem to have done it again. Canadian officials have discussed with Washington the possibility of being consulted if the United States goes ahead, and their talks may ultimately compromise Canada's ability to fight the proposal.

The re-emerging debate over Canada's constitutional future has also sapped a great deal of political will. Ironically, the environment has become something of a political football to be fought over by Ottawa and Quebec, although neither government appears ready to do anything particularly constructive with it. Ottawa's record, or lack of it, is apparent. Quebec's biggest aspiration is less to protect the environment than to change it: the government wants to spend more than $50 billion to continue its James Bay hydro-electric project, which would re-shape an area the size of France in ways that are still poorly understood.

Nevertheless, in spite of the long odds, I am still hopeful. I don't even think the green wave that started a generation ago is finished; a sudden war and a worldwide economic downturn may have temporarily blocked its flow, but I doubt that it will ever be weak again. Examples are all around, from the high level of concern about damage in the Gulf to the public's persistence in seeking out products that are genuinely better for the environment. Despite experts' warnings that interest in the environment comes and goes in cycles, I believe environmentalism is here to stay. Every spill adds to the wave's intensity and every new revelation about environmental abuse sustains it.

We have to remember that the international political mechanisms for protecting the environment are only now being created being created. It may be late, but it won't be too late if the work continues until completed. As a nation, Canada may lag behind because its environmental politics and some of its activists are still too clumsy, too unsophisticated and too reliant on emotion, rather than on the basic rightness of their cause. But parts of the country are grappling with problems and coping surprisingly well, and other countries are finding the pollution they face so intolerable that they're taking action as well.

I still believe that, more than anything, the determined actions of individuals can change the way we treat the environment. And our perspective is clearer. A generation ago, the problems were only predicted. Then the problems became real, but the solutions were sketchy. Now very little is abstract; we know many of the solutions, and we must face up to the sacrifices and trade-offs that are needed to solve our environmental problems. For many of my generation, even the reason so often used to justify these sacrifices is no longer abstract. We always said it was our obligation to pass along a better world to our children. Now these children are here and they will ask us what we have given them.

Unlike earlier generations, we can't say we didn't know anything was wrong.

David Israelson
London, 1991

SELECTED
BIBLIOGRAPHY

Silent Earth is based largely on original research and personal interviews with many of the individuals mentioned in the text; however, the following materials are gratefully acknowledged, as they were particularly helpful.

―――― **Chapter One:** ――――
The Most Polluted Creatures on Earth

Beland, Pierre. "Witness for the Prosecution." *Nature Canada* (Fall 1988): 28.

Dover, Pegi. "Endangered: The St. Lawrence Beluga." *Probe Post* (Spring 1988): 30.

Pippard, Leone and Heather Malcolm. *White Whales: Observations on their distribution, population and critical habitats in the St. Lawrence and Saguenay Rivers.* Ottawa: Department of Indian and Northern Affairs, Parks Canada, 1978.

―――― **Chapter Two: The Great Green Wave** ――――

Atwood, Margaret. *Survival: a Thematic Guide to Canadian Literature.* Toronto: Anansi, 1972.

Briggs, Shirley A. "Rachel Carson: Her Vision and Her Legacy." In Gino J. Marco et al., *Silent Spring Revisited*. Washington: American Chemical Society, 1987.

Carson, Rachel. *Silent Spring*. New York: Fawcett Crest, 1962.

Graham, Frank, Jr. *Since Silent Spring*. Boston: Houghton Mifflin Company, 1970.

Lovelock, James. *The Ages of Gaia: A Biography of Our Living Earth*. New York: W.W. Norton & Company, 1988.

_____ *Gaia: A New Look at Life on Earth*. Toronto: Oxford University Press, 1987.

Paehlke, Robert C. *Environmentalism and the Future of Progressive Politics*. New Haven: Yale University Press, 1989.

Strong, Douglas H. *Dreamers and Defenders: American Conservationists*. Lincoln and London, Nebr.: University of Nebraska Press, 1988.

World Commission on Environment and Development. *Our Common Future*. New York: Oxford University Press, 1987.

—— **Chapter Three:** ——
"Who Wants to Swim among the Gall Bladders?"

Burdick, Alan. "Hype Tide." *The New Republic* 200, no. 24, (June 12, 1989): 15–18.

Marine Pollution Bulletin 19 (March–November 1988). "Mystery of Fouled Beaches: Clues, but No 'Smoking Gun.'" *New York Times*, July 25, 1988.

Warren, Jacqueline M. and Andrew R. Kass. Testimony of the Natural Resources Defense Council before the House Committee on Small Business Subcommittee on Regulation and Business Opportunities, August 9, 1988.

—— **Chapter Four: The Diaper War** ——

Isaacs, Colin. "Harnessing the profit motive to clean up world pollution – it's faster than government." *Globe and Mail*, July 10, 1989, p. A7.

Lehrberger, Carl and Rachel Snyder. "The Disposable Diaper Myth: Out of Sight, Out of Mind." *Whole Earth Review* (Fall 1988): 60.

Manolson, Michael. "Big business is cashing in on environmental worries while industry keeps polluting." *Globe and Mail*, July 10, 1989, p. A7.

Procter & Gamble Inc. "Some Answers to the Most Commonly Asked Questions about the Impact of Disposable Diapers on Municipal Solid Waste." Company literature.

—— **Chapter Five: Just Add Poison and Stir** ——

Ashworth, William. *The Late, Great Lakes*. Toronto: Collins, 1986.

Canada. Environment Canada. *Storm Warning*. 1985. Errata sheet, 1987.

Carroll, John. *Environmental Diplomacy*. Ann Arbor: University of Michigan Press, 1983.

Estabrook, Barry. "What Price Wildlife?" *Equinox* 4, no. 20 (March–April 1985): 78.

Keating, Michael. *To the Last Drop: Canada and the World's Water Crisis*. Toronto: Macmillan, 1986.

—— **Chapter Six: Food, Dangerous Food** ——

Conservation Foundation and International Institute for Research on Public Policy. *Great Lakes, Great Legacy?* Report, 1989.

Goldsmith, Edwin and Nicholas Hildyard, eds. *The Earth Report: Monitoring the Battle for the Environment*. London: Mitchell Beazley, 1988.

Mott, Laurie and Karen Snyder. "Pesticide Alert." *The Amicus Journal* 10, no. 2 (Spring 1988): 20. (Published by Natural Resources Defense Council, New York.)

Proceedings of Large Lakes Conference, Mackinac Island, Michigan, May 1986. 5 volumes.

Report of the Great Lakes Science Advisory Board to the International Joint Commission, October 1989.

—— **Chapter Seven: From Sea to Filthy Sea** ——

"Alaskan Oil Spill." *Marine Pollution Bulletin* 20, no. 5 (May 1989): 200.

Brewster, J. Alan, ed. *World Resources 1987*. World Resources Institute and International Institute for Environment and Development. New York: Basic Books, 1987.

Couper, Alastair, ed. *The Times Atlas of the Oceans*. Toronto: Van Nostrand Reinhold Company, 1983.

Cousteau, Jacques-Yves. *The Cousteau Almanac*. Garden City, N.Y.: Doubleday and Company, 1981.

Egan, Timothy. "Elements of Alaska Oil Spill Disaster: Drinking, Fatigue and Complacency." *New York Times*, May 22, 1989, p. 10.

"In Ten Years You'll See 'Nothing' " (Interview with Exxon Chairman Lawrence Rawl). *Fortune* (May 8, 1989): 50.

Myers, Dr. Norman, ed. *GAIA: An Atlas of Planet Management*. Garden City, N.Y.: Doubleday & Co., Anchor Press, 1984.

—— **Chapter Eight: Smoke of a Furnace** ——

City of Toronto Department of Public Health. *Toronto: State of the Environment*. May 1988.

Garrod, Stephen et al. *The Regulation of Toxic and Oxidant Air Pollution in North America*. Toronto: CCH Canadian Ltd., 1986.

Lees, David. "Club Lead." *Toronto Life* (December 1986): 43–45.

Royal Society of Canada, Commission on Lead in the Environment. *Lead in the Canadian Environment: Science and Regulation.* Final report, September 1986.

Russell, Dick. "L.A. Air." *The Amicus Journal* 10, no. 3 (Summer 1988): 10. (Published by Natural Resources Defense Council, New York.)

Wallace, Barbara and Kathy Cooper. *The Citizen's Guide to Lead: Uncovering a Hidden Health Hazard.* Toronto: NC Press, 1986.

Chapter Nine: Silent Earth

Grey Owl. *A Book of Grey Owl: Pages from the Writings of Wa-Sha-Quon-Asin.* Ed. E. E. Reynolds. Toronto: Macmillan, 1981.

Hodgins, Bruce W. and Jamie Bendickson. *The Temagami Experience: Recreation, Resources and Aboriginal Rights in the Northern Ontario Wilderness.* Toronto: University of Toronto Press, 1989.

Hummel, Monte, ed. *Endangered Spaces: The Future for Canada's Wilderness.* Toronto: Key Porter Books, 1989.

Lampman, Archibald. "Timagami." In *Selected Poems of Archibald Lampman.* Toronto: Ryerson Press, 1957.

MacKay, Donald. *Heritage Lost: The Crisis in Canada's Forests.* Toronto: Macmillan, 1985.

Nikiforuk, Andrew and Ed Struzik. "The Great Forest Sell-Off." *Report on Business Magazine* (November 1989): 56.

Chapter Ten: The Sky's Bitter Tears

Cannon, James S. *The Health Costs of Air Pollution: A Survey of Studies Published 1984-89.* Washington: American Lung Association, 1990. (Pre-publication edition.)

Federation of Ontario Naturalists. Acid Deposition Teaching Kit, 1987.

Green, Mark and Gail MacColl. *Reagan's Reign of Error*. New York: Pantheon Books, 1987.

——— **Chapter Eleven: Congregation of Vapours** ———

Boyle, Robert H. "Forecast for Disaster." *Sports Illustrated* (November 16, 1987): 78.

Gribben, John. *The Hole in the Sky: Man's Threat to the Ozone Layer*. Toronto: Bantam Books, 1988.

McKibben, Bill. *The End of Nature*. New York and Toronto: Random House, 1989.

Miller, Jack. "We'll be warm as toast 50 years down the road." *Toronto Star*, February 13, 1988, p. A1.

Moomaw, William R. "In Search of the Greenhouse Fingerprint." *Orion Nature Quarterly* 8, no. 1 (Winter 1989): 4.

Pearce, Fred. *Turning Up the Heat*. Toronto: Paladin Grafton Books, 1989.

Roan, Sharon. *Ozone Crisis*. Toronto: John Wiley and Sons, 1989.

Rowland, Sherwood. "Can We Close the Ozone Hole?" *Technology Review* (August–September 1987): 50.

Shabecoff, Philip. "Global Warming Has Begun, Expert Tells Senate." *New York Times*, June 24, 1988, p. 1.

Stevens, William K. "Methane From Guts of Livestock Is New Focus In Global Warming." *New York . Times*, November 21, 1989, p. 19.

Udall, James R. et al. "Climate Shock: A Special Report." *Sierra* (July–August 1989): 26.

United Kingdom Department of the Environment. United Kingdom Stratospheric Ozone Review Group, *Stratospheric Ozone*. London: HMSO, 1987.

—— **Chapter Twelve: The Political Edifice** ——

Canada. House of Commons. Proceedings of House of Commons Environment Committee, October 26, 1989.

The Green Plan: A Framework for Discussion on the Environment. Discussion paper released by Environment Minister Lucien Bouchard, March 1990.

Greenprint on the Environment. Presented by representatives of 28 environmental groups to Prime Minister Brian Mulroney. June 1989.

—— **Chapter Thirteen: Success Stories** ——

Transcript of Statement by U.S. President George Bush, June 12, 1989.

—— **Conclusion** ——

Caldwell, Erskine. *God's Little Acre*. New York: Signet, 1961. The quotation in the conclusion is taken from this novel.

INDEX